PELICAN BOOKS
JFK AND LBJ

Tom Wicker was chief Washington correspondent
and head of the Washington bureau of *The
New York Times* from 1964 through 1968. He is
now associate editor of and a columnist for that
newspaper. Born in Hamlet, North Carolina in
1926, and a graduate of the University of North
Carolina, he served as editor and reporter on
several North Carolina newspapers, and worked
for the North Carolina State Board of Public
Welfare. In 1952, the Navy called him from the
reserves for two years' service in Japan and Korea.
He was a Nieman fellow in journalism at Harvard
in 1957-1958. Mr. Wicker joined the *Times* as a
Washington reporter in 1960, first covering
Congress. His two years as White House correspondent included coverage of President Kennedy's
assassination, and led to his book *Kennedy Without
Tears*. Mr. Wicker is well known for his widely
read column, "In The Nation," and is also the
author of the novels *The Judgement, The Kingpin,*
and *The Devil Must.*

JFK AND LBJ

The Influence of Personality Upon Politics

TOM WICKER

PENGUIN BOOKS
BALTIMORE · MARYLAND

Penguin Books Inc., 7110 Ambassador Road
Baltimore, Maryland 21207

First published by William Morrow & Co. 1968
Published in Pelican Books 1969
Reprinted 1970, 1972, 1973

Printed in the United States of America

An excerpt from this book has appeared in
The Atlantic Monthly.

To Arthur Krock
and
James Reston

Contents

Away with the cant of 'measures, not men!'—the idle supposition that it is the harness and not the horses that draw the chariot along. —CANNING

KENNEDY
AND
JOHNSON

*The ear of the leader
must ring with the
voices of the people.
—Woodrow Wilson.*

Lyndon Johnson's father once told him that he did not belong in politics unless he could walk into a roomful of men and tell immediately who was for him and who was against him.* In fact, even the shrewd LBJ has not quite such occult power, but his liking for the story tells us something useful about him: he sets much store by instinct. No wonder, then, that it would be to his instincts—honed in the Texas hill country, sharpened in a life of politics, confirmed in his successful Congressional career—that he would often turn in the White House.

This reliance on instinct enabled Johnson to put on the Presidency like a suit of comfortable old clothes. John Kennedy, on the other hand, came to it with a historical, nearly theoretical view of what was required of a strong President; he knew exactly what Woodrow Wilson had said about the office and he had read Corwin and Neustadt and he was unabashedly willing to quote Lincoln: "I see the storm coming and I know His hand is in it. If He has a place and work for me, I believe that I am ready."

And Kennedy would add: "Today I say to you that if the people of this nation select me to be their President, I believe that I am ready." With eager confidence, Kennedy acquired a

* So Johnson is fond of saying, anyway. An author's note on sources appears on page 279.

Presidential suit off the rack and put on a little weight to make
himself fit it.

JFK, in his pursuit of excellence, and LBJ, with his instinctive grasp of power and responsibility, are the subjects of this
book. It is a work of the imagination that poses an explanation
of Kennedy's bitter and disappointing relationship with Congress, and puts forward the thesis that the expansion of the war
in Vietnam was an almost inevitable but not entirely planned
result of Johnson's succession to the Presidency.

These studies are not documentary records of history or
unassailable truths but imaginative reconstructions of events.
They are efforts to impose, for the sake of wider understanding,
a design and a logic upon those events that could not possibly
have been displayed at the time of their chaotic unfolding. So
that they might be seen from a consistent point of view, the
dominant considerations in these reconstructions have been the
characters and personalities and experience of the participants,
acting within whatever framework the circumstances of the
moment might reasonably have imposed.

To take this point of view was by no means an arbitrary
decision. The general American understanding of politics—
that is, of the way men cope with other men—swings wildly
from a sort of schoolboy's preoccupation with the neatly organized processes and institutions described in civics books
to a devil theory depicting everything that happens as the calculated product either of ideological subversion, economic
venality, or human evil.

The schoolboy view has been held even by Presidents. Two
years after he left the White House, Dwight D. Eisenhower
solemnly declared to a crowd gathered at Rensselaer, Ind., for
Charlie Halleck Day what any civics book will tell you:
"The Congress makes the laws. The President executes them."
This drew a big round of applause, despite its hopeless in-
adequacy.

The devil theory, until quite recently, was primarily the
staple of those Right-wingers who viewed all the acts of the

federal government since 1932 as a sellout to Communism, and those novelists and playwrights who pictured every political choice as one between morality and expedience. Since the war in Vietnam, the strongest current devil theory has been held on the Left, where it is believed that the war is the deliberate, calculated product of an evil President and his evil henchmen, whose aim is to subjugate Asia and wipe out Communism, if necessary in a nuclear war.

In fact, American politics does have an institutional framework, if one more fragile and complicated than General Eisenhower suggested, and it does impose a considerable discipline of due process; and American politics does, of course, have its share of unprincipled men, porcine hypocrites and perhaps even a few subversives. But the most controlling factor in American political life, by all odds, remains the necessity for public figures to win public approval for their public policies. By and large, the public view and morality is imposed on politics and politicians, not the other way around. What the public wants, the public gets, more often than not, and the real problems of American politics are that the public so often wants unworthy things, and is so seldom set straight by anyone who will be listened to.

The first and most fundamental task of the American politician ought to be that of public education—the enlightenment of the electorate he represents, a constituency that in the nature of the case and in the press of its own business will not have the time, opportunity, or inclination that he has to inform itself about the realities of an ever more complex and shrinking world. It is regrettably true that most constituencies operate on the ethic boldly admitted by that weekly publication that once proclaimed itself "The Only Newspaper in the World that Gives a Damn About Jacksonville, N.C."

But representative government is just that, and so is human nature; and their conjunction means that American politicians are doomed to the nebulous position of being both follower and leader. Even so, the public is sometimes sold a bill of goods;

it may be convinced by politicians, for instance, that the destruction of some part of its natural heritage, perhaps its rivers, is necessary to its prosperity; but even this kind of fraud usually has to be perpetrated through a spurious but plausible conception of "the public good." Occasionally, too, some politician strides boldly out in front of his constituency in advocacy of something theretofore generally rejected; and in these cases, too, success or failure will be based squarely on whether or not he can convince enough voters to follow him.

What happens usually is compromise—two steps forward and three steps back, or vice versa, a choice not between good and evil or morality and expedience but between a greater and a lesser good or a greater and a lesser evil or between two interchangeable mediocrities. The compromise is struck like any other deal, on the basis of whatever circumstances are believed to exist at the time—in the political case, with an eye to what seems on the basis of experience most easily justified to the large numbers of people who will have to be convinced that the arrangement was the right one.

Thus, the public atmosphere is always the framework within which American politics function; and it is what politicians spend most of their time trying to divine. When John F. Kennedy was a young Congressman, he was approximately as conservative as his Irish Catholic constituency in Boston—just as when Lyndon Johnson represented the Texas district around Austin, he was as Populistically liberal as was required by the farmers and ranchers who had received aid from the New Deal and wanted more. When Kennedy moved to the Senate, he moved toward the Left, as demanded by modern, industrialized Massachusetts—just as Johnson, when *he* reached the Senate, moved toward the Right to accommodate the conservative oil and other Texas interests with which he had not had to cope in his Congressional district. And when both became Presidential candidates, both tried to recast their political images to appeal to the national constituency; this led to the rich irony of Kennedy compromising on the 1957 civil rights bill because he wanted to add Southern support to that which his liberalism would give him elsewhere, while Johnson took the same compromise position to show Northern liberals that he was not a prisoner of his Southern background.

But if it can certainly be said that circumstances thus are a constant and powerful influence on the general practice of American politics, far less is known about the specific tactics, words and deeds of those who pursue the calling—particularly after they assume the patriotic mantle of government, and even more particularly if that mantle is worn at so high a level (say the White House) that some plausible claim can be made to the additional cloak of "national interest."

The fact is that journalists, television commentators, academicians and others who are not actual parties to political decisions seldom know much about what actually happened or was said or decided—much less *why*—in the Cabinet Room, the committee meeting, the cloakroom, the Boss's limousine, the whispered conference in the corridor, or even on the convention floor. And almost all of what they do know is derived from those who have a special interest in the telling.

The journalist who relies solely on what politicians tell him usually is relying on tainted and self-serving information; even if it is true, it probably is being told him for some reason other than its truth, for some purpose he has to try to comprehend if he is to know the full dimension of what he is doing. So he must be able to put his hearsay information through some sort of a filter, much as oldtime miners washed dirt through wire mesh in order to screen out the heavier, thicker particles of gold.

There are two strands from which such a journalist can weave his screen. One is his own knowledge of life, of human nature, of politics, of the way things work, of what men believe and fear, will do and will not do, of how they can be made to transcend their limits or fall short of their possibilities. The other is what he knows of the politicians—men—involved in the events about which he is curious.

The way of a nation at every stage of its existence [F. S. Oliver observed] is determined by a parallelogram of forces. At the one pair of opposite angles the pull is between the dread of change and the hope that change will make things better. At the other pair, the pull is between the rivalries and ambitions of individual men.

Within any government of laws, that is, and using it as their instrument, there exists a government of men—men fighting and struggling for their interests, their ideas, their necessities, their prejudices, their ideals, their power, sometimes even for their lives. Some dread change, some seek it; some have more or less ambition, and therefore rivalries, than others; all are fallible human beings.

This clash of men cannot be entirely controlled by due process, and non-totalitarian government, as a result, is always of laws *and* of men, usually more of the latter than the former; because if laws and procedures must be controlling in any orderly society, still they have first to be established, and second to be observed or periodically changed. And these are tasks of men.

So if procedures and institutions are to be established, observed, enforced and changed—if law is to prevail—men must first be controlled. Men must be made to understand, made to believe, pushed sometimes to conform, urged sometimes to dissent; they must be led, persuaded, dissuaded, mobilized, dispelled—in short, governed. And all this can only be done by men who can maintain some measure of public approval. This is politics and that, too, is a task of men.

Lord Tweedsmuir thought that task was "the greatest and most honorable adventure," but Oliver, no doubt more realistically, saw it only as "the endless adventure of governing men." And endless it is, since man does not change much. The hope and the dread, the rivalry and the ambition, are always there; the parallelogram persists, even as time alters the conditions in which men live. So leaders like Kennedy and Johnson still must cope, in our time and system, with men and circumstance, much as Pitt or Jackson or Balfour or Kerensky coped in theirs—as best they can, with what they have and know, for as long as possible.

Above all, of course, such leaders of men must cope with themselves; for what *they* are—their hopes and dreads, rivalries and ambitions, character and experience—will largely determine what they do, and how they do it. That is why these studies of Kennedy's greatest defeat and Johnson's severest trial are based fundamentally on ideas about John Kennedy and Lyndon Johnson, as well as on observations of the circumstances in which they performed.

Any such book must be a work of the imagination. This one, manifestly, is not a political history of the Kennedy-Johnson era, nor the "inside story" of anything. These accounts are not intended to be definitive; they are general, not detailed. There is no particular connection between Kennedy's loss of Congress and Johnson's loss of his Consensus, except that both are stories of men who tried to govern others and found their own personalities and circumstances not the least of the trouble.

And if someone else would tell these stories differently, that is only to be welcomed. Who would wish for a single, authorized version of the endless adventure?

PART I

KENNEDY
LOSES
CONGRESS

When I was a Congressman, I never realized how important Congress was. But now I do.—John Kennedy.

1 'Alone, At the Top'

Senator John F. Kennedy addressed the National Press Club eleven months before he was elected President, and gave the following view of the kind of man needed in that office:

Whatever the political affiliation of our next President, whatever his views may be on all the issues and problems that rush in upon us, he must above all be the chief executive in every sense of the word. He must be prepared to exercise the fullest powers of his office—all that are specified and some that are not * * * the President is alone, at the top.

In the same speech, the erudite young Senator quoted Woodrow Wilson's famous dictum that "the President is at liberty, both in law and conscience, to be as big a man as he can*** His office is anything he has the sagacity and the force to make it * * * His capacity will set the limit."

In the long campaign that followed, Kennedy never deviated from this expansive idea of the office and the opportunity confronting the man who would be elected in November, 1960. And in that campaign, he stood for nothing if he did not stand for federal aid to education and for an increase in, and an expansion of the coverage of, the minimum wage.

In the massive record of his campaign statements, more than
two pages are required merely to index his remarks on education. He did not simply advocate federal aid, he promised it:

> Unless we have a good and increasing educational system,
> we are not going to have a strong democratic society . . .
> America needs the Democratic party because the Demo-
> cratic party intends to help the states build classrooms and
> pay for the teachers which are necessary if we are to have
> an educational system second to none. And America can-
> not afford schools which are second to anyone . . . We will
> permit every American child to receive the kind of edu-
> cation which will produce the skills and creativity which a
> growing America desperately needs . . . A Democratic ad-
> ministration will act in 1961.[1]*

Exactly one month to the day after he was inaugurated, Mr.
Kennedy sent his education program to Congress with the confident message that it would provide a "new standard of excellence" available "to all who are willing and able to pursue
it."

In his campaign, he was no less positive or stirring on the
subject of the minimum wage; in office, he was even more
prompt to move in this field than he was in sending up his
education bill.

On August 29, 1960, to reporters in the Capitol, he had said:
"I intend to take this fight to the American people. I am sure
that they will support me in November in my goal of a minimum
living standard of $1.25 an hour for millions of Americans
who work in the large enterprises of our country."

And a month later, on September 29, in Buffalo, in one of
the most ironic footnotes to the campaign and events to follow,
Kennedy declared ringingly: "As long as the average wage for
laundry women in the five largest cities is 65 cents an hour for
a 48-hour week . . . there is a need for our party."

Again and again, candidate Kennedy repeated such pledges

* Footnotes are in a special section at the end of this book.

as he raced across the United States. It was about as surprising, therefore, as the reappointment of J. Edgar Hoover, that President Kennedy asked in his first Economic Message, February 2, 1961, for a minimum wage increase. One month after his inaugural, he sent a special message to Congress asking a program of federal aid to education.

Thus it was that the new President—in his campaign and in his first actions—identified himself, as on few other issues, with aid to education and an increased minimum wage. These were old and familiar propositions in American politics; if the new President really meant, in the words of Wilson, "to be as big a man" as he could be—to be in his own phrase "the chief executive in every sense of the word"—then here was the place to begin. On no other issues had he more thoroughly committed himself; on none did he more passionately paint the need; on none could he either move his program ahead more decisively for the whole, or be held more strictly to account.

Scarcely two years later, Theodore C. Sorensen, the President's brilliant and tough-minded special counsel, one of the prime shapers of his domestic legislative proposals, told an audience at Columbia University: "While it should not be impossible to find an equitable constitutional formula to settle the church-school aid problem, it is difficult for that formula to be suggested by the nation's first Catholic President."

And Kennedy himself wrote in 1963, in his foreword to the book publication of Sorensen's Columbia lectures, a far different view of the Presidency than he had offered the National Press Club in 1960:

The President . . . is rightly described as a man of extraordinary powers. Yet it is also true that he must wield those powers under extraordinary limitations—and it is these limitations which so often give the problem of choice its complexity and even poignancy. Lincoln, Franklin Roosevelt once remarked, "was a sad man because he couldn't get it all at once. And nobody can." Every Pres-

ident must endure a gap between what he would like and
what is possible.[2]

What had happened in the intervening years, to cause this
heightened regard for the limitations of the office Kennedy
had sought so eagerly, with such confidence that it would confide its greatness to a man who would not shrink from it?

What happened, of course, is the story of the Kennedy Administration. But that story was influenced, in no small part,
by events that took place at the outset, particularly the episodes
of the minimum-wage and aid-to-education battles. And those
episodes, like the larger story, were in great part shaped by circumstances that existed the day John Kennedy took office—by
the human and political context circumscribing that particular
man as he took the oath on the Capitol steps on January 20,
1961. It might have been a context that he, more than any
other, had fashioned; but he could not control the minds, experience and imaginations of others, as they sought to see it
for themselves.

But the frustration that would reach John Kennedy, that
would cause him, finally, to see the White House in terms of
its limitations rather than its opportunities, had origins even
earlier than that, in the very nature of things. He might have
envisioned himself being "alone, at the top" but, like Wilson,
he would find out that not even a President moves free of
human entanglement, human needs, human illusions; not even a
President can be independent of those around him.

Kennedy learned at least that lesson right at the start. It was
taught to him, as it had been to some of his predecessors, by the
Committee on Rules of the House of Representatives. And
the committee's challenge to his power disclosed much about
the difficulties that lay ahead—about the world in which John
Kennedy would seek to be as big as he could.

2 *Judge Smith and Mr. Sam*

High noon in the House of Representatives . . . Samuel Taliaferro Rayburn emerged from his rococo corner office on the Principal Floor of the Capitol and moved with stately tread through the Speaker's Lobby. From its walls, former Speakers, transfixed in somber Victorian oils, gazed at him with dark foreboding. The old man—bald, erect, stubby—looked neither to right nor left at the scattering of reporters and members who watched him pass.

He was on his way to the climactic battle of a career that had spanned eight Presidencies and half a century in the House —a battle whose loss would diminish his immense prestige, cripple his power to lead the Democratic majority, and mortally wound the new Administration his party had installed just eleven days before.

The issue seemed too innocuous to threaten such results. Should the House Committee on Rules continue to number eight Democrats and four Republicans? Or should Sam Rayburn's resolution to add two Democrats and a Republican to the Committee be adopted?

The question only seemed trivial. What was really to be decided that day was whether Rayburn controlled the House of Representatives—and thus whether the Democrats and the new President, John F. Kennedy, could control Congress.

Sam Rayburn had been saddened by the bitterness of the struggle, shaken by the perfidy of colleagues. In eight months, he would be dead. That day, he did not know if he would win this last great fight of a lifetime. He only knew that the matter was out of his hands, the issue was close, and he had done his best.

An aide held open the heavy swinging door that gave entrance to the House Rayburn had often called his "greatest love." With unfaltering stride, he entered and started up the steps to the rostrum that had been his for more years than any other Speaker's.

As if at a signal, rows upon rows of men—Republicans and Democrats, liberals and conservatives, friends and foes—came to their feet on the steep House floor in front of him. The sound of their applause, pierced here and there by whistles and shouts, broke in waves around the solid old figure—the straight-shouldered little man who stood blinking and nodding, his gavel in his hand, the lines of age on his face and neck offset by pride and character.

There were hundreds in that House who loved the man they called Mr. Sam. There was scarcely a one who did not respect him deeply. All who cared to learn had been his students. In the drama and tension of the moment, with a spontaneity that the oldest of them could not recall, they had risen in grand and instinctive generosity to yield him his due.

If there was one among them whose handclapping was more perfunctory than any other, he was likely the stoop-shouldered, elaborately courteous, faintly reserved Gentleman from Virginia known to all as Judge Smith. It was not, however, that there was personal enmity between the Speaker and Howard Worth Smith—at seventy-eight, only a year younger than Rayburn but two decades his junior on the hallowed seniority list of the House. There seldom is enmity between seasoned old politicians, who know as much as men can of human weakness and human strength.

As chairman of the Committee on Rules, the Judge had been

on more than one occasion the Speaker's good right arm, a
willing and able lieutenant generally ranked as one of the most
powerful men in a body where power was, if not everything,
an asset surpassed only by the sort of respect Sam Rayburn
commanded.

Power was at the root of the trouble that day. Judge Smith
had too much of it. Shrewd, ruthless, a Southern Bourbon to
the bone, he was the acknowledged leader of the stubborn
Southern Democratic bloc. As the national Democratic party,
under leaders like the new President, continued its steady
progress to the left, Judge Smith had formed an effective coun-
terforce in coalition with Representative Charles A. Halleck
of Indiana, leader of the House Republicans. With Halleck's
help, the Judge had welded his conservative followers—one
fellow Southerner and four Republicans—on the Committee
on Rules into a instrument that had challenged Rayburn for
control of the House's business. For without the consent of the
Committee, it was difficult if not impossible to bring legislation
to the floor of the House for a vote.

At length, the applause for Mr. Sam died and members took
their seats. For the second day in a row, the galleries were
packed with spectators; in the press section above the rostrum,
every seat was taken again and reporters jammed the aisles
and stood against the rear wall. Twenty-four hours earlier, on
January 30, 1961, the great chamber, harshly bathed in television light, had been filled to capacity, the beautiful Kennedy
women had dazzled the populace from its galleries, the floor
had been crowded with Senators and diplomats, justices and the
new Cabinet, as the President—lion of the hour—delivered his
first State of the Union message. But that had been yesterday.

"Almighty God," said the Rev. Woodrow W. Hill of Petersburg, Virginia, acting as chaplain, ". . . we pause at this noon-
day hour to ask for wisdom and strength . . ."

On this second day of drama, only members of the House and
a few kibitzing Senators occupied the floor, and in the galleries other fur-coated women took the place of the glamorous

Kennedys. Students in chino pants, stenographers and lawyers from the independent little world of Capitol Hill, members' families, lobbyists from plush office buildings on K Street and Connecticut Avenue, government officials, ambitious Georgetown hostesses, all Washington's ubiquitous political buffs, had filled every seat and taken every inch of standing room to watch the greatest battle in the House of Representatives since the revolt against Cannonism in 1910.

"Responsibility is great," intoned the Rev. Mr. Hill, "and we pray that it might be matched with wisdom from God, with devotion to duty, and with strength to perform . . ."

The battle, everyone knew, was not just between Mr. Sam and the Judge, though they were the central figures in the drama that shortly would unfold in the historic old chamber of Henry Clay and Thaddeus Stevens, Thomas B. Reed and Uncle Joe Cannon. Rather it was between the new President—untried in office, elected on the most radical platform in history, the first Roman Catholic and the youngest and wealthiest man ever elected President—and those who mistrusted and hoped to frustrate or restrain him: economic conservatives of both parties, segregationist Southerners, party-line Republicans, disgruntled members of an older generation, devout believers in conventional wisdom.

In a real sense, it was a renewal of the Presidential election just past, an election believed by many to have been stolen by the Democrats in the wards of Chicago, the precincts of Texas, and the extraordinary closeness of which was duplicated by the razor-edge division of the House into *tres partes*—174 Republicans, 160 Democrats of the North and West, 101 Southern and border-state Democrats. A closeness duplicated, too, by the deadlock of the vital Committee on Rules—Judge Smith and his five conservatives, opposed to six Democrats generally loyal to Rayburn and presumably to President Kennedy as well.

The national division, as represented in all these ways, was so close that nothing had been decided in the election except who was to occupy the White House, which party and what men were to have legal control. Great power had been formally conferred; but no real mandate had been issued as to what should be done with it, as to what direction it should be given; it was not yet clear to what extent it was power checkmated, power balanced. And these questions could only be answered in the clash of men.

In such a situation, on the last day of January, 1961, none of those who opposed the new Administration were conceding it anything. Charlie Halleck, whose House Republicans had gained twenty-two seats on the day Kennedy was elected, had given his views bluntly in a post-election interview in *The New York Times*. "We're going to have to be reckoned with, not just as roadblocks, but for sanity in government. I'm not going for a lot of radical, wild-eyed spendthrift proposals that will do the country severe damage."

And when the Republican leader was asked if he planned to work with Judge Smith and the Southern Democrats, Halleck had replied that he did, indeed, expect "business as usual" with the Judge.

Now Halleck and Smith were sworn allies in the effort to retain the strongest bastion of their power, the Committee on Rules. Yet, only a day earlier, Kennedy had called for a sweeping, if familiar, program of economic, social and national defense action. That program, and each of its parts, could not even be voted upon in the House without the permission of the Committee on Rules.

It was no wonder that many members, confronted with the Rayburn-Kennedy determination to seize the committee by expanding its membership, silently shared the Rev. Mr. Hill's pointed words—"As we find ourselves being weighed in the balance we pray that we shall not be found wanting."

Few members ever had undergone the sort of political pressures that had been brought to bear in the House in those tension-filled weeks in January that had marked the end of the Eisenhower Era and the beginning of the Kennedy Administration. Many of them believed the votes they would cast that day would be the most perilous of their political careers.

Phone calls had been made by the President and cabinet

officers, seeking support for Rayburn. Attorney-General Robert
F. Kennedy, widely believed to be the new Administration's
political "enforcer," was active. Democratic members of the
House had been summoned "downtown," importuned in hotel
rooms and elsewhere to support the Speaker and the Administration. All the major lobbies were heavily committed on one
side or the other—the National Association of Manufacturers,
the American Medical Association and the United States
Chamber of Commerce, for instance, were backing Judge
Smith and Halleck, while the big labor unions were with Rayburn.

Even some state governors, quietly mobilized from the White
House, were bringing pressure on their state delegations to
support Rayburn and the President. Democratic Governors
Terry Sanford of North Carolina and Orval Faubus of Arkansas
were particularly active, although Sanford failed to produce any
vote switches in the Tar Heel delegation. Like many other
Southern representatives, the North Carolina members had
been "pledged" to the support of Judge Smith long before most
non-Southern members had known there was going to be a
fight at all.

But "pledged" members were not immunized from pressure.
One Gentleman from North Carolina, Alton Lennon, reported
to the press that he was "shocked and amazed" at a hint from
the Interior Department that if he persisted in supporting Judge
Smith, a promised water desalinization test plant would not be
located in his seaside district, after all. Lennon stood fast; the
implied threat was never carried out.

Leaders on both sides openly threatened to send new members, unless they toed the party line, to the Veterans' Affairs or
District of Columbia committees, a fate regarded by most representatives as worse than death. Innumerable phone calls went
to hometown political powerhouses, in an effort to bring long-
distance pressure to bear on wavering members. Anyone
known to have a particular interest in a dam, or a new post
office, or a defense plant for his district was an automatic target

for those who claimed to speak for the Administration. New-comers in particular were threatened from both sides with blighted careers unless they "voted right," and one waverer was summoned to Sam Rayburn's office and given the issue in a nutshell.

"The question under discussion is a simple one," Rayburn ₃aid, ominously. "Are you for the Speaker or for that old man from Virginia?" No politician needed to have that translated.

So in the chamber that day, as the Rev. Mr. Hill concluded his prayer and the House moved to its pending business, there was posed one of those remarkable occasions when great events teeter on the head of a pin.

Kennedy was not on anyone's ballot and was not even officially engaged. Nominally, Sam Rayburn and Howard Smith were the protagonists. There was no moral distinction between the two sides, however profound their political differences. No vital programs or funds or policies would be affected specifically by the vote; each still would have to be fought for, no matter how it came out. A cabinet would not fall or a war begin, nor would Rayburn or Smith lose his office—much less Kennedy. The matter to be decided was merely procedural.

But Howard Smith and Sam Rayburn knew that he who controls procedure often controls substance, and that was what the fight was about. Each, as everyone knew, was seeking the power to control the Committee on Rules—and hence procedure in the House and therefore the fate of the President's legislative program. Thus, in retrospect, it is possible to say that this was the *one* vote John Kennedy *had* to win during his brief tenure in office. More than procedure, more even than the substance of a few or many bills, was at stake; for the real task of politicians is to manage men, to influence them, to produce an effect on them, and the *effect on men* of victory or defeat in the House that day would roll on far beyond immediate consequences.

A defeat on such an issue, at the outset of his Administration, almost surely would be irredeemable for John Kennedy, and not merely in his relations with Congress. It would mark him at once, perhaps forever, as a minority President without the power to achieve the meanest of his goals. No foreign leader, least of all the bumptious one in the Kremlin, would take him seriously; and that could be disastrous.

Victory, on the other hand, would mean opportunity—control of the House, political power, a lesson to opponents that Kennedy was not to be taken lightly. Victory, above all, would not be defeat and defeat was simply unacceptable.

It was not surprising that such an issue should have arisen from the Committee on Rules. Its history, in 1961, was almost a textbook lesson in the entwined workings of men and law—in the way men first make law and procedure, then use law and procedure for their own ends.

The Committee held the immense power to decide what bills, of the thousands introduced each session by zealous members, would go to the House floor for a vote. A measure studied for months in a legislative committee, perfected to the last *whereas* by experts in its subject matter, supported by hundreds of members of the House—to say nothing of the President—could in an hour's time be killed by the Committee on Rules' refusal to send it to the House floor for a vote; and that refusal could be effected, not just by a majority of the Committee, but by a tie vote. It was by precipitating frequent six-to-six deadlocks in the Committee that Judge Smith and his five colleagues imposed their will upon the other 429 members of the House, and the hundred Senators.

On the other side of the coin, the Committee had been known to send to the floor bills that had not received a day's consideration in a legislative committee. By threatening to withhold a measure from the floor, the Committee often could force its sponsors to amend it or rewrite it to the Committee's specifications. Not infrequently, Judge Smith struck a deal. He would send one bill to the floor if those supporting it would withdraw or amend some other measure (or measures).

The Committee, even when it did dispatch a bill to the floor for a vote, had the right to impose the conditions under which the House would consider it. Thus, if a "closed rule" was granted for a measure, members could offer no amendments from the floor; they had no choice except to vote for or against the original proposition.

The Committee could specify, if it chose, that only one amendment would be considered on the floor, and dictate the exact wording of that amendment. The number of hours or days that a bill could be debated was decided in advance by the Committee on Rules. Its chairman even had considerable power to affect the order in which bills the Committee had cleared would come to the floor.

In another field of authority, all House investigations and junkets had to be approved by the Committee. Almost nothing, in short, could be done in the House of Representatives—and thus in Congress, which legislates bicamerally, except in approving treaties and some resolutions—without the consent of the Committee on Rules. Even when both the Senate and the House had passed a measure, the Committee held a final trump. Unless the two bodies had enacted identical bills, it could prevent the House from entering a conference with the Senate to iron out the differences in the two versions. Thus, the unofficial "third house" had the power to veto a measure desired by the President and passed by the two Constitutional houses.

If anyone proposed to change these rules of the game in the House, he first needed the clearance of—naturally—the Committee on Rules. And it was a splendid irony that for all this power not a word of specific authority could be found in the Constitution. The framers of that document granted the House no more than the right to "determine the rules of its proceedings." Like so many other commanding realities of American politics, the immense power of the Committee on Rules rested on usage, custom, practical necessity, political convenience and Constitutional flexibility—in short, on men, not measures —and was therefore almost impossible to reform or restrict.

In the first ninety years of the republic, the Committee on Rules was a special panel with little influence. After 1880, it was a standing committee of varying numbers of members and in 1883 it acquired the importance it still had in 1961. In 1883, the Committee issued its first "rule" for the consideration of a bill—a tax measure—on the floor. Speaker Keifer of Ohio was upheld in ruling that the Committee had the right to do so. That right has not been fundamentally challenged since.

Before that, amid vast confusion, unanimous consent of all members had been required to get one bill, among the many thousands that might be offered in a session, to the floor. As the national population and the House membership grew, this became an impossible situation, paralyzing all action.

To impose order on the chaotic House, the Committee on Rules under the autocratic Speakers Thomas B. Reed of Maine and Uncle Joe Cannon of Illinois was given virtually the power of direction of House affairs—the power it retained in 1961. But Reed and Cannon, who were little inclined to yield to awkward notions of democracy, ruled the Committee absolutely. Its powers enabled them, the elected leaders of the House, to lead.

The revolt against Cannon in 1910 removed him, and subsequent Speakers, from membership on the committee and limited their power in significant ways; but the revolt did not restrict the Committee's intrinsic power or remove it from the Speaker's indirect influence. Until 1937, the Committee functioned at the direction of succeeding Speakers, imposing a tight and generally effective order upon the House. In those years and later, it also performed another function, one perhaps as necessary in a democratic (which is to say imperfect) order. Fiorello H. LaGuardia, long a member of the House, described it with characteristic candor. "Members alibi themselves behind the Rules Committee when pretending to be for certain legislation but not really for it; or in a desire to avoid a vote on highly controversial subjects."

The Committee on Rules, composed as nearly as could be of impregnable members from "safe" districts, was counted upon to keep off the floor bills that would embarrass too many members, bills for which there was vociferous public demand but equally loud opposition, bills of an irresponsible nature that still were hard to vote against (old-age pensions for all, for instance). The Committee was constituted to "take the heat" for members who could not, or feared to. It invariably sent tax bills to the floor under a "closed rule," for example, ruling out in advance mischievous or demagogic amendments.

In 1937, the long-simmering wrath of conservatives outraged by the New Deal boiled over. Franklin Roosevelt's disastrous attempt to pack the Supreme Court, a move that still would have its echoes in Congress a quarter-century later, brought into action the dormant Congressional coalition of Southern conservatives and Republicans that had existed since the disputed Presidential election of 1876. In the House of Representatives, the coalition not only had an informal majority; it took firm control of the Committee on Rules, a control it was to relinquish only in the Republican-led Eightieth and Eighty-Third Congresses.

Not in all the years he had been Speaker, therefore, had Sam Rayburn had the ultimate *power* to *command* the Committee on Rules. Without it, he lacked the ultimate power, if challenged, to command the House of Representatives. Without that, he and the Democrats lacked the power to command Congress. And, in many an instance, the Speaker had found himself helpless to bring the program of his party or of Presidents Franklin Roosevelt, Truman or Eisenhower even to the House floor.

On January 31, 1961, the long and involuted story of the Committee on Rules had come to a dramatic climax. It had become, through its particular combination of institutional function and human political power, virtually a third house of Congress equal, and in some ways superior, to the House and the Senate. It was directly challenging the new President, John Kennedy, for control of Congress, and the challenge was neither idle nor quixotic.

3 Government of Men

"Mister Speaker," said the Gentleman from Iowa, H. R. Gross, "I make the point of order that a quorum is not present." Manifestly, a quorum *was* present, as the House opened for business, that January 31. Few seats were empty. But even those few were too many when every vote would count. And a roll call would give time for a last check on wavering members, a last quick bit of pressure or persuasion in the shelter of the cloakroom.

"Mistah Speakah," replied the Democratic floor leader, John McCormack, in his ringing Boston Irish, "I move a call of the House."

The long roll call began; old-fashioned, as in so many matters, the House still relied upon a clerk to call each of 435 names and wait for an answer. Then the clerk would go through the roll again, calling the first-round absentees. But the shouts of "Here!" were not long in coming. Most members already were in their seats and latecomers were rushing to the chamber.

Few were in any doubt of the importance of the issue. And most knew that whatever claims would be put forward, whatever arguments would be made when the quorum call came to an end, not a single man who answered "Here" would be asked to vote to change the Committee's function, or to restrict its writ. That was not the point at all.

"On this roll call," announced Sam Rayburn in the turkey gobbler's voice that in his late years often approached incoherence, "four hundred and twenty-six members have answered their names, a quorum."

He laid before the House, and referred to the Committee on Banking and Currency, a message from the President transmitting the report of the Commodity Credit Corporation for the year ended June 30, 1960. Then, without a pause, Mr. Sam moved irrevocably into the battle that would preserve or break his reputation and authority, make or break the Kennedy Administration's legislative prospects, reputation and authority. He recognized the Gentleman from Arkansas, James Trimble, a Democratic member of the Committee on Rules who had been designated to control the time of debate.

"Mister Speaker, I call up House Resolution One-Twenty-seven and ask for its immediate consideration," Trimble said. The clerk read the resolution:

> Resolved: That during the Eighty-Seventh Congress the Committee on Rules shall be composed of fifteen members.

Among those who knew him and the political risks he took to support Rayburn and the Democratic party in the secret proceedings of the Committee on Rules, Trimble was one of the more admired members of the House. Soft-spoken, honest, as dependable as a grandfather clock, he was a man of the cloakroom and the executive session who obviously did not relish the prominent role that had been given him. But Jim Trimble was nothing if not loyal.

"This is one assignment I did not seek," he told the House, in his almost inaudible slurred Southern voice. "I have deep affection for all the parties involved in this controversy, and I have deep respect for the rules of the House. I am a Democrat. I have always fought my political battles in the battle-scarred uniform of the Democratic party, and I shall continue to do so.

"However, I have a firm belief in the position that with the majority rests the responsibility. If the Republican party were in the majority here today, and had the Speaker, and they were seeking some means of assuring the leadership leeway to conform to their responsibilities as the majority, I would vote with them on a similar resolution."

There was the issue—as nearly in a nutshell as a gentle, circuitous Southerner, on the political spot, could put it. This was no fight to reform the House or the Committee on Rules. It was a fight to take the Committee, its powers intact, away from Halleck and Smith and deliver it into the hands of John F. Kennedy and Sam Rayburn.

Power—who would have it, who would wield it?

It may seem strange that the question could even arise. How could a virtually anonymous Congressional committee, with no substantive responsibility to supplant its procedural powers, have precipitated such an issue? How could the Speaker of the House who had served longer than any other be so challenged in his own domain? How could a newly-elected President be in such danger, when he so recently had won the most powerful political office in the world?

It may also seem strange, once the showdown was certain, that there could have been any doubt about the outcome. The right of the President and the Speaker to take their program to the floor of the House appeared so overwhelming that one might almost have expected unanimous support for their position.

But none of these things was strange at all—not in a government of men. Offices are not powerful because they exist; men make them so. Rights are not honored because they exist; men compel their recognition. And men like Sam Rayburn and John Kennedy must struggle always, despite their offices and prerogatives, within the circumstances they and others have created.

Sam Rayburn was jealous of his place, like any effective leader. Still, few public figures were as misjudged as was this Texas bachelor so widely considered a muscular and merciless dictator of the Democratic majority of the House. The nation scarcely knew the Rayburn who confessed in rambling, maudlin speeches every two years—upon his biennial re-election as Speaker—that "this House has been my life; it has been my love."

Millions of Americans, rather, had gained their prime impression of Sam Rayburn not as Speaker but from his quadrennial radio and television performances as chairman of the Democratic National Convention. They saw a tough-looking little man, so bald his head appeared shaven like a stormtrooper's. They saw his menacing frown, his curt parliamentary commands. They saw or heard him unhesitatingly gavel through unpopular motions, declare nominations unanimous that were vociferously opposed. When he abandoned the gavel in 1960 to manage Lyndon Johnson's abortive effort for the Democratic Presidential nomination, millions more saw him grimace and snort like a wounded bull when Governor Leroy Collins of Florida—a very different type of convention chairman—hesitated to declare Johnson's nomination as Vice President unanimous over the catcalls of the Democratic left.

Older Americans could remember that it had been Sam Rayburn who had bluntly interrupted Harry Truman in 1945, when the latter first addressed Congress as President and forgot to wait for an introduction. Newspaper stories frequently referred to Rayburn's "iron control" of the House; they spoke of the old man as "tough," "rugged," "iron-willed"—and he could be all of those things. When President Eisenhower sent American troops into Lebanon in 1958, Sam Rayburn highhandedly gaveled the House into adjournment before a single dissident could rise to ask what the President thought he was doing.

But Mr. Sam was not a tough guy and never had been. An iron-willed Speaker with iron control of the House would not have tolerated the obstructionism of the Committee on Rules as long as he had. The hard-gaveling convention chairman of television renown—had he felt justified in being so autocratic as Speaker of the House—would have moved against Howard Smith long before January, 1961.

But Sam Rayburn never had sought to rule the House by power alone. Possessed of a Southerner's talent for maneuver and retreat, he preferred compromises to showdowns, friends to subordinates, and gladly took two steps forward, then one back, to avoid running over a colleague. He had given his heart to his life in the House, to his friends, his party. Sentimental, loyal, one of those men whose strength lies in his character rather than in his intellect, or his vision, he had shown himself most truly in his choked eulogy of his old friend, Alben Barkley: "God comfort his loved ones; God comfort me."

Always, Sam Rayburn had tried to *persuade* colleagues to follow his lead; he had avoided pressure tactics when he could. There was nothing strange about his close relationship with a similar man, Dwight Eisenhower. To countless freshmen members, he had advised that "the best way to get along is to go along," and he was no one-way giver of advice, unwilling to take it himself. Many an anguished member of the House had approached Mr. Sam in trepidation, confessed that some vote the Speaker wanted from him was just too difficult politically to cast—and found that beneath his gruff façade, the old Texan was a warm and understanding man.

While serving both in the House and as Speaker longer than any man in history, Rayburn had compiled an extensive file of due bills, the House's term for those political favors for which, at the proper time, a return favor would be expected. It was through the affection and respect in which he was held, the force of his character, the long experience that had given him wise knowledge of men's hearts, his Southerner's sensitivity to the feelings and rights of others, and his judicious calling-in of due bills that Sam Rayburn ran the House of Representatives.

Only such a man could have endured the kind of Committee on Rules that Judge Smith had built. Sam Rayburn, in fact, had for years given no impression that the restrictions the Committee placed on his leadership were even irritating. Insiders in the House knew that, on measures about which the Speaker had powerful personal feelings, Judge Smith rarely used his powers of obstruction. As for pet Rayburn peeves—the perennial resolution to televise House proceedings, for instance—the Judge could be relied upon to bury them as deeply as the Speaker wanted.

When the Committee on Rules did arouse the rare ire of the Speaker, he sometimes had been able to play a hole card—his long friendship with Representative Joseph W. Martin, the malapropian former Republican leader of the House. Martin seldom failed to come to the Speaker's rescue, when it was politically possible, partly from friendship, mostly because he wanted Rayburn to do the same for him in those unusual years when the Republicans won the House and elected a Speaker. It made sense to Joe Martin, too, that a man had better go along if he expected to get along.

But that was past history on January 31, 1961. Charlie Halleck, the Indiana "gut-fighter," had moved into Joe Martin's old office not far from the Capitol rotunda and, as the new Republican leader, he saw no virtue in going along with Democrats—save Southerners—on anything. When the outspoken Clarence Brown of Ohio, senior Republican on the Committee on Rules, rose to attack the Rayburn resolution in debate on January 31, the galleries knew he was speaking for Halleck and his party's leadership.

"This resolution was designed and introduced for one purpose and one purpose only," Brown growled, in a voice that seemed to spew gravel about the chamber, "To pack the Rules Committee so as to give either one individual or a limited few the power to completely control all its decisions and actions.

"It is exactly similar to the 1937 attempt of Franklin Delano Roosevelt to pack the Supreme Court so as to obtain the favorable decisions he desired."

With the superb aplomb of a carnival barker, the Gentleman from Ohio discussed the complicated rules of the House, insisting that the Committee on Rules really had no power, really was no problem to anyone.

"So actually," Brown concluded confidently, if with murky

logic, "it is only power which is being sought by this resolution
—power to prevent any individual member, as well as any
minority, from a vote, or free expression on legislative bills.
This is power no little group, no Speaker, no President should
seek. This is power no little group, no Speaker, no President
should have."

Brown was right that it was only power that was sought in
the Speaker's resolution and many non-Southern Democrats—
and some Southerners—wished Sam Rayburn had set himself
a higher goal than merely enlarging the Committee. But most
of them also considered it a minor miracle that the old man,
never one to start a fight, had gone as far as he had. It had
taken him, in fact, just two years to declare his war on
Howard Smith, to take a decision against the very grain of his
fifty years of going along and getting along in the House of
Representatives.

Two years before, Rayburn had declined any such action. A
group of liberal Democrats, flushed with their party's landslide
triumph in the Congressional elections of November, 1958,
awoke in the cold winter to the realization that in the coming
Eighty-Sixth Congress their majorities might be larger but the
Committee on Rules would be just the same, only worse. A
tractable Republican member of the Committee, Hugh Scott,
had been elected Senator from Pennsylvania; another, Henry
Latham of New York, had retired. The liberals could not fore-
see that Halleck was going to overthrow Joe Martin's leadership
and seize the reins himself, but they knew the likelihood was
that two dour rural-state conservatives would replace Scott and
Latham on the Committee on Rules,[3] and they went to Mr.
Sam with the problem.

The liberal group wanted to increase the size of the Committee to assure a liberal Democratic majority; they sought to
remove the Committee's power to block Senate-House conferences on bills already passed by both. These steps, they said,
were in the interests of the Northern-Western Democratic
majority in the House. Would the Speaker help?

The Speaker would not. No man was less ideological than he, and a power play like that proposed by the liberals repelled him in his inner nature. He wanted to sit down and talk with an opponent; there was no real instinct for the jugular in Sam Rayburn. Compromise, not principle, was his guiding star.

On January 3, 1959, just before the Eighty-Sixth Congress convened and he made his biennial declaration of undying love for the House, Rayburn conferred with a liberal Democratic leader, Representative Chet Holifield of California. Holifield and his friends, the Speaker said, should make use of various obscure House rules to get around Judge Smith. If that didn't suffice, he might help them do something substantial about the Committee later in the session. For the moment, all he would promise was to use his good offices with Judge Smith to get legislation to the floor.

No one ever accused the old man of failing to try to keep that promise—or any other. By May, 8, 1959, United Press International reported that the Speaker had threatened to "bypass" the Committee on Rules unless it cleared a $2.1 billion housing bill "pretty soon." On January 28, 1960, soon after the second session of the Eighty-Sixth Congress opened, *The New York Times* reported that Judge Smith had called a committee meeting only "to forestall the possible success of a pending [discharge] petition to get the civil rights bill out of his committee." Ultimately, in the latter case, the Judge responded to what was really a *fait accompli*—a discharge petition lacking only a few needed signatures. Rather than have the civil rights bill so rudely wrested from his grasp, he sent it reluctantly to the House floor, where it was passed.

But this was an awkward way for the liberals to have to proceed. And despite such occasional successes, by the time the crucial summer of 1960 and the national nominating conventions rolled around, it was clear to all—except, apparently, Sam Rayburn—that he could not deliver legislation to the floor as he had promised the liberals in January, 1959. With Democrats anxious to be off to Los Angeles for their convention on July

11, the Committee on Rules still was "considering" three politically vital bills—federal aid to education, an increase in the minimum wage with Senator John F. Kennedy's name on it, and another housing measure. The school bill actually had been approved by both House and Senate, the first time in American history that both had so voted, but the Committee was refusing to permit a conference to iron out minor differences, thus imposing its will on both houses.

The Committee even bottled up for a time the Kerr-Mills bill, a conservative proposal to provide medical care for the aged through Federal-State grants. Judge Smith feared that the Senate eventually would substitute for it the controversial Social Security financing plan. Among minor bills—important, however, to numbers of Representatives—frozen in the Committee were measures to assist educational television, provide federal aid for community library services, and increase the pay and retirement scales of foreign service officers.

Earlier in 1960, members of both parties had had to go the tortuous route Rayburn had recommended—another discharge petition—to get out of the Committee a bill to increase Federal pay scales. And liberal Democrats had resorted to the rarely used Calendar Wednesday procedure to pass a depressed areas bill, which was promptly vetoed by Eisenhower.

Irate political pressure built up around the imperturbable Committee and its laconic chairman. Members anxious to get to California or Chicago for the conventions, Democratic leaders striving to create a legislative record to support their future nominees, lobby groups like the National Education Association and organized labor, even Vice President Nixon, exerted all their force to get action on one or another of the pending bills. Nixon was working hard behind the scenes to produce just one Republican vote for the school bill from among the four members of his party on the Committee. They all knew he was to be the Republican Presidential candidate but they would not give him the one vote that would have broken the deadlock in favor of the bill—the one vote that would have handed him much credit for its enactment, and stolen a campaign issue from the Democrats.

Nor could Sam Rayburn budge the Committee. On June 29, he conferred with Judge Smith as one potentate with another. The Judge's response was quick and emphatic. The Committee on Rules voted that day on the housing bill and set it aside on the usual six-to-six tie vote. The Committee also refused to reverse its earlier ban on letting the school bill go to a Senate-House conference. It relented just enough to send the minimum wage bill to the House floor, and the press gave Rayburn credit for squeezing that much out of Judge Smith. But angry Democratic liberals knew that the Judge had voted to clear the wage bill as part of a deal. In return, he had exacted a pledge from Representative James Roosevelt of California that the Education and Labor Committee would drop for the rest of the year a labor-supported bill that would have permitted construction workers to picket an entire building site.

Resentment against the conservative coalition so powerfully in control of the Committee was rising and spreading as Congress left Washington for the national political conventions, but the evidence of that resentment was plain only to those who knew how to sniff the airs blowing through the Capitol.

The library services bill and the pay raise for foreign service officers, for instance, had been taken from the Committee on Rules and passed by "suspension of the rules," a procedure requiring *a two-thirds majority* of the House in each instance. In these cases, the Committee clearly had overstepped itself and the House had revolted.

Representative Gerald Flynn of Missouri—to give another sample of the Congressional atmosphere—had attacked the Committee in a radio speech for "stifling the forward-looking, progressive legislation." The Olympian Judge Smith had taken the unusual step of replying publicly to this brash freshman member, ordinarily a man beneath his notice. Perhaps the Judge had been made nervous when the House only narrowly passed (by 182 to 167) a bill to pay the moving costs of Virginians being displaced by Washington's grandiose new Dulles International Airport; they were all Judge Smith's constituents and it was the sort of bill a senior member of the House usually whips through on a quick voice vote, without a word of dissent, almost as a personal privilege.

More importantly, Holifield's liberal group had begun to stir again. Representative Frank Thompson of New Jersey, Richard Bolling of Missouri, John Blatnik of Michigan, Stewart Udall of Arizona—all were convinced that a drastic check had to be put upon the power of Howard Smith. They gave Speaker Rayburn credit for trying but none believed any longer that even his best efforts could sway the Committee on Rules when it did not want to be swayed.

Rayburn kept his own counsel. Some who knew him were not hopeful. On July 10, the day before his party's convention opened in Los Angeles, the Speaker left Washington late in the day, hopeful that Lyndon Johnson would "stop Kennedy" and become the Democratic Presidential nominee. For a few minutes, just before his departure, I talked to him in his quiet office, hoping to be able to write about his intentions regarding the Committee on Rules. He would say nothing for publication but talked somewhat wearily for my ears alone.

He chose first, with scrupulous fairness, and in almost academic detail, to point out that the Committee on Rules *could* be bypassed. There was, for instance, suspension of the rules.

Under this procedure, the House gets an opportunity to vote but under conditions requiring a two-thirds majority for passage of the measure, a practical impossibility on all but innocuous measures.

Two other possible routes past the Committee on Rules in 1960 were equally difficult, as Rayburn outlined them. One was a discharge petition: if an absolute majority of the House signed a petition demanding that a certain measure be brought to the floor, the Committee was discharged of further jurisdiction. But such a majority was hard to get on any controversial measure, and a discharge petition usually was opposed by powerful senior members, careful of the prerogatives of other committees in Congress, and of their elder colleagues.

The third possibility was quaintly referred to as Calendar Wednesday—special days, two of which were set aside each month, when chairmen of legislative committees might call for a House vote on bills being held by the Committee on Rules. But each chairman had to take his alphabetical turn (by title of his committee) and might get only a few Calendar Wednesday chances in a session. Worse, a bill called up in this fashion had to be debated and voted upon on the same day, making it vulnerable to parliamentary delaying tactics, of which House veterans like Judge Smith had an impressive repertoire.

A fourth alternative had been tried, and found wanting, in 1949 and 1950, after the Republican-controlled Committee on Rules of the Eightieth Congress had applied a sledge-hammer to much of President Truman's program—blocking Universal Military Training, a labor bill, amendments to the Social Security Act, and a civil rights bill. This experiment allowed a chairman of a legislative committee the right to call for a House vote on a measure approved by his committee, if it had been held by the Committee on Rules for twenty-one days or more. Under that rule, eight major bills were wrested from the Committee's death grip and passed by the House in the Eighty-First Congress.

Nevertheless, the twenty-one-day rule was resoundingly defeated, 247 to 179, when supporters sought to impose it on the Eighty-Second Congress in 1951. Members of the House had become disenchanted with it when they realized that the rule diminished the Committee's ability to protect them from having to stand up and be counted on controversial measures.

The death of the rule cut away, for a moment, much cant and pretense, and gave a flash of insight into government of men. For if few members liked the autocracy of the Committee on Rules better than other members, a half-century earlier, had liked the dictatorship of Uncle Joe Cannon, even fewer wanted to be exposed to the popular pressures of the House and the populace without the shield the Committee could raise between them and the people they represented. Few members wanted any part of more democracy in the House. It could be too embarrassing, and too dangerous.

The death of the twenty-one-day rule in 1951 disclosed something about Sam Rayburn, too. He had lifted not a finger to save it; quite the contrary. Rayburn disliked having the Committee block measures that he supported but he disliked even more the idea of having committee chairmen, supported by the House, being empowered to call for a vote on bills that he did *not* want to come to the floor. It was better to have his power restricted than to hand it over to someone else.[4]

Having lovingly explained the rules to me, that summer afternoon, Mr. Sam turned, without rancor, to the subject of Howard Smith.

"Just before we recessed," he said, "he came around and wanted to know if there was anything I wanted him to do that he could do." The Speaker chuckled, appreciating the humor of the offer without deriding it. "I've always gotten along with Howard Smith," he said.

I suggested that a growing number of Representatives did not feel so kindly toward the Gentleman from Virginia. Many wished to curb his powers and those of his Committee. Did the Speaker feel that way? Would he help do the job?

Rayburn's lips pursed. His hands touched. He leaned back in his chair, looked at the ornate ceiling of his office.

"The boys are serious this time," he said. There was a moment's silence. "Of course, they won't get anywhere."

They would not get anywhere, I understood, because Sam Rayburn would not help them get anywhere.

But in the abortive post-convention session of August, 1960, the rebellious liberals found even more cause for anger. "The only legislation I will consider," Judge Smith, true to his pact with Jimmy Roosevelt, told his Committee, "is the minimum wage bill. If you try to bring up anything else, I'll adjourn the meeting."

The Committee on Rules did clear the minimum wage bill for House-Senate conference; but although both houses had enacted a bill, not even Senator Kennedy, the Democratic Presidential candidate, could work out a conference version on which both could agree. Already, the Senate had narrowly defeated Kennedy's proposal to substitute the Social Security medical care plan for the Kerr-Mills bill, in part because Judge Smith had made it plain he would not permit a conference to reconcile a House-passed Kerr-Mills bill and a Senate-passed Social Security bill.

There was the record. Minimum wage—dead in conference, after being bargained out of the Committee on Rules. Medical care—dead in the Senate, under the shadow of the Committee on Rules. Depressed areas—dead by Eisenhower's veto, after being torn out of the Committee on Rules by the difficult Calendar Wednesday procedure. School construction—dead in the Committee on Rules. Housing—dead in the Committee on Rules. Obviously, even if Kennedy replaced Eisenhower in the White House, a major obstacle to all this unpassed liberal legislation would still remain untouched.

On August 26, as the Eighty-Sixth Congress passed into history, one by one, Representatives arose in the House to assail the clear and unmistakable enemy of their causes. They were liberals, members of the active Democratic Study Group. By and large, they were enthusiastic supporters of Kennedy for President, and they knew that the prime legislative issues of his first years in office would be precisely those upon which the hand of the Committee on Rules had fallen most heavily in 1960. They were vigorous men with blood in their eyes. But they were not of the hierarchy of the House—liberals almost never are—and the central question remained.

What did Sam Rayburn think now? Would he go along, as he had been unwilling to do in 1959? Without him and his great prestige, it would be useless to attack the Committee on Rules; even with him, it would be difficult enough to bring along the powerful elders of the House. The adamant stand Judge Smith had taken in the August session was against what was generally regarded as his party's best interest. Rayburn was a Democrat, first and last; the Judge's affronts to him might be accepted, but could the Speaker put up with what he was bound to regard as a betrayal of his party and its candidates?

He could not; his tolerance of Howard Smith had turned to outrage—but it was to be months before that was known. In the excitement of the Presidential campaign, few thought of such a mundane matter as the Committee on Rules. Nixon mentioned it once, at Richmond on October 4—"as a member of the House I opposed curtailment, and I'm against it now." The Democratic platform called for a change, but Kennedy did not raise such a dull issue; the Democratic candidate was talking about other things more interesting to a public largely ignorant of Congressional procedure and of the men who controlled it.

Then, suddenly, after the closest election of the century, Kennedy was the President-elect. To a far greater degree than it had when he was a Senator frequently frustrated by its powers, the Committee on Rules would affect the course of what he wanted to do. Did he favor a change to give Rayburn —and thus himself—more certain control of the House? That, Kennedy said at Hyannis Port on November 10, was "a matter of judgment for the House."

Kennedy was only exercising a President's time-honored deference to the Constitutional independence of the legislative branch. In fact, he was not only in favor of a change; he was insisting on it. If anything were needed in addition to the August outrages to prod a party regular like Sam Rayburn into action, it was the expressed need of a Democratic President. From the moment of the election of John F. Kennedy, the battle between Mr. Sam and the Judge was inevitable. One or the other might rule the House, but not both.

4 'No Purgin' No Packin''

Howard Worth Smith ambled down the aisle toward the well of the House. He was slightly stooped from his seventy-seven years but not at all from submission to the North, the liberals, the Speaker, the New and Fair Deals, the New Frontier, the young upstarts in the party of his fathers, or the twentieth century. His patrician hands, shuffling the pages of a speech, seemed nervous without his customary long cigar. He peered almost benignly over the spectacles, slipping down his nose, that made him look not unlike Andy Clyde, the old comedy star. The faintly antebellum air that clung to him was a reminder that until World War II interrupted his source of supply, the Judge had habitually worn wing collars.

Able, shrewd, ruthless, a master parliamentarian, a witty but somewhat aloof man in private, the Judge had earned his title by early service on the Sixteenth Circuit bench in Virginia. In the House, after service since 1931, he had earned a different quality of respect from that universally accorded Sam Rayburn. The Gentlemen of the House loved and respected Rayburn and coveted his favor; they feared and respected Smith and deferred to his power.

His years as chairman of the Committee on Rules had disclosed to the full the Virginian's qualities of strength, wit, ruthlessness, the innate conservatism that put him fundamentally out of step with a world of big business, big unions, big government and big plans. His words on a given matter were apt to be final.

Washington's Fine Arts Commission once accepted and submitted to Congress a plan for a Theodore Roosevelt Monument on Theodore Roosevelt Island in the Potomac River, just off the foot of Constitution Avenue. The proposed monument was, putting it mildly, of contemporary design, and the artist's abstract conception—a number of interlocking rings, not unlike a gyroscope—was, at least, puzzling.

The plan, like almost everything else in Congress, eventually came before Judge Smith's Committee on Rules. Would the Committee permit the House to vote on whether the monument should be erected on the island? Committee members puzzled at length over the design, the explanations of its symbolism, the sponsors' protestations that it was truly in the free spirit of T.R. and of the undeveloped island where it was to be erected. From one member after another, understanding neither the work nor art, came expressions of bewilderment and dismay. Still, they hesitated; they were not sure; the final consensus had not been reached—until Howard Smith spoke the mind of the Philistine:

"If we're going to have a monument to Theodore Roosevelt," he said, "why can't we just have a statue of a man carrying a big stick?"

The sponsors knew for whom the bell had tolled. They folded their design and slipped away. No more has been heard of the gyroscopic monument and the government now has built a mammoth bridge across Theodore Roosevelt Island to Judge Smith's Virginia. The island now is adorned with a monumental, thirty-foot-high, stone and bronze replica of T.R.; only the big stick is missing from the Judge's vision.

The Judge was regarded in the House as a fighter, and if he was not so boastful about it as Charlie Halleck was, he did not conceal it either: "I am a conservative and I have been scrambling and scratching around here for thirty-two years now and I have always found that when you are doing that, you grasp any snickersnee you can get hold of and fight the best way you can."

When events allowed, Judge Smith was subtler than that. The Gentleman from Kansas, William H. Avery, a member of the Committee on Rules, told admiringly how Smith as a presiding officer firmly cut short long-winded meetings with a device

> . . . very mildly reflecting his concern, by dangling the gavel over the block and permitting it to slightly bounce without actually bringing it down to a conclusive crack. . . . The Committee members have all learned to recognize the tapping sound as a signal to conclude the questioning just as soon as possible.

What's more, Avery said, the virtuoso chairman could get the same effect just tapping on an ashtray with the pipe he occasionally smoked. But another member of the Committee was less impressed. "You have to respect the Judge and I always say nice things about him in public," he confided, but "the truth is he's a hard, mean old man."

Certainly on the subject of the Committee on Rules, Judge Smith was unyielding. Asked his opinion of the theory that the Committee should be a "traffic cop," sending bills to the House floor in orderly fashion, he replied shortly: "My people didn't send me to Congress to be a traffic cop." Once, after sending a housing bill he opposed to the floor under conditions that virtually guaranteed its defeat, he conceded with some pride that his Committee had dictated "probably the most drastic gag rule that I have seen presented in my time here in the House."

Again, while stalling a civil rights bill, Judge Smith had disappeared from the Capitol entirely, leaving his Committee without the power to call itself to order, much less take action. Some days later, intelligence drifted across the Potomac from

Virginia that a barn on one of Judge Smith's dairy farms had burned and that he was on the scene, inspecting the damage.

"I knew Howard Smith would do most anything to block a civil rights bill," said Mr. Sam, in a rare witticism, "but I never suspected he would resort to arson."

The Speaker's amiability did not affect Judge Smith when Mr. Sam approached him about making a change in the Committee's makeup. He threw down the gauntlet. "No purgin'," he said in the soft, deceptive tones of Virginia, "no packin'."

Knowing all of this, the Gentlemen of the House settled back attentively as Smith adjusted the lectern, shuffled his papers, almost inaudibly put his preliminary remarks behind him. There was no quarrel, he said, between himself and the Speaker; if there was it was on Rayburn's side. And he would repeat a pledge he had made when he first became chairman of the Rules Committee.

"That is, I will cooperate with the Democratic leadership of the House of Representatives, just as long and just as far as my conscience will permit me."

The House broke into laughter—and not all on the Democratic side. The qualification of conscience, most members believed, would not permit Judge Smith to go far in cooperation with Kennedy and Rayburn. But as the laughter died, the character of the quiet, dignified man in the well of the House came clear.

"Some of these gentlemen who are laughing maybe do not understand what a conscience is," Smith said. "They are entitled to that code and I think I am entitled to mine."

Quiet settled on the House. Few doubted Judge Smith's sincerity, any more than they doubted Rayburn's. The House knew the Virginian for many things, but not for perfidy. Sam Rayburn had conceded many times that Howard Smith kept his word. The only thing you had to watch, the Speaker confided to colleagues, was the Judge's genius for legalisms and loopholes that would give him an honest "out."

In his quiet, almost disinterested voice, Judge Smith gave

the House his reasons for opposing Rayburn's plan to "pack"
—his term—the Committee on Rules. The Committee had
killed only ten per cent of bills coming before it, he said;
legislative committees killed about ninety per cent of the
fifteen-thousand-odd bills introduced in the House in any one
Congress. His proposals for compromise had been refused,
but h~ renewed them anyway.

"One other thing," Smith said. "There has been some talk
about my going out and milking cows once or twice." This
was a reference to his famous device of secluding himself on
one of his Virginia dairy farms, leaving his Committee unable to call itself to order. "Well, I will make this statement,
that so far as I am concerned there will not be any delay,
any undue delay on any call that the leadership makes to
hold hearings in the Committee on Rules." It was a promise
not to do precisely what Smith and the Committee always had
done. Of course, if the committee was expanded, Smith continued gently, in the tones of a man tried beyond endurance,
"I make no commitments."

Why not wait, he asked reasonably, suavely, until the Committee "did something that the House thought it should not
do" in this Congress before penalizing it for what it might have
done in the last? What did those who insisted on expansion
really want? "Is it an effort merely to humiliate one chairman
of one committee in this House? Well, if it is, nobody can
humiliate me except the people who have elected me to Congress sixteen consecutive times."[5]

And then Judge Smith stated the issue as no one doubted he
saw it:

> When I am asked to pledge aid to the passage of any re-
> solution or bill in this House that I am conscientiously op-
> posed to, I would not yield my conscience and my right to
> vote in this House to any person or any member or under
> any conditions . . . if there is any other member here who
> thinks he ought to yield his conscience and the views of his

constituency to the will of somebody who is not a member
of that committee, then he ought to vote the other way.

It had been a simple and effective speech and a sincere one.
In many ways, despite his conservative views on twentieth-
century legislation, Howard Smith represented the best of Congress—honor, dedication, great ability in the related crafts of
legislation and politics, and a sound knowledge of the weaknesses and strengths of men.

But the matter had gone too far. No personal sincerity and
certainly no blandishments from Howard Smith could avoid the
showdown that had become inevitable when Kennedy emerged
the winner from the breathtaking 1960 election.

In that campaign, a number of Southern "Democrats" had
bolted the Kennedy-Johnson ticket and worked for Nixon or
for unpledged electors—that favorite pipedream of dissident
Dixiecrats longing for 1876 all over again. Prominent among
them were Otto Passman of Louisiana, then the keeper of the
key to the foreign aid cash drawer, and a quartet from Mississippi—Jamie Whitten, John Bell Williams,[6] Arthur Winstead and William Colmer. The last of these was the second-
ranking Democrat on the Committee on Rules, Judge Smith's
spear-carrier in the coalition with the four Republican members.

On November 13, five days after the election, obviously
"planted" newspaper stories suggested that the "Democratic
leadership" was considering a purge of Colmer from the Committee and his replacement with a liberal—both as punishment
for bolting and as a means of giving Rayburn control of the
Committee on Rules. The liberals were at work. Two days later,
the risible Williams fired back. Purge Colmer, he said, and
Southern Democrats would vote with Republicans to organize
the House. But, he said, if the Committee on Rules was merely
expanded, the Southerners could learn to live with that situation.

John Bell Williams was by no means a power in the House

or even among Southern Democrats—extremists seldom are. Still, he had outlined what eventually came to be Rayburn's course, and suggested the Speaker's motivation. No proposals but "purgin' or packin'" ever were considered seriously by Rayburn and his supporters.

On December 20, when the President-elect met at Palm Beach with Rayburn, Johnson and Mike Mansfield, the Senator from Montana who would be the new Majority Leader, the Speaker assured Kennedy that he would win control of the Committee. He did not say how and Kennedy did not ask. He believed the Speaker—that mythical dictator of the House—capable of handling the matter unaided.

To reporters, Rayburn gave no hint of his position. He denied, *pro forma,* that the Committee on Rules even had been discussed. That, he said, was "utterly" a problem for the House and J.F.K had taken a "wise position" at Hyannis Port when he refused to involve himself in it.

The handwriting on the wall nevertheless was plain to the experienced reporters trailing the President-elect. For, in a news conference, the four leaders announced the following top-priority legislative program for the first session of the Eighty-Seventh Congress:

1. An increase in the minimum wage.
2. Federal aid to schools and colleges.
3. Area redevelopment.
4. Housing.
5. Medical care for the aged through the Social Security system.

One needed to remember no farther back than the previous August to divine how the Committee on Rules would deal with these familiar proposals. It surprised no one, therefore, that on Christmas Day, *The New York Times* reported that "Democratic leaders" planned an early showdown on the Committee issue. Rayburn had "told colleagues" that he would lead a fight to expand the Committee. A purge was unlikely, however, and the Speaker was unalterably opposed to restoring the twenty-one-day rule.

That made sense to old Rayburn watchers. Expanding the Committee would not attack the hallowed seniority system. It would not make obvious examples of the party bolters, or—so he said—wound the delicate nerve tissues of prancing Confederates like Williams. It offered little danger of turning Southern Democrats into official Republicans. If a man like Sam Rayburn were to act at all against Smith and his Committee, expansion seemed eminently suited to his softshoe tactics.

There was one catch—a big one. Expanding the Committee from eight Democrats and four Republicans to ten Democrats and five Republicans would require a change in the standing rules of the House. That could be got through the Committee on Rules by instructions from a Democratic caucus, which Rayburn would control, to party members on the Committee. But it would give Charlie Halleck and the Republicans, if they chose, an opportunity to enter the battle on the House floor and to join hands in the familiar coalition with Judge Smith and the Southern Democrats against a rules change. It would give the coalition a final chance to prevail.

In a two-hour conference with Smith on New Year's Day, 1961, Rayburn learned that the Virginian would agree to no change at all—"no purgin', no packin'." On January 2, Rayburn confided to the liberals what seemed the most surprising decision of his career—he was going to purge Bill Colmer from the Committee on Rules and replace him with a more accommodating Democrat.

News of that magnitude is not long in filtering down to the Washington press; when this item became known, Washington's New Year hangovers faded into general consternation. Not since the Senate had refused to seat Theodore Bilbo of Mississippi had anyone flown so cavalierly in the face of the South, the seniority system or the laissez-faire of American party discipline.

But Rayburn's strategy was typical of the man. By threatening to purge Colmer—an action he had the votes to push through a Democratic caucus, if he insisted—he planned to force some of the Southern Democrats to sue for peace. They would not, he reasoned, hold still for a purge that would threaten the South's Congressional stronghold, when a compromise was available. Once enough Southerners came to this view, the Speaker could demand Judge Smith's acquiescence in the expansion plan, his original goal. With his forces divided, the Judge would have little choice but to assent.

It well may be asked why, if the threat of a purge was as powerful as all that, Rayburn did not plan to go through with the purge itself. John Bell Williams' bluster was patently empty —and echoed by few other Southerners. Few of them wanted to desert their party formally and finally, sacrificing their Congressional and other seniority, and move into Halleck's Republican ranks. No one loves an apostate. Besides, in 1961, the South still was too solidly Democratic in local and district elections for most members to risk a Republican label.

It was known, moreover, that a number of Southerners who had taken large political risks to support the Catholic, supposedly liberal Kennedy, would shed no tears if Williams, Colmer and others who had deserted him were punished. The purge would be a strong and perhaps needed stroke of party discipline. And though senior members of Rayburn's party, like the cadaverous Clarence Cannon of Missouri, were outraged by the idea of purge as a threat to the seniority system and their own domination of the House, in any showdown between the Speaker and Howard Smith, most would be forced to choose Rayburn, Kennedy and party regularity.

The truth is that Rayburn was one of these seniors—one of them in spirit as well as in age. He did not want to purge anyone or question seniority or shake the system and would not if there was an acceptable alternative. At the crucial moment, he was not ruthless enough to push ahead upon the hard path of discipline and power; as always, he sought an easier way.

For nearly a week, turning these events over in his mind,

Judge Smith made no move; a good general shifts ground only when there is something to be gained by it. Then he countered probingly. He visited the Speaker in the corner office on the Principal Floor and outlined his own compromise. He would support a resolution that would change the rules to eliminate the Committee on Rules' power to block a conference between Senate and House on bills approved by both. And he would give Rayburn a guarantee to send to the floor the five major bills Kennedy and his Congressional leaders had called for at the Palm Beach meeting. This was not good enough and Rayburn rejected it in some anger.

"Shit!" he burst out to an aide. "The President may want forty bills!"

But the meeting gave Rayburn an opportunity to pursue his strategy; he again suggested expansion of the Committee as an alternative to the purge. Judge Smith could hardly mistake the message. Mr. Sam also increased the pressure on the Judge; not only Colmer was going to be purged, he said, but Williams, Winstead, Whitten and Passman would lose their committee posts, too.

If Judge Smith would not take the bludgeon-like hint the Speaker had dropped, there were other Southerners who would —for instance, the influential Gentleman from Georgia, Carl Vinson, then the second most senior man in the House but second to none in prestige and to few in power. From his long experience of Sam Rayburn, he knew what the Speaker really wanted. And neither he nor any of the other senior Democrats in the House—men like Cannon and Representative Francis E. "Tad" Walter of Pennsylvania—wanted to see a purge shake the foundations of the seniority system that had brought them to power. Among the Southerners, Vinson knew, there was sizable sentiment for compromise rather than for a showdown they were sure to lose.

On January 10, Vinson called a secret caucus of influential Southerners. The purge could be halted only by compromise, he said; and the only possible compromise was Rayburn's earlier plan to expand the committee. With Howard Smith speaking out adamantly in opposition, the Southerners came to an agreement that compromise was necessary.

Rayburn's strategy had worked, it seemed. On January 11, the delighted Speaker called a special news conference to announce that, after all, he had chosen "the painless way and the way to embarrass nobody if they didn't want to be embarrassed." In fact, he had chosen the way that came nearest to embarrassing him.

For although Vinson was believed able to sway enough of Judge Smith's Southern troops to assure passage of the expansion compromise, the inescapable fact was that Sam Rayburn's lifelong search for accommodation had led him to seek a rules change rather than an intraparty disciplinary move. In a rules-change vote on the floor of the House, Halleck and Smith could combine Republican and Southern Democratic forces. Instead of a vote in the Democratic caucus that Rayburn could not lose, he was going to have to face a vote on the floor that he might not win. The old Texas compromiser, ready as ever to avert a fight, had compromised himself into the hardest battle of his career, and in the process, he had put Kennedy's chances for legislative success squarely on the line. And more than that, although it could not be realized until the closeness of the battle became apparent, the prestige and power and prospects of a new President were going to be put at stake almost before he could move into his office.

Rayburn moved swiftly to consolidate what he thought was his position. He called a Democratic caucus for January 18 and announced that for the first time since 1949 it would be a "binding party caucus." This device had been common in Woodrow Wilson's day but had fallen into disuse. At a "binding caucus," if two-thirds of the party voted to support a given proposition, then all members would be obliged to vote for that proposition on the House floor. Those who refused, it was explained by Walter, the leader of the Democratic caucus, would lose their seniority and committee assignments. The explanation was necessary, for many younger Democrats had never heard of the procedure.

Obviously, if Rayburn could win a two-thirds vote in caucus, and thus force a unanimous Democratic vote on the floor, there would be no way for Judge Smith and the Southerners to coalesce with Charlie Halleck unless they bolted the Democratic party for good. Watching and waiting, Halleck and his Republican leaders met on January 13 and took no position on the rules fight.

But Rayburn's strategy now depended upon Vinson's being able to deliver enough Southerners at the caucus to assure a two-thirds vote in favor of expanding the Committee, so that the party could be forced to a unanimous stand on the floor. Doubts began to develop at once as to whether Vinson could do it. On January 15, John McCormack expressed pessimism; in the circumstances, that was a damaging hint. Behind the scenes, Vinson himself, Walter, Cannon and other seniors soon were urging moderation on Sam Rayburn. They had found unexpected opposition. A number of Democrats, they told the Speaker, "resented" being bound by a caucus vote. Actually, they said, a bigger vote in support of the expansion plan might be won without the binding provision, because some members who would support Rayburn on the Committee issue still would not vote to "bind" themselves or anyone else. Even Judge Smith, without the coercion of being bound by a caucus, might look more kindly on the expansion plan—or so it was argued. Besides, his trusted advisers told Rayburn, they believed as many as forty Republicans ultimately would vote with him on the floor. He would not really need a unanimous Democratic vote to change the rules.

What was happening, in hindsight, is not hard to discover. Hardshell Southern conservatives had been quick to perceive that, in an open vote on the House floor, they might yet, in alliance with Halleck, retain control of the Committee on Rules. Conservative lobbyists from the United States Chamber of Commerce, the American Farm Bureau Federation, the

National Association of Manufacturers and the American Medical Association were at work, pointing to the latent power of the coalition to defeat a rules change that they said would "open the floodgates" to liberal legislation. And in the South, strident newspapers were creating a false picture of the Committee on Rules as the last barrier against Communistic civil rights legislation. In fact, the Committee rarely had blocked a civil rights bill since filibustering Southern Senators had a better opportunity to do that. But the idea in the South that the struggle to purge Colmer or expand the Committee was really a civil rights fight was one of the major reasons the issue developed into a bitter collision on the floor of the House. That idea made compromise difficult even for those Southerners—and there were many—who agreed in their hearts with Sam Rayburn's effort to win control of the Committee on Rules.

One day before the "binding caucus," unsure of the two-thirds vote that in any case he no longer seemed to need, Rayburn announced that the binding plan would be dropped. He would seek endorsement of the Committee expansion, but Democrats would be free to vote their consciences on the House floor. It will never be known whether he could have won the two-thirds vote at a "binding caucus," but the point is that Sam Rayburn *should have known—and before he announced that such a caucus would be held*. Rather than a hard-and-fast headcount, he had accepted the loose assurances of Carl Vinson, and his own wishful thinking. With great interests at stake, that kind of battle intelligence is not enough. So when Rayburn announced one course of procedure, then backed away from it, he advertised to the House of Representatives and to Howard Smith the sudden weakness of his own position; and they got the message.

One more ingredient was needed in the brew of trouble Mr. Sam had boiled for himself, and on January 19, Charlie Halleck supplied it. He and the thirty-three other members of the House Republican Policy Committee voted unanimously to oppose the Rayburn resolution to expand the Committee on

Rules. Representative John Byrnes of Wisconsin, chairman of the policy committee, compared the resolution to Roosevelt's effort to "pack" the Supreme Court. "Republicans," Byrnes pledged, "will always fight to preserve the integrity of the Congress."

That was just one day before John F. Kennedy became the thirty-fifth President of the United States.

5 *Headcount*

It was no secret in Washington that the pugnacious Halleck had worked like a beaver to defeat Rayburn. There was even one report that he had physically "shaken up" the Gentleman from Nebraska, Glenn Cunningham; but publicly, Halleck had remained quiet, and as he arose from his seat on the day of the debate and strode grimly down the aisle to make the closing argument for the opponents of the Rayburn resolution, there was a stir of surprise in the galleries. It had been thought that Halleck, as a potential Speaker himself, would not argue openly against giving the present Speaker control of the Committee on Rules.

But Charlie Halleck, whatever his other qualities, was not a man to conceal his position on anything. The resolution, he bawled with customary bellicosity, was "unwise, unjustified, untimely, unnecessary and, therefore, unsupportable." He had had an "avalanche of mail, most of it handwritten . . . from the people of this country, right-thinking people by the millions" and he was "convinced they are afraid that this effort signals a collapse . . . they are afraid the floodgates will be let down and we will be overwhelmed with bad legislation."

Halleck wound up to a burst of applause from the Republican side of the chamber. The House stilled expectantly.

"Mister Speaker," Trimble said, "I yield the balance of the time on this side to the Gentleman from Texas."

There was another ovation as Sam Rayburn handed his gavel to the Representative from Oklahoma, Carl Albert. Then the old man, ramrod-straight, came down from the rostrum into the well of the House—a place he seldom visited except to acknowledge his biennial election as Speaker.

The issue, Rayburn said in his gobbler's voice, was a simple one. "We have elected to the Presidency a new leader. He is going to have a program that he thinks will be in the interest of and for the benefit of the American people.

"I think he demonstrated on yesterday (in the State of the Union Message) that we are neither in good shape domestically or in the foreign field. He wants to do something about that . . ."

The President would have many proposals, Rayburn told the quiet House, "and after the legislative committees hold hearings, after executive session, when every 'i' is dotted and every 't' is crossed, and when the chairman comes to the Committee on Rules—and I do not say Rules Committee, because that is not the proper designation; it is the Committee on Rules—comes to the leadership of the House and wants a rule after all of that consideration, I think that the Committee on Rules should grant that rule whether its membership is for the bill or not. I think this House should be allowed on great measures to work its will, and it cannot work its will if the Committee on Rules is so constituted as not to allow the House to pass on these things."

What was more, he continued—with some asperity—neither "the Gentleman from Virginia nor any other member of this House can accuse me of ever packing any committee for or against anything." But if there was going to be talk about packing, why, "away back in 1933 we had a tremendous contest in this House. One side won. They put up a man for membership on the Committee on Rules; our side put up their man, and we at that time packed the Committee on Rules with the Gentleman from Virginia!"

It was an audacious and effective thrust. I'd never pack a committee, Rayburn had claimed—but the last time I packed one, I packed it with Howard Smith! The House rocked with laughter, while Judge Smith sat quietly. But the laughter died quickly, without breaking the tension. The moment of decision was fast approaching—a laughing matter to no one in that House.

Mr. Sam's head was high. He knew the House was listening. He had resisted all Smith's threats and blandishments and stratagems, all Halleck's bluster. Just before entering the chamber that day, he had confessed to an aide that he did not know whether he had the votes to win. But he had tried hard, risked old friendships, suffered much, in serving his party and his President as well as he knew—and now the last word, at least, was his.

"Let us move this program," the old Speaker told the hushed House. "Let us be sure that we can move it. And the only way that we can be sure that this program will move when great committees report bills, the only way it can move, in my opinion, my beloved colleagues, is to adopt this resolution today."

And all time having expired, the call of the House was ordered.

Abbitt . . . Abernathy . . . Adair . . . Addabo . . . Addonizio . . . Albert . . . three consecutive nays, three consecutive ayes. The first six names were symbolic of the close vote that everyone knew was to follow. Then came six straight votes for Halleck and Smith—but that was an accident of the alphabet. As the tally clerk settled into a steady drone of names, it was apparent that the House was dividing almost exactly in half.

That was appropriate to the times and the situation. Kennedy's popular margin of 113,057 had been the smallest in seventy-two years; he had carried only twenty-four states to Nixon's twenty-six. While winning the Presidency, his party had lost two seats in the Senate, twenty-two in the House. It had elected fifteen governors to twelve for the Republicans.

And though the Democrats commanded handsome paper margins in House and Senate, inevitable defections of Southerners and other conservatives sharply reduced the party's expectations in Congress. In short, the House was not much closer on the issue of expanding the Committee on Rules than the country was on the general issue of urban, mostly Democratic, liberalism vs. non-urban, mostly Republican, conservatism.

Blatnik . . . Blitch . . . Farbstein . . . Feighan . . . Inouye . . . the House was hushed, the galleries still. There was only the drone of the clerk's voice, the shouted replies; at leadership tables on both sides of the aisle, heads bent over tally sheets. Not a few members were keeping score for themselves.

The mere sound of that American medley of names rolling through the House was proof enough of Kennedy's reaction to the close situation in which he had found himself. He had not yet been dismayed. He had accepted the challenge. Less than a week after he and the cool young men around him had come to power, they had been plunged into a legislative war—total and to the death—for which they were ill-prepared and not yet organized, in which the advantage of surprise lay with their opponents, in which their ambitious program could be lost before it was presented, that could deal them a mortal wound at home and in the world.

The session of August, 1960, was seared on Kennedy's memory; after that he never wavered in his determination that the Democrats must move to win control of the Committee on Rules. At the Palm Beach meeting five days before Christmas, he brought heavy pressure upon a reluctant Speaker Rayburn. But the Speaker's ultimate willingness to take the lead reassured the President-elect. He took no part in Rayburn's strategical decisions, nor did any of his aides; they assumed that the old man—a member of the House longer than most of them had been alive—could win the battle on his own. And as a fourteen-year veteran of Congress, Kennedy knew better than to give the appearance of openly interfering from "downtown" in Capitol Hill's business.

On his Inauguration Day, January 20, 1961, Kennedy still had no knowledge that this first battle was so near to being lost. Consequently, he had taken no action to help Rayburn, and he got a rude shock at his first meeting with the Democratic legislative leaders in the White House on Tuesday morning, January 24.

What alarmed the President was not that Mr. Sam was somewhat pessimistic and that he predicted, at best, a close roll call on the prescribed day, Thursday, January 26. It was rather that the old man was unable to give him a precise headcount—an accurate reading of how many were for, and how many were against, and who was undecided on, expansion of the Committee on Rules.

In the eyes of the shocked Kennedy and his White House political staff, the machine-like victors of another roll call at the Democratic National Convention—a roll call in preparation for which they had left no stone unturned in nearly three years of grinding work—it was almost the cardinal sin not to have an up-to-date headcount, and its absence could mean only one thing. Here was not the hardheaded and effective leader of a disciplined House majority that Kennedy had expected; here was not a flint-hearted master of his own House; above all, here was none of the file-card-and-adding-machine precision of Kennedy's own clockwork victory at the Convention.

Kennedy at once ordered Lawrence F. O'Brien to see what could be done. O'Brien, the genial Irishman who had organized, in a matter of days, the effective Kennedy campaign in the West Virginia primary, was to be the President's special assistant for Congressional affairs. But he hardly knew the House, had as yet little influence there, and had taken no part in the crucial preliminaries of the struggle.

O'Brien moved swiftly and in the Kennedy pattern. His first action was to take, by every means available, an up-to-date headcount. In this undertaking, the liberal forces working under Bolling, Thompson and others were of great help; their efforts were more organized than Rayburn's. The appalling result of O'Brien's inquiries was the plain intelligence that Speaker Rayburn was going to lose the battle by seven or eight votes. No more than twenty-two (certainly not forty) Republicans would support him; that left perhaps 152 Republicans that Halleck could throw in on Judge Smith's side. Only 218 were needed for an absolute majority. The Judge need keep his grip on only 66 Southerners to achieve such a majority.

O'Brien and Kennedy were not men to place much political trust in Providence. They saw at once that the Speaker did not have the votes to win. They believed he *had* to win. *They* had to win. There was only one solution. Time was needed for a West Virginia-type rescue operation that would engage the new Administration to the fullest—and the sensitivities of Congress and of Sam Rayburn could not be spared.

Kennedy and O'Brien proposed to the Speaker that the vote be put off until January 31. He demurred—in the White House view because he was tired of the distasteful struggle and ready to vote, win or lose. But Kennedy knew he could not afford to lose, and he brought effective personal pressure on Rayburn for a postponement.

When the Speaker reluctantly announced the five-day delay on January 25 ("I don't think we will be in any worse shape by Tuesday," he said. "I still think we are going to win."), it was of course, interpreted in the House as a further sign of weakness.

"The New Frontier is having trouble with its first roundup," Charlie Halleck jeered.

It was reported that a Rayburn man had conceded that the vote, if taken as scheduled, might have gone either way by three "and that's too close for comfort."

Postponement, however distasteful to Rayburn, was in any case a risk the White House believed necessary. It momentarily gave the opposition a psychological lift but it gave O'Brien and

Kennedy five precious days in which to join their considerable resources of energy and power to those of Rayburn and the Congressional leaders supporting him. In those final five days, the fiercest of the many pressures of January, 1961, were brought to bear in the House of Representatives—by Udall, for instance, and by the Southern Secretary of Commerce, Luther H. Hodges of North Carolina.

Up to then, Rayburn's forces had been curiously divided. On the one hand, almost independently of him, Thompson and Bolling were working tirelessly, directing a well-organized liberal effort, persuading, bringing pressure, threatening, pleading—above all, keeping accurate track of where the members of the House stood, of who would vote for what. On the other hand, without much liaison with these energetic men, Rayburn was calling in his own due bills, speaking paternally to his Democratic colleagues, making the issue virtually one of personal loyalty. So were elder colleagues and close associates like the Representative from Louisiana, Hale Boggs.

"My boy," Rayburn would say to a cornered Democrat, "you're going to stay with me on this one, aren't you?" Or, to an older member—"We've got to give this young man in the White House a chance to move his program."

A Representative from Florida, James A. Haley, was approached in this manner, and discreetly reminded that in 1958, at some personal discomfort, Speaker Rayburn had made an electioneering trip into Florida on his behalf. Haley could hardly remember it. Besides he was pledged to Smith. It was one of many incidents that the Speaker considered a personal betrayal.

On a slightly different plane was the case of a Texas colleague, Representative Joe M. Kilgore. Months before Rayburn had made known his intention to expand the Committee, Kilgore had said in a radio address that he was opposed to tampering with the Committee on Rules. Rayburn could also regard Kilgore as indebted to him, for many favors, but, understanding as always, he conceded that Kilgore already was "on the record" and therefore honorably excused from paying up.

O'Brien regarded such a soft approach as ill-suited to the desperation of the hour. Hand in glove with the harder-hearted young liberals, in five days he ran a tough new check of every Democrat in the House. They were left in no doubt at all as to where the White House stood, what it wanted. Patronage, preferment, party loyalty, power—these were O'Brien's weapons. But he was operating in near secrecy and there were no more than vague rumors in the Capitol and elsewhere that the White House had "intervened."

For his part, Kennedy moved cautiously. At his first news conference, January 24, 1961, the same day Rayburn announced the postponement, the President answered a question with another. "Shouldn't the members of the House themselves, and not merely the members of the Rules Committee, have a chance to vote on these measures?"

It was "no secret," the President told the reporters, that he wanted Rayburn to win control of the Committee. But he was careful to point out that the Senate and the House were the judges of their own rules, and that Rayburn was anxious for the House to settle its own affairs without Presidential interference. He concluded: "The responsibility rests with the members of the House and I would not otherwise attempt in any way to infringe upon that responsibility. I merely give my view as an interested citizen."

The reporters laughed and Kennedy laughed with them. They knew he was much more than an interested citizen. For one thing, there was the widely publicized activity of Secretary of the Interior Udall, still as interested in reshaping the Committee on Rules as he had been while a member of the Eighty-Sixth Congress.

Udall had put in personal telephone calls to at least four Republican members of the House, asking them to vote with Rayburn. Since the Department of the Interior has much to do with the water, reclamation, power, conservation and park projects so dear to the West, his motive was obvious—intimidation. Halleck screamed foul, but not even the members Udall had called accused him of openly threatening to hold up projects in their districts.

"Halleck styles himself as a gut fighter who plays the game to the hilt," Udall said later, "but he doesn't like it when someone else plays the game to the hilt." All he had done, he said, was to suggest to the four that their projects might later encounter difficulties with Rayburn's supporters in the House. After all, "Congressmen have memories."

From across the Capitol rumbled one of the few comments to emerge from the Senate on the titanic struggle in the House. Udall's intervention, said the fluent Senator from Illinois, Everett McKinley Dirksen, "was in the nature of serving notice on all New Frontiersmen—check your guns and your voting records at the door, the project line forms on your right." It seemed only a mild Dirksenian overstatement, and it was a question whether Udall had helped or hurt the cause. His calls angered members of the House; all four of those he is known to have called eventually voted against Rayburn. How many Democrats stayed in line because of the tacit threat he had implied never will be known.

Halleck was having little less trouble holding Republican feet to the fire. One liberal Republican, John V. Lindsay of New York, was openly backing Rayburn on grounds that the ancient alliance with the Southern Democrats "in the long run is contrary to the principles and best interests of the Republican party." Other urban Republicans—Seely-Brown and Sibal of Connecticut, Fino and Halpern of New York, Florence Dwyer and Cahill of New Jersey, took the same stand.

Representative Thomas Curtis of Missouri, often a loner, had a different reason for bolting Halleck. Without the "phony excuse" of the Committee on Rules' intransigence, he said, the Republicans soon would be able to demonstrate that the Democrats were simply too divided to legislate. And the jovial Representative from Massachusetts, William Bates, explained his decision to support Rayburn with the jaunty remark that he voted liberal one week and conservative the next and the expansion vote would fall "in my liberal week." A Halleck threat to withhold Republican campaign funds did not frighten the impressive new Representative from Pennsylvania, William W. Scranton, whose economically depressed district needed liberal legislation as much as any in the nation.

The House of Representatives became a furnace of such pressures. Thompson, Bolling, O'Brien, other White House aides, a number of other active members of the House, worked without letup. A valuable member of the team was Representative Bob Jones of Alabama. Carl Vinson's support for speaker Rayburn gave some cover for any Southerner who wanted to take the same course; but it was the untiring work of Bob Jones, more than that of any other Southern member, that extracted dissident votes from Judge Smith's erstwhile followers.

After Kennedy's press conference statement backing the Speaker, the Rayburn men picked up several votes to a total of 213. It was enough to win most battles in the House—but if all the "uncommitteds" voted with Smith and Halleck, they would poll 216 (six of the 435 members of the House were regarded by both sides as certain absentees on voting day).

No politician likes to vote when the sides are as even as all that. Few votes ever are taken in Congress without the proponents and opponents knowing in advance who will win. When the issue is in doubt, usually both will cast around for some means of delay. The battle for the Committee on Rules was no exception.

Both sides sought compromise. Smith put forward again his promise to clear Kennedy's five major bills, and his offer to relinquish the power to block Senate-House conferences. If that wouldn't do—and Rayburn again rejected it out of hand—Smith said he would agree to the expansion in return for a guarantee that the two new Democratic members of his Committee would be "mutually acceptable" to Rayburn and himself. The Speaker, agreeing with a colleague that "there ain't no such men," threw that down, too.

Before the Rayburn forces could label these offers a sign of weakness on Judge Smith's part, Rayburn himself sent Vinson and Walter to Smith with a proposal. He would drop the expansion plan if the Virginian gave him a written agreement to clear any Kennedy-proposed bill that the Speaker personally requested. Judge Smith sent back the word that his offer to clear Kennedy's Big Five stood; he would yield no further. That was the end.

Rayburn called a news conference on January 28 and announced that "there has never been any basis between me and Mr. Smith for compromise that I know anything about." There was no turning back. But the Speaker would say only that he had "good prospects." And he added, wryly: "I think the vote is not going to be overwhelming either way."

Itching to get into the fray, personally, Kennedy made several telephone calls to Capitol Hill, mostly to friends like Thompson. Word of this drifted out, as did news of O'Brien's activities. On the day before the vote, most newspapers reported that the Administration had intervened openly to save Rayburn and its prospects. That day, Kennedy went personally to the House—"my oldest home" in Washington—for his State of the Union Message.

Only one instance of direct Kennedy action is known. At a meeting in his office, he announced his intention of calling Harold D. Cooley of North Carolina, dean of that state's eleven-man delegation. Ten of them were pledged to Judge Smith— and since the new Secretary of Commerce, Luther H. Hodges, the new Undersecretary of Agriculture, Charles Murphy, and the new Administrator of the National Aeronautics and Space Agency, James E. Webb, were Tar Heels, Kennedy thought he deserved better of Cooley's troops. Hadn't their state cast its electoral votes for the new President and his program?

Rayburn begged the President not to call Cooley. The news inevitably would leak, he said, and that might cause more harm than good, like Udall's activity. But Kennedy's blood was up. In Rayburn's presence, he put through the call. Even that did

not shake Cooley[7] and the only vote Rayburn and Kennedy
ultimately got out of North Carolina was that of loyal Herbert
Bonner—who believed that Speaker Rayburn's North Carolina
campaign trip had saved the state for Adlai Stevenson and the
Democratic party in 1956.

Kennedy might ignore Sam Rayburn in such an instance but
the Speaker remained the keystone of the Administration's
hopes. Without him, there could have been no fight at all.
And as Churchill said of Jellicoe in the First World War, he
was the only man who could have lost the war in a single
day. His errors of leadership and strategy had made the struggle
unnecessarily hard; his methods of rounding up votes were un-
equal to the task. But without his name, without his prestige,
without his final resolve—agonizing for him—to fight Howard
Smith, nothing could have been done.

And as tension rose like ground mist in the House and the
long roll call of January 31, 1961, drew to its close . . . *Ullman*
. . . *Utt* . . . *Vanik* . . . and the galleries waited in silence, only
the occasional shuffle of a foot or a gasp at some unexpected
vote sounding through the chamber, it was apparent that Kennedy had needed all his influence, all Rayburn's prestige, the
hard frontline work of Bolling and Thompson and Jones, every
Republican like Scranton and Lindsay and Curtis—every
nuance of power he could exert; if he salvaged control of the
Committee on Rules and its vast Congressional authority, it
would be by a margin no greater than his hairline victory over
Nixon three months before.

Yates . . . *Younger* . . . *Zablocki* . . . *Zelenko* . . . the last man
answered "aye" and a muffled, windy sound rose from the galleries, as if all the spectators had breathed out at once. Sam
Rayburn leaned over the rostrum and asked for the totals.

Two hundred fourteen for expansion, a clerk whispered; two
hundred nine against.

The clerk began calling the names of the eleven members
who had failed to answer—and who could reverse the first
round result. Cannon, with almost visible reluctance, gave
Rayburn the two hundred fifteenth vote—three short of an ab-

solute majority. A "no" and an "aye" followed—then two more quick "nos." Two hundred sixteen to two hundred twelve. The Gentleman from Minnesota, Fred Marshall, voted "aye" and put the Speaker within one vote of a majority.

The stout and perspiring Representative from Mississippi, Frank Smith, stepped out of the cloakroom and answered to his name. He had pledged his vote—one that could have killed him politically in his Delta district—to Sam Rayburn, if that vote was needed to win the Speaker's battle. Now, Frank Smith, sure of the outcome, was able to vote "no," making it two hundred seventeen to two hundred thirteen—and no more names to call.

There was still the possibility of vote switches and the crowds in the galleries muttered when Representative Edgar Chenoweth of Colorado sought recognition. But Chenoweth merely announced a "pair" with old Joe Martin, who was sunning himself in the Caribbean. Faithful to his friend Sam Rayburn, unforgiving of Charlie Halleck, the man who had overthrown him as the Republican leader, Martin would have voted "aye" if present. So Chenoweth withdrew his "no" vote to balance Martin's absence, and was recorded as "present."

That was all.

By five votes, 217 to 212, for the first time in eighteen years as Speaker, Sam Rayburn controlled all the machinery of the House of Representatives. So, theoretically, did John F. Kennedy.

"We won," Mr. Sam, smiling and happy, told the reporters crowding around, "and I am satisfied."

"As far as I know," Judge Smith told a questioner, "I am still chairman of the Committee on Rules."

He promptly proved it. He announced that there would be no available chairs at the Committee table for the additional members Rayburn and Halleck had sent him—Representative Carl Elliott, of Alabama, a Southern moderate responsive to Rayburn's leadership, and Representative B. F. Sisk of California, Democrats; and Representative William Avery of Kansas, the new Republican member. The Judge's riposte amused Washington but when Elliott's Alabama constituency sent him a chair even bigger than the Judge's, Smith capitulated and provided standard furniture for the newcomers.

The day before Washington's birthday, the sly old Judge moved again. He confronted the expanded Committee with the question whether to send to the floor the usual resolution that would open House sessions to live television, and another that would halt "backdoor spending," a method of supplying agencies through Treasury loans without appropriations. That was hardly the sort of legislation Sam Rayburn—he annually blocked both resolutions—had had in mind during the January battle, and his new eight-man majority on the Committee was put in the embarrassing position of "bottling up" the resolutions over the opposition of Judge Smith's seven-man minority, who voted to clear them.

The Virginian, obviously enjoying himself, later brought up a resolution for a study of national fuel resources. Rayburn fumed. A Texan always sensitive to anything affecting oil interests, he had wanted the resolution buried. His new majority was forced to block another Committee action.

Judge Smith said reporters would have to decide for themselves whether there was a "new coalition" afoot. "I thought," he added slyly, "that when they packed the Committee earlier this year, the purpose was to make certain the House would have a chance to express its will on such matters. The reverse seems to be true."

Clarence Brown chimed in: "I said on the floor of the House when the resolution to pack the Rules Committee came up that only one thing was sought, the power to control the Committee's decisions. The correctness of that statement was demonstrated today."

So it had been. Now the question was, what would Kennedy do with it? The liberals had won their fight. The way was open. They looked expectantly to the young President for the leadership that had been promised, that they believed they had made possible.

6 *Look Away, Dixieland*

The omens seemed favorable. Kennedy's minimum
wage bill, as an example, sped with only minor
amendments through a subcommittee, the House Education
and Labor Committee, and the Committee on Rules, all by
March 21. The new leadership in the White House obviously
had the pressure on, or so it might have seemed to those who
did not closely follow the involuted ways of the House of
Representatives.

In fact, the minimum wage bill was moving at unusual speed
for two reasons that had nothing to do with Kennedy. Gravel-
voiced old Graham Barden of North Carolina, a tenacious
Southern conservative and chairman of the Education and
Labor Committee since time immemorial, had retired from
Congress in despair at the twentieth century. A prime opponent
of the minimum wage bill Kennedy had sponsored as a senator
the year before, Barden had been replaced as chairman by the
ineffable Adam Clayton Powell of New York who, despite his
soaring irresponsibility, was firmly committed to the Kennedy
bill.

This guaranteed that there would be none of the delay in
committee that Barden had been a master at provoking. And
just as responsible as this development for the speed with which
the bill moved was the fact that, the year before in the same

committee, all the same witnesses had been heard and all the
same arguments made and all the same charges leveled. This
was a rematch, not a new fight, and no one's heart was in the
preliminaries. The sooner the showdown the better.

But the apparent ease with which the minimum wage bill
was moving only helped to conceal the fact that President Kennedy was in trouble with Congress. He had barely survived the
Rules Committee fight; a storm was brewing over his education
bill; and those who bothered to count heads in the House knew
that the wage bill itself was moving swiftly through Committee
to a probable disaster on the House floor.

Kennedy's excellence as a campaigner and his personal
charisma were in some ways the cause of the misplaced opti-
mism. Kennedy supporters, confident of that charisma and of
his ability to operate in the "strong" tradition that he extolled,
had little doubt that from the "bully pulpit" of the White
House, he and they would remake the country. They were ex-
pecting more than he could possibly deliver.

Kennedy himself, as his actions suggest, was too astute to
believe his own "image." He remembered clearly that a closely
divided House had rejected, only a few months earlier, a
minimum wage bill similar to the one he was proposing, and he
knew there were now twenty-two *more Republicans* on the roll
call than there had been then. Charisma or not, John Kennedy
had run behind his ticket, failed to pull marginal Democratic
members of Congress into office again, and therefore his party
had lost ground in the House at the last election.

In the case of the minimum wage bill, which was immediately at issue, the net loss to Kennedy was forty-four seats;
for each of those twenty-two Republicans had taken the seat
of a Democrat who had supported the bill the year before.

But had not so experienced a legislator as Richard Bolling
of Missouri said he would rather have "the powers of the
Presidency" on his side than those twenty-two lost Democrats?
Had not the Committee on Rules been packed, and every other
early voting test been won by the Administration?

They had, and for these and similar reasons, Kennedy was still very much in his honeymoon period as Congress confronted his first major measures—education and the minimum wage. Despite the closeness of the Rules Committee vote, there was as yet little recognition that in fact the close division of the House represented, if inexactly, *a close division of the country*. What actually impended in the Eighty-Seventh Congress, because of the situation in the House, was a struggle at every turn that would be as close and hard-fought as the 1960 election between Eisenhowerism and Kennedyism, as difficult as the battle for the Committee on Rules.

It was of parallel importance that, as Kennedy took office, no visible and unmistakable national crisis confronted the country; he himself believed, for instance, that the voters would gladly have re-elected the soothing standpatter, Dwight Eisenhower, if they could have. The economy was in something of a recession, it was true, but still most Americans had "never had it so good." The foreign scene was not a happy one, but neither was it grimly menacing. There was, in good measure, peace and prosperity. Kennedy was by no means in the position of Franklin Roosevelt, taking office in the depths of the Depression, when almost any expedient would have been acceptable, any action welcomed, and "fear itself" was the powerful ally of a confident man who knew how to dispel it.

Yet, Kennedy had campaigned on the most liberal, activist platform in history. He had promised action and more action "to get this country moving again." He had pledged himself to be a strong President "in the forefront of the battle." He had swept the most publicized liberal intellectuals of the country—men like Arthur Schlesinger Jr. and John Kenneth Galbraith—into the Administration with him, after their years of thunderous dissent from Eisenhowerism. He had in short, aroused expectations—or fears—of the kind of assault upon political orthodoxy, conventional wisdom and social lethargy that Roosevelt had delivered in 1933.

But who was demanding it? The 113,000-vote margin over

Nixon was scarcely a mandate at all, let alone a mandate for remaking the country; while it was a remarkable personal victory for Kennedy, the voters actually had given the Republicans an increased number of seats in Congress. And what circumstances existed for all to see and fear that warranted sweeping new developments and venturesome new programs? Every item in Kennedy's five-point priority legislative program had been rejected or drastically cut in the preceding Congress —and the fact that the voters had made the Eighty-Seventh Congress even more conservative showed something less than public outrage at the record.

Thus, Kennedy had staked his fortunes on his pledge "to get this country moving again"—when there was no real public evidence that the country believed it was standing still, no overwhelming demand for new movement, and in some ways there were greater obstacles to new movement than there had been a year earlier. Yet, Kennedy himself had made movement and change his criteria, and he had aroused great anticipation among those who shared his views and considerable fear among those who did not.

Senator Joseph S. Clark, Democrat of Pennsylvania, told me just before the inauguration that he expected in the next hundred days to experience the most exciting times of his political life. Halleck had already growled *his* defiance of what he expected: "a lot of radical, wild-eyed, spendthrift proposals." Men like Clark were bound to be disappointed by what Kennedy actually proposed and could achieve; Halleck was sure to react against the most innocuous Kennedy proposal as if it were a child of the Kremlin. Thus, what really faced Kennedy at the outset of his term was the live prospect that, his campaign and election having created one effect upon men—the sense that he was committed to sweeping change—his actual performance in office now would create another—the impression that he could not deliver.

Kennedy and legislative assistants like Larry O'Brien and Henry H. Wilson of North Carolina were well aware of their tenuous strength in the House, at least after the Rules Committee fight. But their efforts to deal with the situation had a built-in flaw.

Kennedy had appealed in his campaign primarily to, and had been elected almost entirely by, the industrial Northeast, with its dominant urban liberalism. Now that he was in office, his power base was the group of urban liberal Democrats from these states; together with Western and border-state Democrats, they numbered about 150 members. This was a problem, because it was a relatively narrow base, almost seventy members short of a majority of the House. But there were about twenty Republicans liberal enough to be lured across party lines. Even so, it was little wonder that in Kennedy's mind, as events showed, the threat to his goals in Congress seemed to consist primarily of the determined, shrewd, powerful band of Southern Democrats that split his paper majority to the breaking point. He needed about fifty of them for an absolute majority on any vote. His strategy, as it developed, was to buy them—a policy that was bound to dismay and alienate the urban liberals he had to count upon more than anyone else.

Kennedy had had no choice, as we have seen, but to fight the Southerners for control of the Rules Committee, and he had won. After that, however, the liberal new President conciliated the South; the man who had pledged to get the country moving again through strength in the White House was forced to compromise.

He omitted civil rights legislation from his 1961 program, and on purpose. He remained aloof from a struggle in January, 1961, to eliminate the filibuster from Senate proceedings. He was hardly in office before he increased cotton support prices. He channeled ample patronage southwards, provided defense contracts in profligate supply, permitted a disproportionate share of area redevelopment funds to be made available for Southern projects, and spread flattering attention on Southern leaders. In the spring of 1961, he dropped in by helicopter to honor Harry F. Byrd's birthday picnic at Berryville, Virginia,

although the Senator had not supported him in 1960 and
annually used the picnic to heap imprecations on a federal government of which the President was the central figure. In one
way or another, each of these steps, and others, was taken at
the expense or to the discomfiture of his urban liberal supporters. As he evidently saw it, Kennedy had to risk the faith
and loyalty and interests of those who would naturally support
him in order to buy the votes of those who would not.

It is easy to see why Kennedy took this course. The Southerners held the balance of power in the House (and many of
the important committee chairmanships in both houses). They
had been defeated in the Rules Committee fight only because
of the peculiar nature of the issue, and because Rayburn,
Vinson and Jones had been able to divide their personal loyalties. Yet, trying to please hard-sell Southern legislators was
scarcely the way to get the country moving again, although
it was in the same pattern as Kennedy's controversial choice of
Lyndon Johnson for Vice President.

Whether as a result of the Southern menace or not, Kennedy was not even demanding much in the way of innovation.
Every one of his five priority bills—minimum wage, education,
area redevelopment, housing, medical care for the aged—was
as familiar in Congress as Sam Rayburn's bald head. Democratic liberals were for these programs, had been for them
for a decade or more; but did the new young liberal President,
elected in the image of F.D.R., have nothing more to offer
than the same old programs that had been fought over throughout the Fifties? Between the apparent paucity of his ideas and
his obvious conciliation of the South, Kennedy was diluting
the enthusiasm and loyalty he needed from the urban liberals
who made up his power base.

At the time, for instance, it seemed shrewd politics for Kennedy to have omitted a civil rights bill from his program, while
Administration leaks discussed at every opportunity the "executive action" that was planned in this field. Two rights bills
had been passed in the late Fifties, and the need seemed less

pressing than once it had; in the Senate, a civil rights bill was sure to provoke a long filibuster, delaying other legislation, and there was no assurance that the filibuster could be broken; and the Southerners would be driven even farther into opposition if the new President moved in that direction. There seemed a good deal more to be gained by leaving the issue alone than by raising it.

In retrospect, this analysis is questionable. Fighting for a strong civil rights bill, whether it could pass or not, would have done a great deal to shore up the notion of Kennedy as a vigorous liberal and to hold his supporters together in loyalty and enthusiasm. The measure might even have passed, because it would have been hard for the Republicans to refrain from supporting it; and the Southerners were alienated anyway and had been from the beginning—by the Kennedy campaign and rhetoric, by the Rules Committee fight, and by a legislative program that, however it looked to liberals, seemed radical to Judge Smith and his followers.

It may be hindsight, moreover, but it is nonetheless true that Kennedy's failure to send up a strong rights bill was another link in a long chain of cynical or blind American refusals to act either swiftly or adequately in correcting a century of injustice to Negro citizens. And even in Kennedy's brief term, the nation would begin to suffer the consequences of that shameful neglect. Thus, those of his liberal supporters who protested his retreat from civil rights legislation, and were quietly lectured on the political realities, may have seen the necessities of the time more clearly than their leader.

Kennedy had more personal difficulties, too. He had spent fourteen years on Capitol Hill, but the last four had been primarily dedicated to winning the Presidency, and he had never been—as most members become—part of the Congressional world. That world is not only separate from the rest of Washington; its politics were not the national elective politics in which Kennedy had become adept. In that Kennedy domain of delegates and primaries, Lyndon Johnson, for instance, had been lost; but on the Hill, Johnson had a surer sense of the way things happened, and the way to make them happen, than the man who had beaten him at Los Angeles. One of Kennedy's troubles, Johnson observed to friends soon after the Inauguration, was that in Congress the new President "had the minnows but not the whales."

In translation, Johnson meant that Kennedy did not have the assured support of, or an easy rapport with, the Congressional giants of his party—Rayburn and John McCormack of Massachusetts in the House, Robert S. Kerr of Oklahoma, Richard Russell of Georgia, John Stennis of Mississippi, and other "whales" in the Senate. These men had seen Presidents come and go; they had their own power bases in Congress and at home, even in the Pentagon and elsewhere in the bureaucracy; they did not have to defer to young John Kennedy except in courtesy to his office.

Kerr, in fact, running on the same ticket with the Catholic Kennedy in Baptist Oklahoma, had had active reason to fear the association. Kennedy had lost the state by more than 150,000 votes, a landslide that Kerr had had to "turn around" in order to get re-elected himself. Kennedy's coattails meant nothing whatever to him or to, say, Russell of Georgia or Hayden of Arizona.

Kennedy recognized the importance of these men but it was not easy for him with his wry and detached spirit to defer to them in the way they might have wished; the visit to Byrd's picnic was an exception. As one astute student of Congress has put it, men like Kerr usually must be appealed to through their self-images; they must be treated for what they believe themselves to be. This is a far different thing from being appealed to through self-interest—the usual promises of patronage or preferment or federal money in one's state or district, or the occasional threats to withhold these things.

All members of Congress, sooner or later, expect such appeals to their self-interest; but the "whales" like Kerr and Russell can seldom be won with that appeal alone. Public and private recognition of their own sense of pride and place is likely to matter more to them in the long run. Nothing could be more damaging, for instance, than to send an underling to see a man like Kerr on important Presidential business; he believes he rates a Presidential phone call and receiving it will do more to sway him than any more tangible "conciliation." The underling's arrival may mortally offend him.

Kennedy also had been, as a colleague put it, the only "intellectual playboy" in the Senate; it had its other intellectuals, like J. W. Fulbright, and its other playboys, like George Smathers of Florida, but it had no intellectual playboy but John F. Kennedy, and this tended to make other Senators a little nervous about him. They liked him, surely envied him, even admired him—but they were not entirely certain that he was to be taken seriously; they were not sure that he really cared about things that to them seemed crucial. His wit and gaiety were not customary in the Senate, and so even after he entered the White House there were those among his sober-minded colleagues who doubted that he would really work at the job any more than they believed he had worked in the Senate.

One elderly Senator recalls, for instance, presiding over a night session. "There was Johnson down there on the floor, working like hell, pushing bills through," he said. "I looked up in the gallery and there were Jack Kennedy and George Smathers sneaking out with a couple of girls. Johnson and the rest of us were still in there working while they went on the town."

Kennedy was President now and it is hard for politicians not to take any President seriously. But this Congressional attitude was a difficulty for him; it might make a difference, sometime in the future, when a hard-pressed senator was trying to decide whether to follow the President on a difficult political course; it might make a difference at some future moment when only a tough and hard-driving leader could expect to be followed. It

might make a routine act of political expedience or accommodation on his part look like something worse.

Kennedy had never held executive office and was inexperienced, but there can be no real preparation for the White House
in any prior office. It seems of greater moment, in retrospect,
that he came there with a highly developed determination to
be a "strong President" at a time when he had small opportunity to be such a President; with an opposition the conciliation of which was both difficult and sure to disquiet his own
supporters; with the limitation—as well as the blessing—of a
public identity of vigorous liberalism placed on him by his
campaign to "get this country moving again"; with a suspiciously conservative Congress on the Hill; with the hopes or
fears of those who watched him at a dangerous peak; and with
an undercurrent of mistrust, disdain or scorn just barely visible
among some of the members of Congress who could help or
hurt him most.

These were major difficulties and they put Kennedy in
serious trouble in Congress before he ever sent a bill there;
the bills themselves were bound to make it worse. The Rules
Committee fight had made his weakness plain to anyone who
studied it, and the speedy course of the minimum wage bill
through the Education and Labor Committee would not conceal it much longer—only until it reached its ordained showdown on the House floor with the resurrected alternative that
the Eisenhower Administration and Barden had backed the
year before, and with which they had fought Senator John
Kennedy to a standstill.

This was a remarkable document called the Kitchin-Ayres
bill, after a pair of sponsors who were the personification of
the Republican-Southern Democratic coalition—Rep. William
H. Ayres of Ohio, a jovial, chain-smoking, conservative Republican with a talent for invective and publicity, and Rep.
Paul Kitchin of North Carolina, the son of a former Democratic floor leader in the House, an ex-F.B.I. agent, a committed Southern conservative in the smooth new bankers'-gray

model that had replaced most of the more interesting gallus-snappers of years gone by.

The Kitchin-Ayres bill proposed to raise the minimum wage to $1.15 in one fell swoop, rather than to $1.25 in three annual steps, as the President advocated; it sought to include 1.3 million workers not then protected, about a third as many as the Kennedy bill; and these newly-covered workers would get a minimum of only $1 an hour, instead of gradually being stepped up to $1.25, as Kennedy proposed, or even to the $1.15 Kitchin and Ayres were asking for those already covered.

But none of these were differences central to the fight; events were to show that all could be compromised. The real struggle centered about the interstate commerce clause of the Constitution,[8] that artfully stretched and tortured phrasing upon which rested so many twentieth-century reforms, including the right to impose wage-and-hour standards on private employers.

The legal problem for President Kennedy was so to define "interstate commerce" as to bring under federal wage-and-hour standards the largest number of workers possible. Taking particular aim on the nearly ten million "uncovered workers" in retail and service enterprises, he set as a criterion the annual dollar volume of business of such enterprises. Any retail firm doing an annual volume of $1 million a year was to be considered obviously in the stream of interstate commerce, and therefore subject to the regulation of Congress, either because of goods purchased from across state lines or because of goods sold that then moved across state lines.

Kitchin and Ayres, aiming in the opposite direction—to provide new coverage for as *few* then-uncovered workers as possible—wrote a definition of interstate commerce restrictive enough to have won the favor of Calvin Coolidge. They proposed to extend the wage floor and hours ceiling only to workers in chain enterprises that had five or more establishments in two or more states. What effect such a definition—and precedent—might have on future interpretations of the previously flexible commerce clause, liberal lawyers shuddered to think.

This difference in definition of interstate commerce was basic, although otherwise both bills represented compromise.

In the bill he had unsuccessfully pushed as a Senator, for instance, Kennedy had set his "dollar volume standard" of interstate commerce at five hundred thousand dollars annually. As Preside⸜ t, he raised it to one million dollars, obviously to exclude many smaller enterprises and thus many uncovered workers. This was a sop to those who wanted no new coverage at all, or as limited coverage as possible, but it was not to have that effect. Conciliation often makes things worse, and this one did.

The Kitchin-Ayres bill was a compromise also designed to win the support of men who wanted no new coverage or no increase in the minimum, or neither, but who were willing to give a little to get a lot. It also was designed to appeal to those conservatives who were politically forced to back some increase and expansion, but who wanted both held to the lowest possible level. They could accept the Kitchin-Ayres increase and extension, which were not large; more important, they knew that its restrictive definition of interstate commerce, once embodied in the basic Fair Labor Standards Act, whatever its effect on other legislation, would put a virtual end to further extensions of minimum wage coverage after 1961.

On the other hand, since Kennedy had already changed the level of the dollar-volume standard of interstate commerce that he proposed, his opponents saw instantly that, in the future, the wage floor could be extended to uncovered workers by the simple expedient of lowering the required dollar volume —perhaps to $500,000, perhaps to $250,000 in annual business. Thus, Kennedy's conciliatory move turned out to be an alarm bell to those he had sought to win over, and a disappointment to his own backers.

If the departure of Barden and the capture of the Rules Committee had given Kennedy initial momentum, they could not alter the fact that an effort to increase the minimum wage and particularly to expand its coverage was essentially an interest-group struggle of the most violent kind, and one in which the opponents of expansion had a special advantage.

Despite the great stress the Administration bill placed on retail workers, in other paragraphs, as plain as legal terminology could be, there were stated additional inclusions of this class of worker, that type of enterprise—telephone exchange employees, for instance, or employees of auto and farm implement dealers. More workers would be brought into coverage; those already covered would have to be paid more. Almost without exception, Kitchin-Ayres presented a lesser threat to various powerful interest groups—retail and industry associations, for instance, local Chambers of Commerce, organizations of managers and employers.

The opposition to the Administration bill was not confined to employers whose employees would be directly affected by it, or to their trade organizations. Opposition was aroused, too, among employers already paying their workers $1.25 an hour or more, or whose work force already was protected by the $1 wage floor and forty-hour work week.

Many felt that if the $1.25 floor was established, a $1.50 or $2 floor would not be long in coming. Those in a given industry or trade who were already paying substantial wages feared that, if they were to keep the cream of the available workers, and if competitors were to be forced to pay 25 or 50 cents an hour more, they would have to raise their own wage scales by a comparable amount. Besides, organized labor was supporting a minimum wage increase, and some management believes that whatever labor backs must be bad for business.

Thus, a broad spectrum of the interest groups of the nation worked against the Kennedy bill. Turning—as such groups usually do—to their representatives in Congress, they produced great pressure for its defeat. And the obvious way to defeat it was to accept the Kitchin-Ayres bill, with its lighter immediate impact, its political advantages (it was, after all, an increase and an expansion) and its implicit promise that it would end minimum wage extension once and for all.

It may be supposed that the Kennedy bill would have had an equal and opposite effect, that those who would benefit by the bill would produce pressures equally strong. Where such persons had their own strongly organized interest groups, they did bring effective pressures. The lobbying power of organized labor was strongly mobilized for the bill. But in hundreds of Congressional districts, labor unions have no power, while employer groups, trade organizations, powerful individual businessmen, are everywhere.

Powell and other New York Representatives, for instance, were under union pressure to win the inclusion of non-tipped hotel and restaurant workers in the Administration bill; but that bill's sponsors would not listen. They had troubles enough already, and the opposition of hotel and restaurant owners' associations was too powerful for the relatively weak unions involved, whose stronghold was in New York City. Florida and other resort areas, in particular, *opposed* this inclusion—and the Administration most needed Congressional votes in areas *outside* of New York City, whose Representatives had little political choice but to support the more liberal approach, with or without the inclusion of restaurant workers.

It is a striking fact that, other than for the efforts of organized labor, the people who would be directly benefited by the Kennedy bill seldom were heard from. A Kennedy lieutenant heavily involved in the battle also had served in a legislature in which three state minimum wage battles had been fought. Never once—in those three fights or in the 1961 Congressional battle—was he approached or pressured by a single individual who stood to gain if the minimum wage bill in question was enacted.

The reasons are obvious. People who earned less than $1.25 an hour were those least politically interested; this is borne out by the known difficulty of getting low-income groups to register and vote, as attested by officials of both parties. Such people usually are poorly educated and do not pay much attention to political and government affairs in the newspapers; they may not even know someone is trying to benefit them. If workers were members of active labor unions, they were not likely to be paid less than $1.25 an hour in 1961; if they were not union members and did earn such low wages, they were likely to be totally unorganized, uninstructed in political matters, without an association or leader to speak for them, and either unwilling or not knowledgeable enough to express themselves directly to a legislator.

Thus, the numerous interest groups *opposed* to the Administration bill were outspoken, organized, active, effective. Those who might have been expected to support it—save labor unions—were inarticulate, unorganized, inactive, ineffective. (One interesting exception ought to be noted. A number of employers, already paying wages above the proposed $1.25 minimum, apparently were being hurt by "sweatshop" wages paid by unorganized competitors. These employers did not want to cut the wages they paid, and they saw in the minimum wage proposals a golden opportunity to force up the wages of their competitors. Kennedy lieutenants concede that the help they got from this unique interest group was considerable.)

Thus, Kennedy was deeply involved in the complex and shifting events of a government of men. That he controlled the Rules Committee and no longer had Barden to contend with had served the valuable purposes of preventing delay and getting his bill to the floor. Once there, the problem was transformed; it became a matter of raw power, of which side had the votes, of which could best influence, appeal to, coerce, persuade and finally control, men. And on the floor, the outlook for the President was not a bit better than it had been when the same battle had been fought a year before. It quickly became obvious that his bill could not possibly overcome the lure of Kitchin-Ayres.

By the time the House debate opened late on the afternoon

of March 22, there were, in fact, such undeniable indications that the Kennedy bill was in deep trouble that Secretary of Labor Arthur Goldberg felt it necessary to issue a denial; the President, he said, was "standing by the bill reported by the House Education and Labor Committee."

But Goldberg was not convincing and rumors swept the House, all based on a fact that soon came to be acknowledged: the Administration did *not* have the necessary votes; its bill could not pass, and both sides soon knew it.

The jubilant Ayres, collaring reporters in the House lobby, said the obvious support for his bill "convinced the President that the Congress wants and intends to vote for (Kitchin-Ayres) coverage." Bald and hustling Jimmy Roosevelt of California, official sponsor of the Administration bill and zealous as always in New Dealish causes, conceded he didn't have the votes to pass the President's bill. Neither, he insisted without evidence, did Ayres have enough support to pass his.

It was a situation ripe for a compromise move and no one saw that more quickly than the Swamp Fox, canny old Carl Vinson of Georgia—who probably acted with at least the tacit consent of his close friend, the greatest compromiser of all, Sam Rayburn. Vinson, a link to the Southern support that Kennedy men believed vital to passage of the Administration bill, introduced a third measure, predictably enough "splitting the difference" between Kennedy and Kitchin-Ayres—a compromise between the compromises. It was the instinctive solution of a thorough-going Congressional man.

Vinson's bill would have accepted the Administration's proposed pay scale and overtime provisions, both for workers already covered and for those to be newly included. But it also would have accepted the Kitchin-Ayres formula of "five or more units in two or more states" as the criterion for enterprise in interstate commerce. There was little doubt that the forces behind Kitchin and Ayres would have accepted this formula, since it would have yielded them their most important goal. But Goldberg's late-afternoon statement stopped what might have been an Administration stampede to the Vinson bill; he and Kennedy would not swallow the Kitchin-Ayres interstate commerce definition.

Debate—as usual in the House, rambling, incoherent and of little interest to anyone save the orators—continued next day. In mid-afternoon, Kennedy, at a news conference, scouted rumors that he would back a compromise and called for passage of a bill "as close as possible" to his proposals. He pointed out that his proposed hourly rate totaled only fifty dollars a week and added: "I think anyone who is paid less than that must find it extremely difficult to maintain themselves and their families. I consider it to be a very minimum wage . . ."

Therefore, said the son of Joseph P. Kennedy and the heir to much of his fortune, he found it ". . . difficult to know why anyone would oppose seeing somebody, by 1963, paid $1.25 in interstate commerce."

Clue-seeking reporters found no mention of new coverage in the President's remarks, except in his general support of the House bill. And almost as Kennedy spoke, in Speaker Rayburn's office off the House floor, the familiar forces of compromise—the most fundamental ingredient of interest-group politics and government of men—again were making themselves felt. But not in Carl Vinson's terms.

7 *Washing Out the Laundries*

Word quickly spread that something was happening in the Speaker's office. Rayburn was there. Arthur Goldberg was there. Larry O'Brien, plenipotentiary from the White House, was there. Garrulous John McCormack, the Democratic floor leader, was there. So were Carl Albert of Oklahoma, the assistant floor leader, Richard Bolling, Jimmy Roosevelt, Powell, several Labor Department technicians and the Swamp Fox.

First out of the meeting, grinning a little, flourishing his cane, came Vinson. "I'm only a seatwarmer," he told the waiting reporters, grandly waving aside their questions.

Next out of the meeting came all the participants but the Speaker. They gathered in the big, busy outer office, while Rayburn's clerks and aides kept on working at their desks. Reporters and lobbyists mingled in the corridor outside, peering through the open double doors at the small group conferring in the northeast corner of the big room. Goldberg was writing on a pad held on his knee. Occasionally a conferee would look up, see the watching reporters, grin self-consciously, and turn back to the earnest discussions.

Finally, out of the meeting came what was to be known in Congressional parlance as the "Albert compromise"—so-called because the assistant leader, a man of singular prestige who commanded wide affection in the House, had been selected as its sponsor. A few minutes later, in a hastily called news conference in the House lobby, Carl Albert—short of stature but known back home in eastern Oklahoma as the "Little Giant from Little Dixie"—disclosed what was afoot.

Albert would offer a bill that would retain Kennedy's dollar-volume criterion for interstate commerce, but which would nonetheless reduce the number of newly covered workers from 4.3 million to about 3.8 million. Its major exclusion provided that single units of chain enterprises, if such units grossed less than $250,000 yearly, need not pay the minimum wage even though other units in the parent chain had to, and regardless of the chain's total volume.

In addition, it provided what Jimmy Roosevelt, lurking at the edge of the news conference, said was a "sound interstate commerce connection" by exempting any enterprise of any dollar volume of business if less than twenty-five per cent of its annual gross volume of business was derived from purchases or sales of goods that moved across state lines. The practical effect of this stroke, Roosevelt confided with gleeful indiscretion, was nil, since almost no enterprises, otherwise affected, could claim the exemption.

The sole concession the Albert "compromise" made to the Kitchin-Ayres concept was to accept its plan to pay the newly-covered a flat $1 an hour, with no provision for later increases and no requirement for overtime. Obviously, then, the Albert plan could not hope to attract the hard-core supporters of the Kitchin-Ayres concept, for above all, they were committed to the "five or more units in two or more states" concept, and would take nothing more liberal. What the Albert proposal was constructed to do was to wean away from Kitchin and Ayres a vote here, a vote there, part of this bloc, some of that delegation—by making concessions to the particular interest groups with which they were most intimately concerned. By excluding those small units of certain chains, the opposition of some legislators presumably could be removed since businessmen constituents could be mollified. In the closely divided House, everyone knew that even ten votes switched might make the difference. The Albert "compromise" was essentially a lure for the Administration approach, not a middle way between the two conflicting concepts.

Three questions arose immediately:

Was it lure enough—did the concessions go far enough to win the necessary vote switches? Administration leaks like Roosevelt were quick to make it known that other "sweetening" amendments could be offered on the House floor if it became necessary.

What about Vinson? His support for Albert seemed necessary. Bolling, the most articulate of the Democratic strategists in the House, liked to say that the way to carry the day for the Administration was to "split Vinson from Judge Smith," for that also would be to split the usually cohesive Southern Democratic ranks between the two patriarchs; some would thus back the Administration rather than all following Smith in opposition.

Would Kennedy and Goldberg actually stand by the Albert compromise? After all their pledges, could they afford to reduce coverage by a half-million Americans and bring in the new workers (indefinitely) at the $1 figure they were deriding as inadequate for those already covered?

Albert was guarded. Perspiring, obviously not too familiar with the complex provisions of his own bill, he said, "I don't think you can say this is the Administration bill." Then what was it? Not wisely, Albert said he believed Kennedy would support it as the best that could be passed in the House but that he would not necessarily accept it as the final action of Congress.

That made the Administration strategy all too clear. Kennedy, already set in the course of conciliation, would retreat as far as he had to go to get a bill through the House, stopping short only of abandoning the basic precept of his bill, the dollar-volume formula for defining enterprises in interstate commerce. Then, in the friendlier Senate, he would seek his original measure with good prospects for success. In a Senate-House conference, where Adam Powell and not Graham Barden would dominate the House conferees (and even choose them), he would then seek a much stronger bill than the one that he hoped to squeeze through the House.

Albert's admission of this plan provided one more point of attack for the nimble Ayres and his supporters. To those who might waver toward the Albert compromise, Ayres cried that they would only open the way for the ultimate passage of the Administration's bill—lock, stock, overtime pay and extended coverage. In the desultory floor debate—every member knew the important decisions, save the final one, were being made off, not on, the House floor—argument ranged from simple threat to complex economics to humanitarian pleas. If hotels had to pay more to elevator operators, they would install automatic elevators and fire the operators. Business buying power would be reduced as higher wages cut profits. That would force more unemployment. The increased buying power of individuals getting pay raises would be absorbed in higher retail prices, forced by higher retail wages.

On the other hand, who in good conscience, in a time of high prices and substantial unemployment, could vote against raising a shopclerk's pay from $40 to $50 a week? That would leave him takehome pay after taxes of only $39.40 a week.

John J. Rhodes of Arizona pointed to the so-called "balloon effect." Employers, he said, would be forced to retain established wage differentials between lower and higher paying jobs; if they had to raise the pay of workers in their lower classifications, they would have to raise their better-paid employees too, thus bringing on a wage spiral that would cause an inflation which would eat up the pay increases, to say nothing of profits. Roosevelt, busily managing the Administration bill and answering all arguments, countered that the Republican-sponsored minimum wage increase of 1955 had had no such inflationary effect.

To those who assaulted the dollar-volume criterion as having little to do with interstate commerce, Roosevelt made a tough reply. The Kitchin-Ayres "five or more units in two or more states" formula would impose minimum wage standards on many small retail chains but would exempt such one-state, one-unit retail giants as J. L. Hudson of Detroit and Rich's of Atlanta. It was a formula designed to benefit the wealthy and soak the struggling, Roosevelt argued.

Charlie Halleck raised another point popular in the precedent-conscious House. The Albert compromise had been written virtually on the back of an envelope; yet, the Kitchin-Ayres bill actually had been passed by formal vote of the House the year before, though not finally enacted by both houses. "Let's stick with something that's been proved and tried," Halleck growled.

But the representative concerned for elevator operators (or perhaps for hotel operators) had hold of the essential point. Major steps like the 1961 Fair Labor Standards Amendments are seldom taken on the basis of economic theory and projection, even more rarely on humanitarian grounds, and not always on precedent. They are forced by men's interests and opposed by other men's interests; in the long run, the real question is whether Congress wants to benefit elevator operators or hotel operators; and that, in its turn, depends on who has the power that lies, ultimately, in the votes of men.

No one was more aware of that fact of American political life than the calculating young men who were still settling into their offices and burning midnight oil at the White House. That they were willing to act upon it was made clear as the crucial day of the House debate—March 24—opened. No sooner had Carl Albert explained to the assemblage the provisions of his compromise than the Swamp Fox rose in the well of the House, stumped to the microphone, hung his cane on the edge of the rostrum and threw in a "sweetener" that obviously had strong effect, plus the backing of the White House.

Not for nothing had Vinson emerged grinning from the hasty conference in Rayburn's office.

The amendment was read by the clerk. Vinson listened impassively. He had five minutes to explain the amendment but he was contemptuous of the privilege.

"I will merely say," the old Georgian rumbled, "that this amendment takes out all the laundries."

Derisive laughter and several catcalls rose from Vinson's left, the Republican side of the crowded House. The Swamp Fox waited like a comedian for the laughter to die, then smoothly tossed out his punch line.

"It washes laundries clean out of the picture," Vinson said.

The whole House rocked with laughter. The old man sat down, grinning broadly. With a tremendous roar, mostly from united Democrats, the House gave voice-vote approval to his amendment. For differing motives, Southern and Northern Democrats, for once, had voted as one. And since they were so united, it was plain that the Administration had no objection to the amendment—indeed had inspired it as another concession to the Southern votes to which it looked for victory.

Laundry workers were worth, by Bolling's estimate, "ten or twelve votes"; that is, he believed there were that many representatives under heavy pressure from big laundry operators to grant them exemption from any new minimum wage and overtime provisions. Most of these representatives—not one of whom ever was identified by Bolling or anyone else—were Southerners, it was hinted; and although no one mentioned it that day, most of the estimated 150,000 laundry workers so cavalierly thrown out of the Administration-backed compromise bill were Negroes.

Those had been fine words in Buffalo, uttered in John Kennedy's well-honed campaign voice: "As long as the average wage for laundry women in the five largest cities is 65 cents an hour for a 48-hour week . . . there is a need for our party."

But Kennedy was dedicated to the possible, not to the perfect; government of men can operate no other way. "Progress is made through reasonable compromise," John McCormack was to say to his colleagues later that day, and if "reasonable compromise" meant the sacrifice of thousands of black laundry women not much farther removed from slavery than their grandparents had been . . . well, a few more votes in the House perhaps could win a higher wage for millions of other Americans. The laundry women *would* be washed out.

The laundry women, throughout the rest of the minimum wage battle, became a focal point of debate, strategy and the newspaper accounts of what was happening. In retrospect, however, both the shrewdness and the ruthlessness of their exclusion probably were overestimated. For one thing, it never has been shown by anyone that the tactic actually won ten or twelve or any other number of votes, other than Vinson's; nor was it really designed to do so. Rather, the exclusion was part of a *general retreat* on the part of the Administration toward a total bill more acceptable to conservatives, particularly Southerners. As such, it may have been useful; but since the real crux of the battle lay in the two opposing formulae on interstate commerce, which never were fundamentally changed on either side, it could only have been a peripheral usefulness. In the long run, exclusion of the laundry women became most of all a dramatic symbol of the Administration's willingness to compromise, retreat, seek opposing votes. It was designed to influence men, not buy them.

For another thing, the Administration's approval of Vinson's amendment apparently won his unwavering support; but, as will be seen, having "split Vinson from Judge Smith" did not produce the effect among Southerners that Bolling had confidently predicted. Conciliation sometimes encourages the blackmailer only to raise his price.

As for the ruthlessness of the move, one fact in mitigation should be pointed out. Among all the workers considered for inclusion, none were more vulnerable to automation than laundry women. If their wages went up substantially, it was probably more true in their case than with most classes of workers that laundry operators would promptly cut their working forces and put in machinery to do their jobs. Experience had shown, for instance, that where state minimum wage laws had increased laundry wages, institutions like hospitals had promptly installed their own laundry machinery rather than pay the higher bills that resulted. Thus, the Administration could and did argue plausibly that it was preserving laundry women's jobs, if it was not increasing their wages.

On March 24, in the House, however, it appeared that Vinson and the Administration had scored a spectacular and brutal coup. Ayres and Halleck countered immediately. The Representative from Florida, A. Sydney Herlong, a conservative Democrat, quickly rose with an amendment that would "sweeten" the Kitchin-Ayres bill and perhaps hold some of the Southerners Vinson obviously was trying to lure to Albert's support. Herlong's amendment would exempt from the minimum wage those bus and truck drivers who transported fruit and vegetables to market or to a processor within one state; or who transported transient fruit and vegetable harvesters from farm to farm within one state. Republican whips helped push the amendment through, 161 to 133. The Southerners had exacted their tribute from both sides.

It was a faintly alarming portent but observers in the press gallery and the House lobby pointed out to each other that only 294 members had voted; the result could hardly be a fair indication of how the overall battle would go when all members of the House were on the floor.

The arguments had been made, the votes had been bought—both sides hoped they would stay bought—and the decision was at hand. But there now intervened both government of law, through the labyrinthine workings of parliamentary procedure and the rules of the House, and government of men, through the organizational weaknesses of the House Democrats.

Carl Albert was the key figure in the party "whip" system. As the assistant leader, it was his responsibility to round up

his colleagues at the time of voting, to see to it that they were
out of their offices and committee chambers, out of the Capitol
Hill bars and restaurants, the House Office Building gymna-
sium or cafeteria, out of the House barber shop, out of the
clutches of constituents and lobbyists, and safely on the House
floor—the only place they could cast their precious votes.

Democrats being as unruly as they are, Democratic "whips"
always have trouble. In the House of Representatives, Albert
had a special problem. The Democratic whip system had been
organized with no concession whatever to the fact of the
Southern Democrats, a force then so plainly alienated and
devoted to its own peculiar interests that it constituted what
could only be described as a third party.

The whip system was set up to permit Albert and his aides
to make a few quick telephone calls to state and regional
"whips"—other Members of the House—who worked under
them. These sub-whips, in turn, called the dozen or fifteen
members for whose presence on the floor they were responsible. In a few minutes, theoretically, Albert could alert and
mobilize all 258 Democrats for a crucial vote.

In fact, of those 258, 131 were from Southern and border
states (the figure depends on which states are considered
"border"), and so were the sub-whips responsible for them.
One of Albert's sub-whips on March 24 was none other than
Paul Kitchin of North Carolina, co-sponsor of the opposition
bill! It was a fatal weakness and it meant that Albert could
not count on his Southern and border-state sub-whips to
mobilize for him those members in their charge who might be
willing to follow the Administration or at least Carl Vinson;
rather, Albert's supposed lieutenants might be actively working for Halleck and Judge Howard Smith, co-captains of the
Republican-Southern Democratic coalition. Paul Kitchin, for
one, was doing just that, and understandably so.

Early in the day, Ayres had offered his and Kitchin's famous
substitute bill, terming it hyperbolically "the only thing that
could prevent the federal government from eventually taking

over every enterprise in the United States." Albert then had offered *his* substitute, not for the Administration bill, but for Kitchin-Ayres. Vinson had thrown in his amendment and seen it accepted as part of the Albert substitute; Herlong had got his into the Kitchin-Ayres package, which Albert sought to replace.

The result was a highly complex parliamentary situation. Under House rules, Albert was in a situation where there had first to be a choice between his substitute (as amended when Vinson "washed out" the laundry workers) and the bill offered by Kitchin and Ayres (as amended by Herlong). The one of these two that was selected then would be pitted against the original Administration bill. If it was Kitchin-Ayres, everyone in the House knew that Halleck and Ayres had enough publicly committed and unchangeable votes to win. The one thing the Administration could not afford at any time was a roll-call showdown between its original bill and Kitchin-Ayres. The *raison d'etre* of the Albert substitute was to prevent such a showdown by posing one instead between Albert and Kitchin-Ayres.

The Administration was nonetheless at a disadvantage that derived from two provisions of the House rules. One was that even if Kitchin-Ayres was knocked out by the Albert compromise, the minority—the Republicans—would be entitled under the rules to a last try, a so-called "recommittal motion." If approved, such a motion would send an approved bill back to the Education and Labor Committee with instructions to substitute something else for it, and that something else obviously would be the Kitchin-Ayres bill.

The other applicable rule was that the vote between Albert and Kitchin-Ayres—the crucial vote—would be taken by "tellers." A "teller" vote is a clever House device that enables members to vote for or against a proposition without recording their names on the record. Members in favor of a measure march up the center aisle and are counted by a "teller," but not by name; then members opposed to the measure go through the same procedure. This kind of voting is almost always in order on amendments and substitutes, which are considered by the House as a "Committee of the Whole." Its value is that a member can cast an unrecorded vote against some crucial part of a bill; later, on a recorded roll call, he can cast a public vote, for display to his contituents, in favor of what is left of that bill. In secrecy, he may have eliminated its "guts" or blunted its point; in public, he can "make a record" by voting for the shell that remains.

The essential tactical disadvantage of the Administration that arose from these two rules of the parliamentary situation was that if the Albert compromise was defeated in its secret, teller-vote showdown with the Kitchin-Ayres bill, it was completely eliminated from further consideration. Members would never have to be recorded publicly on the hard, meaningful choice between these two artfully constructed packages. The recorded public showdown would be between Kitchin-Ayres and the original Administration bill.

On the other hand, if Kitchin-Ayres was defeated in the teller vote, the Republicans still could—and would—bring it to a roll-call vote via a recommittal motion. Members then would have to go *publicly on the record* on the hardest choice that lay before them—whether to approve the Albert package with its dollar-volume concept of interstate commerce and its fairly extensive new coverage, or the Kitchin-Ayres package with its restrictive definition of interstate commerce and its limited new coverage.

As always in the interest-group jungle of politics in the House of Representatives, there were small numbers of men on both sides who wanted to vote a particular way, or who believed it was politically advantageous in their districts to do so, but who were under irresistable pressures from one or more powerful interests (a big campaign contributor, a dominant local politician) to vote the other way. Others were personally committed to a particular course (perhaps owing a favor to the Speaker or to Halleck, or simply believing that course to be right) that they feared would damage them politically. A politician in such a cross fire eventually may choose or be forced to take a public stand; but his first instinct is likely to be to find a way out—to have it both ways.

For the small numbers of Republicans who for any number of reasons felt obliged to back the Administration, but who did not in private want to do so, Charlie Halleck could point the way out. Vote for Kitchin-Ayres on the teller round, he could say, and if you can't do that, don't vote at all; no one will ever know. That will help knock the Albert compromise totally out of the picture, and no harm done to you. Halleck had the votes, he could argue, to win the showdown that would follow between the Kitchin-Ayres bill and the original Administration bill, even without help from the waverers. On that roll call, Charlie would understand if they had to "make a record" by casting a meaningless vote for the doomed Administration bill. But if it came to a close, decisive roll-call between Kitchin-Ayres and Albert, he would have to call on every Republican to go down the party line, on the record; who wanted that?

The Kennedy men could make no such diabolical argument. To the equally few Democrats obliged to vote publicly against them but perhaps willing to help in secret, they could not guarantee the necessary elimination of the Kitchin-Ayres bill. If a wavering Democrat voted secretly for the Albert compromise on the teller round, and it won, he would be faced later on with a certain roll-call choice between Albert and Kitchin-Ayres on the recommittal motion—the one dilemma he hoped to avoid. A teller vote for the Albert substitute might commit him to stand up and be counted publicly on the only decisive question there was; but a secret teller vote for Kitchin-Ayres—or no vote at all—might eliminate the troublesome Albert bill altogether and confront him only with the meaningless roll call between Kitchin-Ayres and the doomed Administration bill.

This apparently small tactical disadvantage may have been

crucial in the House on March 24, 1961. In hindsight, it may seem the Administration should have planned for that contingency, that it should have had a series of prepared positions to retire to, so that in the event of defeat for Albert other more conservative substitutes might have been offered. In fact, there probably was not time for such orderly, planned combat.

Only as the hour of decision approached had it been made clear that the original bill was hopeless; the Albert bill itself was jeered on the floor as hasty, jerry-built, patched-up—and so it was. The aristocratic Republican from New Jersey, Peter Frelinghuysen (Peter Frozenhosen, irreverent colleagues called him), referred with icy disdain to the quick development of the Albert compromise and its log-rolling Vinson amendment as a "travesty of the legislative process." Written only yesterday, he pointed out, it already had been amended today and never had been studied by a committee.

Moreover, President Kennedy was, for the first time, a partial victim of his own rhetoric and political posture. The legislative situation in the House should have been plain from the start; to him, it may have been. An original bill perhaps even more restricted than the Albert compromise, but perserving the dollar-volume principle, would have been far better *legislative* strategy. But that is not the same thing as *political* strategy.

As a result of his impassioned campaign pledges, the commitments he had made to organized labor, the stand he had taken so powerfully and stubbornly as a Senator, Kennedy could not easily propose or support less than he had. Already, he had compromised enough, in developing his legislative program and in placating the Southerners, to arouse the alarm and even the anger of important liberal elements in the Democratic party; already he was being accused of acting like a "young Eisenhower." He could not have retreated farther, on so publicized an issue, one that evoked all the old New Deal memories, without severe structural damage to that impression of himself as a "strong" President, in the F.D.R. tradition, that he had been at such pains to construct, and to the liberal support that had been so important a cause of his electoral victory. The real question—as we shall discuss—is whether he already had compromised too much.

Thus, in disadvantageous circumstances he had helped to create, Kennedy came to one of the decisive moments in his brief struggle with Congress. Carl Albert moved to the right-hand side of the middle aisle of the House. Across from him, grinning and garrulous, was Ayres. As the bells of the House rang their clarion messages through the southern wing of the Capitol and the two sprawling House buildings, William E. "Fishbait" Miller, the House doorkeeper, took his accustomed position at the door of the Democratic side of the House lobby. Elevators rose and sank, carrying sardine-like loads of Representatives; members hurried from the office buildings through the gray, clinical tunnel under Independence Avenue and the Capitol's south grounds; the House restaurant began to empty; barbershop business dwindled. Fishbait Miller hurried Democrats through the lobby to the House floor with a quick whispered explanation of the issue; Republican aides held the doors at the opposite, G.O.P., end of the lobby.

But there is not much time to mobilize a full-strength voting force for a "teller" vote. As Albert's forces filed slowly up the aisle and he touched each upon the shoulder, reporters in the gallery began to point three things out to each other; they knew there would be no name-by-name record of such votes and that they had to get their information on who did what by eye-witness methods. One thing they saw was that few, if any, Republicans, were going through the line for Albert; only Representatives Paul A. Fino and Seymour Halpern of New York, William T. Cahill of New Jersey and Chester Merrow of New Hampshire were spotted. Another was that, despite Vinson and the laundries, a sizeable number of Southern Democrats were staying in their seats, either to vote later for Ayres or to refrain from voting altogether. Finally, experienced galleryites saw that it was going to be a relatively light vote for such a controversial issue—the fruit of the lax Democratic whip system.

The last man filed through to be touched by Carl Albert. He held up his arm, turned to the rostrum where Representative Francis E. "Tad" Walter was presiding. Albert's slightly hoarse voice was barely audible in the galleries. "A hundred seventy-five," he said, and Bill Ayres nodded in agreement.

Then it was Ayres' turn to count his supporters. One by one they came, mostly from the Republican side of the aisle—Republicans ranging from Old Guard curmudgeons like H. R. Gross of Iowa to bright young "modern" types like Scranton of Pennsylvania, then widely believed to be the most promising newcomer on either side of the House.

Ayres counted steadily. Southerners drifted in noticeable numbers from their seats on the Democratic side, joining the Republican band. Obviously, it still was not a large vote; even more obviously, it would be a close one. The last man drifted through; triumphantly, Ayres bawled, "One eighty-six."

But Albert was not done. Formed up and waiting were a few more supporters of his "compromise." He beckoned them eagerly and they marched up the aisles. It was quiet as a library in the House as the Little Giant from Little Dixie touched each. The last man passed—the tenth man. Albert looked for more. There were none.

"On this vote," Walter announced, "the noes have it, a hundred eighty-six to a hundred eighty-five." The Kennedy Administration had suffered its first major reversal by exactly one vote.

A long day's work lay ahead, but the battle in the House was over. Quickly, on another teller vote, Ayres, Halleck and Judge Smith pushed the Kitchin-Ayres bill through as a substitute for the Administration bill; the count was 205 to 162. Since only four fewer members voted than in the first teller ballot, the attractiveness of the Albert compromise over the original Administration bill could be fairly measured at just about 23 votes—the difference between 185 for Albert on the first vote and 162 for the Administration bill on the second. Add those 23 to the 186 Ayres had obtained on the first ballot, subtract the four abstainers, and one arrives at the exact 205 total Ayres achieved on the second vote.

Obviously the Administration tactic of retreat, by concessions to representatives concerned for particular interests and interest groups, had been well-conceived; it simply had not been nicely enough calculated to pick up the final one or two votes that would have won the victory. But there was another element in the defeat and a chastened Carl Albert, feeling himself partially to blame, pointed it out to reporters. The "whip" system had signally failed to turn out the Administration's potential.

On the attendance roll call that had opened the day's events, 412 members had answered to their names. But only 371 had marched up the aisle in the crucial teller vote between Albert and Kitchin-Ayres; at least 37 potential votes had been missing. Tad Walter, a staunch Administration man, had been in a position to see from the rostrum who had voted and who hadn't; later he called a few names. One was Rep. Cleveland Bailey of West Virginia, second-ranking Democrat on the Education and Labor Committee, an ardent supporter of higher minimum wages for his mountaineer constituents. Bald, belligerent old Bailey, who had once taken a swing at Adam Clayton Powell, had been at lunch in the House restaurant, for some reason unaware that the tellers were counting votes; had only he arrived to tie the vote, Walter could have broken it in favor of Albert. There were others as delinquent, each of whom, in effect, might as well have voted for Ayres.

But the Albert bill was dead and now impended the clinching roll call, on which the House would formally and publicly approve its choice between Kitchin-Ayres and the Administration bill—the showdown the Albert "compromise" had been designed to avoid. Whips on both sides, given more time, labored mightily and turned out a total of 419 voters; six other Representatives were present but "paired" and not voting. The final count by which the House chose Kitchin-Ayres over the Kennedy bill was 216 to 203.

The closeness of that vote—seven switches would have carried it for the President—was of small comfort to the Administration forces. It only emphasized to them the opportunity they had missed on the first teller vote. They did not believe Ayres, Halleck and Smith could have mustered 216 publicly recorded votes for their bill in a roll-call match against the Albert compromise. If 23 votes was truly the difference between the attractions of the Albert plan and those of the original Kennedy bill, then that final, clinching roll-call vote might have been 226 to 193 for the Albert bill . . . might have been! If only the Administration had delivered its full voting strength in the first teller vote, what a different story there would have been. So went the argument, but it was academic.

Less academic was the vital fact that while Albert estimated that "only five or six" Republicans had supported him on the teller vote, twenty-six Republicans voted on the roll call *for* the Administration bill against the Kitchin-Ayres substitute. Had the other twenty or so simply missed the teller vote, like Cleve Bailey? Or had they deliberately "made a record" by voting publicly for the Administration's more liberal bill on the recorded roll call, after abstaining on the more-or-less secret teller vote that actually decided the issue?

Administration men darkly alleged the worst. Accused Republicans, like Lindsay of New York, replied heatedly that they had supported the original Administration bill but had not been willing to back the more limited Albert "compromise" with its exclusion of Negro laundry workers, its flat $1 minimum and no overtime pay for the newly-covered.

On the other side of the aisle, 74 Democrats (all but Fred Marshall of Minnesota from Southern or border states) supported Kitchin-Ayres on the clinching roll call. They joined 142 Republicans in a classic exercise of the Southern-Republican coalition.

8 *The Church Takes a Stand*

In the end, the record shows, Kennedy got his minimum wage bill. He pushed a measure quite similar to his original bill through the more liberal Senate, where the Democratic majority was sixty-four to thirty-six and the coalition could not function, or at least not so well. From that moment on, procedure and the control of it by men played squarely into the Administration's hands.

In the House-Senate conference to reconcile the Kitchin-Ayres and the Administration bills, for instance, Adam Clayton Powell, as chairman of the Education and Labor Committee, could handpick Democrats to serve as House conferees and they outnumbered and overpowered Ayres and his supporters. The Senate conferees also were favorable to the Kennedy bill. And with a Democratic President in the White House, Ayres could not threaten a veto of the Administration bill. Moreover, his unrecorded one-vote victory in the House had puny standing beside the sixty-five to twenty-eight recorded vote for Kennedy in the Senate; the senators could even point out in conference that their chamber had already defeated, sixty-three to thirty-four, a substitute bill—put forward by Everett McKinley Dirksen—that was a duplicate of the Kitchin-Ayres bill. Ayres never had a chance, and the conference sent back to House and Senate a bill that in some respects was even more favorable to the Administration than the one defeated in the House.

There, too, the procedural situation had changed, and men worked in altered circumstances. For one thing, the crucial vote in the House on March 24 had been between Albert and Kitchin-Ayres; a lesser vote followed between Kitchin-Ayres and the original Administration bill. In either instance, there were alternatives, either of which would result in some increase in and extension of the minimum wage. Nobody had to vote outright *against* doing something for the workingman.

On May 3, when the conference report came to the floor, there was no real alternative. The Senate had decisively rejected Kitchin-Ayres; so had the conference; Kennedy undoubtedly would veto it if some miracle revived it; and the only choice was between (1) the Administration-backed conference report, or (2) no increase and extension at all. Even the Republican Policy Committee was on record favoring such an increase and expansion, though not to the extent of the conference report; could it risk the onus for preventing them?

The processes of the House, once so favorable to Ayres and Halleck, now favored Kennedy in an even more important respect. This time, there would be no teller vote; the balloting on the conference report would be publicly recorded by House roll call.

Albert's testimony that only "five or six" Republicans had supported him on that crucial, unrecorded teller vote of March 24 must not be forgotten. Nor can the fact that on the later, recorded vote between the Administration bill and Kitchin-Ayres, *twenty-six Republicans* backed the Administration. The obvious conclusion was that there were some, at least, among the Republicans who had opposed Albert on the secret teller vote and then "made a record" for the more liberal minimum wage bill on the roll call, because they feared to be recorded against increasing and extending the minimum wage.

Some of the Southerners were in the same position as these Republicans. On the only roll call they could be sure of, they felt impelled either to "make a record" for raising the minimum wage for home consumption, or to go down the line with the President. This time, there was no place to hide.

As the roll call inexorably recorded what there was of democracy and what there was of power in that House, seven Republicans who had lined up against the Administration on March 24 deserted Halleck to back the conference report—the only possible minimum wage bill. So did Thor Tollefson, Republican of Washington, unrecorded on March 24. So did twenty-five of the twenty-six Republicans who had backed the original Kennedy bill against the Kitchin-Ayres substitutes on the clinching roll call of March 24. Where these thirty-three Republicans had been in the crucial hour of the teller vote between Albert (a less liberal bill than the conference report) and Kitchin-Ayres is a matter of conjecture. But on May 3, they showed themselves either personally in favor of, or politically forced to support, a minimum wage increase and expansion; hence they had nowhere to go but into the Administration ranks.

Equally important were the shifted positions of eighteen Democrats—sixteen of them from the South. They had been for Kitchin-Ayres on March 24; they supported the conference report on May 3. Three Southerners, unrecorded the first time, also backed the Administration. Exactly which of these votes was cast because there no longer was a teller vote or a Kitchin-Ayres bill in which to take refuge, is a matter of conjecture. What was certain was the passage of the Administration bill, 230 to 196.

Again, as in the battle for control of the Committee on Rules, Kennedy had managed a nominal victory. Four months after the wage bill went into effect, 2.5 million Americans began to receive more money in their paychecks and two years later, 2.6 million received a further increase; later, about 2.4 million would take home more cash at the end of the week. None of them, of course, were laundry women.

But the real question was: What had been *the effect upon men*?

In the House of Representatives, it was widely believed that the new President and his aides had botched the original fight. Embarrassing compromise still had not produced victory; and in view of the ease with which the conference report had been passed, the question was even raised whether the compromises had been necessary. For if defeat in the House could not have been avoided, there had been little necessity for washing out the laundry women in a vain effort at conciliation. And at the crucial moment the Administration had not even been able to turn out its vote.

In the House view, Kennedy had been forced to retreat from his original position, nevertheless had taken a shattering defeat by the margin of one vote that somebody surely should have rounded up, and had been rescued only by his huge majority in the Senate and by the fact of Powell's chairmanship of the Education and Labor Committee (and hence his control of the House conferees on the wage bill).

There had been, moreover, enough distasteful logrolling throughout to cause the caustic liberal columnist, Doris Fleeson, to comment that the result was ". . . a bill aimed at including the maximum number of workers but the fewest possible employers . . . The trading which has gone on, if extended to all the Kennedy program, would doom it to faint praise."

The brilliant promise of 1960 had been that great deeds were on the way; the first practical dealings with Congress had shown that there might be none. The long weeks of the minimum wage battle, moreover, had not been isolated from other events. The new President was locked in another struggle, of far deeper meaning, that had brought about a mighty collision of the racial, religious, geographical and economic interests of the country.

There seemed to be nothing particularly startling about the Kennedy education bill, except to those who were convinced that the President was a wild-eyed radical. Throughout the postwar period, there had been periodic efforts to provide federal aid for the American school system—locally supported, locally controlled, growing (in what was probably a majority view of the matter in 1961) each year more inadequate in its physical plant and less responsive to the needs of the mind and spirit. Each effort—even one backed by the late "Mr. Republican," Robert A. Taft of Ohio—had foundered on one rock or another of entrenched interest. The issue of whether federal aid should go to segregated schools, to Catholic and other religious schools; whether wealthy states should contribute to the schools of the poorer; whether, if they did, the poorer or the most populous states should have the most aid per child; whether the federal government would follow its investment in education by seeking "control" of local school systems; whether it was not the states' "right" to finance and administer schools; whether the nation could afford vast outlays for this purpose when the budget was out of balance and the national debt rising—each of these factors, some or all of them in combination, had been too much for any President or any Congress to overcome in the fifteen years preceding John F. Kennedy's entrance into the White House.

All of those factors came together at once in the education debate of 1961; and it was obvious at the beginning of that year that they all would, certainly that they all could. It has to be asked again, as in the case of the legislative situation generally, why anyone thought that 1961 was to be the year when so many forces would be overcome and a federal education program would be at last embarked upon. And the same answer must be given. It was to be the year because John Kennedy had said so in his strong campaign; because he himself so patently believed that a Wilsonian Presidential effort could get anything done. In the zeal and euphoria of campaign and victory, in the captivating performance of the young champion, to ever-hopeful liberals and ever-zestful Democrats, reasonable doubt came to seem old-fashioned, defeatist, conservative, unvigorous—in a word, Republican.

But Kennedy, himself, as we have seen, was too aware of his narrow victory not to trim his sails as soon as the election was over. His caution was obvious in the education proposals he submitted in a special message to Congress on February 20. The main section was a three-year program of grants to the fifty states, totalling $2.3 billion or $766 million a year, to be used at the state's discretion for school construction, teachers' salaries, or both. But the Kennedy "task force" in education— one of those ferociously dedicated groups that had got up an estimate for the President of what a sincere liberal intellectual would do in various fields of the public welfare, if he only could—had recommended a few weeks before that the Administration spend almost twice that much ($1.46 billion a year).

Ten days before the Kennedy message went to Congress, reports "leaked" off Capitol Hill to the national press that Abraham Ribicoff of Connecticut, the new Secretary of Health, Education and Welfare, had outlined for Congressional leaders a school bill that would have provided $900 million a year in grants to the states. Almost immediately, the bargaining had started; Southerners and other conservatives put pressure on the Administration to reduce the size of the outlays, increasing the heavy pressures for "fiscal responsibility" always brought on any Democratic President. The result, as seen in the formal message Kennedy sent on February 20, was the reduction of the grant request to $766 million a year. It was not lost upon Democratic liberals that this was, despite the campaign oratory, less than the $900 million a year that had been proposed in 1960 in a bill passed in the Senate—a bill that John F. Kennedy had voted for and frequently chided the Republicans for helping to squelch in the House Committee on Rules.

But now Southern Democrats won a limited point in the early discussions. Ribicoff, in his informal outline of the education bill on February 10, said the money would be distributed according to a formula of $30 per pupil per year, based on the average daily attendance of children in each state's schools. In low-income states—mostly Southern—an additional $15 per child would be provided; in big-city schools with special language and other problems, an additional $15 per child also would be provided.

Influential Democrats from medium size-and-income states contended, in informal talks with Ribicoff and other Administration officials, that this was too generous to the Southern states. As a result, the formal Kennedy proposals of February 20 were sharply altered, although they were still, in the view of many Democrats, favorable to the hard-bargaining South.

The $766 million a year was to be distributed on a new sliding scale formula, with each state to get a minimum of $15 per child in average daily attendance. An "equalization" factor was to adjust each state's grant according to its income, with low-income states benefiting most. At the top of the scale was to be Mississippi, the poorest state, getting $29.67 per child; at the bottom would be wealthy states like New York and New Jersey, receiving the minimum $15; an in-between state would receive something between these extremes—Indiana, for instance, was scheduled for $18.51.

This illustrates one of the prime problems of legislating in a federal system. New York and other big states would provide the lion's share of the tax money to finance the program; Mississippi and other poor states—some of them openly defiant of the federal government on matters like school desegregation—were scheduled on a basis of need to get a greater proportionate share of the money.

The states were to have control of spending the grants. In the Kennedy message, nothing was said about any effort to keep the money out of segregated school districts; and Ribicoff went further. He told a news conference the Administration was opposed to withholding funds from segregated schools. He and Kennedy obviously were bowing to the Congressional fact of life that the Southern Democrats would fight, en masse, any bill containing such a restriction. And, as usual, Kennedy was willing to bargain for Southern votes at the expense of his allies' sensibilities.

Other provisions of the program Kennedy sent to Congress

with abundant confidence—providing for college scholarship grants, loans for the construction of college academic facilities, and expansion of an existing program to help colleges build dormitories and other housing accommodations—brought the total proposed cost of the package to $5.625 billion. But it was always upon the grants to the states for secondary and elementary schools that attention was centered.

On a number of points of possible opposition, Kennedy had not yielded. He called for federal aid in paying teachers' salaries, despite the known opposition of Speaker Rayburn. Ribicoff, risking minor Southern wrath, said the college scholarship program would not be available in states where it would be administered in a manner discriminating against Negroes.

But none of the frequent concessions, none of the less numerous refusals to compromise, were so important as the single question of whether the grants to the states could be used to assist Roman Catholic and other religious or private schools. Again, Kennedy's personal circumstances were difficult to evade.

Nothing had been more discussed or more prominent in the campaign than that the Democratic candidate would be the first Roman Catholic President of the United States. Reviewing the endless discussions of this point, one is struck with admiration at how convincingly Kennedy made the case that he would not be influenced by his Church, and that no one should be barred from office because of his religion. And reviewing his years in office, one finds no reason to doubt that religious belief and discipline had no effect whatever upon his Presidential conduct and judgment.

But in another sense, the fact of his Catholicism made a crucial difference. The point had been indelibly made in the public mind that John Kennedy was a Roman Catholic, and he never forgot that fact; had he not done more than anyone, in his insistence on meeting the religious issue squarely, to create that public awareness? As a politician fighting for office, Kennedy had dealt with the religious issue as forcefully and publicly as with the minimum wage or education, and while as President he would not be influenced spiritually or intellectually by his religion, neither would he escape the effect upon men of their knowledge that he was the first Roman Catholic President.

Within the new Administration, on the question of federal aid to religious schools, a substantial fight was waged in secrecy. Ribicoff, the earliest of the Kennedy supporters, the most experienced and supple politician in the Cabinet—save Udall the only Cabinet member who had had Congressional experience—argued one side of the question. In Ribicoff's opinion, the school package could not pass unless there was in it "something for the Catholics."

It was a purely political view. Connecticut, his home state, was heavily Catholic. Ribicoff's experience was largely based on the conditions of the industrial East, where Catholic political power is formidable. Ribicoff, in addition, had made a career of accommodation and coalition; until his nomination to the Kennedy Cabinet, he had never been fully identified as a "liberal" but had made his way with a foot in every camp, and a jaundiced eye upon the adamant stand.

Thus, as he calculated the chances of the education program that was so heavily his responsibility to achieve, it seemed plain to him that if in the closely divided House of Representatives (where he once had served with facility) many conservative Southern Democrats would oppose federal aid to education on racial and states' rights grounds, and large numbers of Republicans, led by Halleck, would oppose it on economic and political grounds, the main hope for its passage lay with the Democrats of the Eastern industrial states.

But Catholic political strength was centered in these states, so that Catholic opposition to a bill in which there was not "something" for Catholic schools, in the Ribicoff view, surely would divide and diminish that necessary base of support. He may have been influenced not only by his personal liaison with influential Catholic leaders but by a speech made by the

late Cardinal Spellman of New York in January, 1961. Spellman had said: "It is unthinkable that any American child be
denied the federal funds allotted to other children which are
necessary for his mental development because his parents chose
for him a God-connected education."

That speech did not arouse much comment or apprehension.
The issue of federal aid to Catholic schools had lain dormant
for more than ten years, since a celebrated fight in 1949. When
a school construction bill moved torturously through the House
in 1960 (ultimately to meet frustration in the Committee on
Rules), Catholic Representative Roman L. Pucinski of Illinois
offered an amendment to provide aid to parochial and private
schools; it was promptly ruled out of order as "not germane"
by Representative Tad Walter of Pennsylvania, a Catholic,
who was presiding, and the ruling was not even appealed. In
the same year, when Wayne Morse offered an amendment to a
somewhat similar Senate bill, with the aim of authorizing loans
to private schools, the amendment was defeated by forty-nine
to thirty-seven and the bill passed the Senate anyway. The
"church-state issue" did not seem to excite people anymore.

In his campaign, for instance, Kennedy had repeatedly opposed the provision of federal aid to Catholic schools, on
Constitutional grounds, and the evidence was that both the
church hierarchy and a huge majority of Catholics had voted
for him anyway. Cardinal Spellman was regarded, in any
case, as more outspoken and rigid in his political views than
other church leaders.

Ribicoff thus found no encouragement at the White House.
He persisted, submitting at one point a memorandum proposing
several methods by which private schools might be federally
aided, within the Constitution. One method was that of tax
relief to parents who paid both public school taxes and private
school expenses. Another was for specified types of loans, to
be provided through an expansion of the popular National
Defense Education Act of 1958—a measure passed in the
wake of the first Soviet Sputnik.

Ribicoff was powerfully opposed, particularly by Robert F. Kennedy, Sorensen, and Douglas Dillon, the new Treasury Secretary. The President sided with them, making the decision against Ribicoff inevitable. The two most powerful influences upon that decision were the Administration's early ebullience and the public's awareness of Kennedy's Catholicism.

The White House still believed, in those first weeks in office, that it could pass an education bill and it saw little reason—in the recent historical record—to fear Catholic opposition. But even if it had feared that opposition, the President's religion surely would have impelled him on the same course of no compromise with the Catholic view.

As the first Roman Catholic President, elected over the protests of leading Protestant clergymen and in a contest that had divided Protestant and Catholic voters, regardless of party, Kennedy and his advisers believed he literally could not accept—just weeks after his inauguration—a program of aid for Catholic schools as a part of his highest-priority legislative proposal. To do so would at least *appear* to negate every assurance of impartiality and freedom that he had given in his campaign, in such open discussions of church and state as he had had with the Houston Protestant ministers—and that was true no matter how convincing might be the case for a public policy of aiding Catholic schools. By recommending such aid, either as a matter of conviction, of merit, or of expedience, the President would have shattered public confidence in his integrity and intentions, re-aroused the issue of a Catholic in the White House, and produced even sharper religious divisions in the country at a time when it was becoming plain that he still had to build a broad base of popular support for all that he wanted to do.

Even in practical political terms, such staggering losses would have been compensated by no important political gain; for Kennedy already had won the Catholic vote to about the extent that any man could. No politics, no merit, no expedience seemed to override the central fact of Kennedy's

religion and the limitations it imposed on him; in so far as the
school bill was concerned, the President was a prisoner of those
limitations and would remain so until the end.

Ribicoff recognized these problems—although he, at least,
feared that the heavy Catholic vote could fall off or turn
against Kennedy when he ran again in 1964. In fact, he did
not propose that the President come out for aid to Catholic
schools. What he wanted was for the Administration to submit
a *public school bill* but to *leave the door open* for Congress, in
the event of heavy Catholic pressure, to adopt one of the means
he had proposed for giving "something to the Catholics." He
recommended that the President "let Congress perform the
marriage" if nuptials became necessary.

Again, ebullience and the President's religion combined to
defeat Ribicoff. The Catholic issue probably wouldn't arise;
but if it did, the President would have to stand forthrightly
where he had stood in the campaign. True, that could be
politically risky. Better not to take the chance; better to slam
the door at the outset.

Slam it Kennedy did, and hard. In his Education message
to Congress he cited what he called "the clear prohibition of
the Constitution" against aid to Catholic or other non-public
schools. It was a closed issue, the message made clear; there
would be, there could be, no such aid. At his next news conference, on March 1, the President drove the point home and
the nails in the door. "There isn't any room for debate on that
subject. It is prohibited by the Constitution and the Supreme
Court has made that very clear. Therefore there would be no
possibility of our recommending it."

The President not only had slammed the door and nailed it
shut; in Ribicoff's view he had gratuitously raised and emphasized the Catholic issue. He had tailored a bill that could
be accepted by the race-conscious Southerners in his own party,
and that would be no more offensive than necessary to the fiscal
conservatives and states' righters in both parties. Perhaps there
was an ample case to be made for that. But the tender political

bones of Abe Ribicoff had not ached without cause, however right or wrong he might have been on strategy. The very day of the President's news conference, that fact began to come ominously clear.

A chance remark by garrulous old John McCormack, then the Democratic Majority Leader in the House, led to the first disclosure of the storm that was about to break over the Kennedy school bill. McCormack, a Boston Irish Catholic who for years had worked closely with the so-called "hierarchy" of his Church, confided almost casually to Rep. Frank Thompson Jr., a liberal Catholic Democrat from New Jersey, that a number of Church leaders were meeting in Washington.

Thompson, an energetic and voluble former Navy officer, had just started his seventh year in the House. Such junior liberals ordinarily disposed of little influence in a body then heavily weighted toward senior conservatives. But Thompson was a more practical and accommodating politician than run-of-the-litter liberals. He had become a hard-boiled legislator, astute in the ways of the House, and had achieved some prominence in 1960 by guiding through it the ill-fated bill to provide federal aid for local school construction—only to see it lost in the Committee on Rules.

As a member of the House Education and Labor Committee, Thompson had come into the Kennedy circle in 1959, during the epic battle that resulted in the Landrum-Griffin labor bill. He headed the Democrats' National Voter Registration Committee in the 1960 campaign, with such success that the new President offered him a Cabinet office in the incoming Administration. Thompson chose to remain in the House and Kennedy told him, in a meeting at Palm Beach before his inauguration, that he would be the sponsor of what everyone thought would be the Administration's "historic" education bill.

It was in that capacity that Thompson—an outspoken, anti-clerical Catholic, long aware of McCormack's high church connections and not particularly charmed by them—pricked up his ears at the white-haired Bostonian's remarks about a meeting of Catholic leaders. Smelling trouble, Thompson got in touch with John D. Morris of *The New York Times,* a Catholic reporter he knew and trusted. Morris also scented smoke and went to work; the result was a dispatch to *The Times,* dated March 1, 1961—the day of the President's news conference remarks, ten days after the education bill was sent to Congress. "The highest prelates of the Roman Catholic Church," Morris was able to write, had met in Washington that day to plan a fight on the Administration's school bill.

Meeting as the administrative board of the National Catholic Welfare Conference, eight bishops and archbishops and Francis Cardinal Spellman of New York, James Cardinal McIntyre of Los Angeles, Richard Cardinal Cushing of Boston, Albert Cardinal Meyer of Chicago, and Joseph Cardinal Ritter of St. Louis had gathered in downtown Washington.

The Catholic leaders denied briefly that such a meeting had been held but Morris reported that it had been moved up a month, from the routine schedule, in order to deal with the educational problem. And when his account appeared in *The Times* of March 2, together with the President's news conference remarks, the issue appeared to have been joined. That day, the Church confirmed its position.

Archbishop Karl J. Alter of Cincinnati, a participant in the Massachusetts Avenue meeting, called a news conference and read a "summary" of the views arrived at in the hierarchical meeting. The text was as follows:

1. The question of whether or not there ought to be federal aid is a judgment to be based on objective economic facts connected with the schools of the country and consequently Catholics are free to take a position in accordance with the facts.

2. In the event that there is federal aid to education we are deeply convinced that in justice Catholic school children should be given the right to participate.

3. Respecting the form of participation, we hold it to be strictly within the framework of the Constitution that long-term, low-interest loans to private institutions could be part of the federal aid program. It is proposed, therefore, that an effort be made to have an amendment to this effect attached to the bill.

4. In the event that a federal aid program is enacted which excludes children in private schools those children will be the victims of discriminatory legislation. There will be no alternative but to oppose such discrimination.

This remarkable document rewards analysis, for in it the church hierarchy had not only stated a case; the bishops and cardinals also had laid down a shrewd political line and charted for themselves a clear, tough-minded course. To those who read it and who understood the interplay of interests in the legislative process, it was plain that the Church leaders were not, in the vernacular of Washington, "making a record" simply to please their constituents. They meant business and they knew how to go about it. In their hearts, some reporters and some legislators believed that, from that day forward, the Kennedy school bill was dead.

9 *The Education of JFK*

In the first paragraph of its statement, the hierarchy rested its case on "objective economic facts"—and on this ground the prelates could put forward sound arguments. At that time, there were 10,300 elementary and 2,400 high schools in the nationwide Catholic parochial system; five million or more students were taught in them by 102,000 teachers, 40,000 of them laymen. Plainly, "education" in the United States was an incomplete term if it did not include this huge and important school system. Moreover, reliable statistics showed that classroom and teacher shortages were even more acute in the parochial than in the public schools—and Catholic ability to remedy these deficiencies was even less than that of local and state governments.

Perhaps even more important, in the eyes of men like Thompson who knew the Church and its people, was the statement in the first paragraph that Catholics were "free to take a position in accordance with these facts." In context, that seemed to mean that the hierarchy was not making it a matter of "faith and morals" for Catholics to follow their lead; members of the Church could make up their own minds on the basis of "objective economic facts."

Paradoxically, that probably brought the cardinals and bishops more effective Catholic backing than they would have received had they made support for their position obligatory for members of the Church. There is always a broad streak of anti-clericalism among the diversified Catholic population of a country like the United States. Thompson believed many Catholics would have resented being told they had to support the hierarchy as a matter of Catholic doctrine. He believed he could refute, on the bases of theology, tradition and the historical positions of the Vatican, any attempt by the cardinals to make that assertion. By weakening their doctrinal position, he was convinced he could erode their political position. But the hierarchy did not fall into that error.

Instead, in paragraph two, they declared their deep concern for "justice" for Catholic school children. Catholic parents, many paying public school taxes as well as parochial school expenses, bound by their faith to provide what Spellman had called "a God-connected education," as conscious as anyone else of the educational deficiencies of schools in the United States, could respond passionately to such a plea for "justice."

Nor were they the only ones. Lutherans, for instance, supported a parochial school system with more than 150,000 pupils. Thousands of other American children attended various private and church schools. Although a spokesman of the National Lutheran Council later opposed federal aid to such schools, there obviously was a strong case to be made by Catholics and other parents of non-public school children on the following lines: If the federal government wanted to improve the quality of education, thus lifting the standards and prospects of generations to come, it could not adequately do so by improving only the public schools. Even if the problem of equity were set aside, the main question remained: how could "education" be improved in the fullest sense, if the millions of students in non-public schools were left out of the improvement program?

Even in practical, immediate terms, the hierarchy had a defensible position. Charles H. Silver, president of the New York City Board of Education, testified later to a House subcommittee that 450,000 of his city's 960,000 elementary and high school students attended private and parochial schools. If New York had to establish public schools for all, Silver pointed out, the program would require capital outlays totalling about $1 billion, plus additional yearly maintenance and operating costs of $200 million.

Parents of children in private and parochial schools therefore were relieving New York city of an enormous financial burden—while still helping to pay the vast public school costs it did carry. The pattern could be repeated in other areas, particularly the big cities. Silver said it was "unthinkable" to confine federal aid to the public schools alone and "would do a disservice to our city."

Parochial and private school officials could make another practical point. If states receiving the proposed federal grants used them to make substantial increases in teachers' salaries, teachers might be "priced out of the market" for non-public schools, unable to match federally-aided salaries. Was it the purpose of federal aid to education to put some of the oldest and best schools in the country out of business, or at a sharp disadvantage? And if that happened, were the local, state and federal governments prepared to take on the financial burden of providing additional schools and teachers for dispossessed private school pupils?

All these problems were summed up in the cardinals' simple and effective appeal for "justice" to "Catholic school children"; similar "justice" for non-Catholic private and parochial school students was invoked by implication.

But the Catholic hierarchy went further and attempted to establish a position in the Constitution as well as in equity, economics and education. Long-term, low-interest loans, they said, would be "strictly within the framework of the Constitution." That, too, was a legally arguable—if not thoroughly established—proposition. At the outset, it wisely dismissed the question of whether parochial and private schools should have outright federal grants, a question the Catholic leaders rightly

—if reluctantly—believed had been settled against them by Supreme Court decisions. And it gave them an argument of "moderation"—they were not asking all-out aid for their schools, only a limited, repayable, particular form of aid, much less than the benefits the President had proposed for the public schools.

So far, in their shrewd "summary," the cardinals and bishops had displayed nothing but sweet reasonableness, discretion, moderation—but in the last three sentences the mailed fist of political power crept out of the ecclesiastical sleeve. An amendment to provide aid to non-public schools was proposed for the Administration's education bill; without it, the churchmen said, that bill would be "discriminatory legislation" and they would have no alternative but to oppose it.

Here, in short, was not merely a persuasive argument for aiding parochial schools; here was a flat statement that any form of school aid that did not provide it was discriminatory and would be opposed by the powerful Roman Catholic Church. The hierarchy would not let its position stand or fall on its own merits; the Church leaders said flatly that they could accept *no other position*. President Kennedy, on the day before, had said as flatly that he could accept *none but his own directly contradictory position*. Compromise, it appeared, had been ruled out in advance. Both sides demanded total victory.

But men are not irresistable forces or immovable objects; when they crash against one another, they do not necessarily shatter. Politics, like war, consists of maneuver as well as power. The weapons are men's minds, hearts, aspirations and interests. As a general seeks to turn an opposing army's flank or lure it into a trap or starve it out, a politician probes, feints and beckons his opponent; and each, if he is any good, charges frontally only when he is surprised or trapped or finally in command of the field. The political and religious generals of the education battle of 1961 quickly found the only possible chance to avoid a disastrous collision. The Catholics did not want to defeat the school bill; they wanted it to pass with aid to their schools included. The Administration did not wish simply to frustrate Catholic hopes or to uphold the separation of church and state at all costs; it wanted, above all, an effective school bill that could pass Congress and the courts, without political disaster for the President. In short, both sides wanted to pass federal aid to education, not to defeat it; and in that fact lay the possibility of *rapprochement*.

Silver put it aptly in his testimony. There had to be, he told the House subcommittee, a "diligent search" to provide school aid *and* satisfy the Catholic aspirations, "consistent with our national principles." No more complex, subtle and demanding task ever had been laid before 535 fallible men—or the equally important 536th fallible in the White House.

As if to illustrate the many facets of the education issue, Speaker Sam Rayburn pointed almost immediately to another complication. Mr. Sam's daily news conferences were always enigmatic affairs—monosyllabic, cryptic, demanding of experienced House reporters that they learn to read his expressions and catch his innuendo as well as understand his gobbler's voice. On March 7, the day the President sent the Speaker and the Vice President a draft bill embodying the education proposals he had made in his message, Rayburn was asked for his views on the draft. He replied typically: "I think that we can get along with a good school construction bill."

To "get along" in Rayburnese meant "pass"—and since that was usually the old compromiser's first concern, it was clear to veteran Rayburn translators that he was saying that a school *construction* bill was his preferred course. But there was not enough elaboration to make the rest of his meaning clear.

Rayburn had steadfastly opposed, even at his legislative meeting with the President in Palm Beach the previous winter, the idea of federal aid for paying teachers' salaries. If he was simply reiterating that belief, then the Administration had a major defection on its hands. But Rayburn students thought they saw more in the old man's cryptic sentence than that— and knew too much, anyway, of his devotion to the Democratic party. They made further inquiries of his confidantes and it was widely reported the next day that the Speaker believed the way to handle the suddenly crucial religious question was to limit the school bill to construction only—a "bricks and mortar" bill, as it was known on the colloquial Hill.

This view was based on the belief that what the Catholic prelates really wanted was help in paying their teachers more money, and in obtaining more teachers; as evidence, their disinterest in real and effective opposition to Thompson's "bricks and mortar" bill of 1960 was cited. Such a limited bill in 1961 might bypass the Catholic issue altogether.

But whatever Rayburn had in mind, the net effect of his statement was to raise another question about the school bill's prospects. If Rayburn meant to oppose an important section of the President's program, either from conviction, or strategically, or both, that program, as such, was in deeper trouble than had been thought.

Kennedy apparently was standing his ground. Mike Mansfield, the Senate Majority Leader, emerged from the White House to say that the President's "position remains the same." As evidence of the sincerity and persuasiveness of that position, the Senator pointed out that, in 1960, he and Kennedy had split in voting on the Morse amendment to provide loans to private schools; Kennedy had opposed it, Mansfield—also a Catholic—had backed it. Now Mansfield said he would go down the line with the President.

But Catholic pressures were coming down heavily on Congress, through a flood of mail generated by the prelates, and through men like McCormack and Pucinski, who espoused their positions from the inside. Conservatives in both parties and other opponents of aid to education watched gleefully as the "religious issue" brightened their chances. Within a week, the statement of the bishops and cardinals, and their effective follow-up pressures, had generated genuine fear among Congressional proponents of school aid—not fear of Catholic retaliation at the polls, but fear that if the comprehensive Kennedy bill was not to be deadlocked, some concession would have to be made to the Catholic interest, just as Ribicoff had predicted.

On March 8, the day after Rayburn and Mansfield spoke out, Kennedy held another news conference—before the Bay of Pigs, he met the press almost weekly—and trimmed his sails. He began by urging Congress, on national television, not to let the church-state issue kill a needed program. He insisted that grants to private and parochial schools were unconstitutional, and hinted a veto of any bill that contained such a provision. He gave it as a personal view that "across-the-board" loans to these schools also were unconstitutional. By "across-the-board," Kennedy apparently meant loans that could be used for any purpose, by any school.

But then—in the words that counted—he drew a clear distinction: special-purpose loans for, say, building college classrooms or purchasing scientific equipment might be permissible. In fact, as a Senator, he had supported the National Defense Education Act of 1958, which had provided for just such special-purpose loans to private schools. He pointed out that "There's obviously room for debate about loans because it's been debated."

But special-purpose loans, the President made clear, were a "separate issue" from his general aid-to-education program. Then he made his point clear: "I definitely believe that we should not tie the two together."

There was the opening for compromise, and the Catholic leaders would surely recognize it. If someone introduced a bill to authorize special-purpose loans to private and parochial schools, the President had said, that might be all right—and the hint was strong that he would not oppose it. But grants and across-the-board loans were impossible, and even special-purpose loans could not be tied to his general aid program.

The decision to make this retreat, one of the crucial moves of the battle, obviously was taken because the Catholic pressures and the growing unrest in Congress had had their effect on the Administration—in which Ribicoff already was an advocate of "something for the Catholics." One Congressional source, intimately involved in the struggle, attributes the President's decision to retreat to the fact that "Sorensen caved in." Ted Sorensen, indeed, had been one of the chief architects of the Administration package and was perhaps, with Arthur Goldberg, at that stage the most influential adviser on domestic legislative policy. If Sorensen joined Ribicoff, and if their inner pressures were added to the rising outcry from the Church and some members of Congress, the basis of decision within the Administration was changed radically.

Two major questions arise from Kennedy's precipitous—there is no other word—retreat. Had the President contributed to the necessity of it by his early, adamant stand against any aid to the Catholics? Ribicoff had feared all along that Kennedy was painting himself into a corner—that by placing himself at the outset so publicly, so repeatedly, so voluntarily, in opposition to the Church, he would arouse the hierarchy and the issue. Had Kennedy not slammed the door and nailed it shut, the bishops might not have knocked upon it so sharply and might not have been so zealous in bringing heavy public pressures down on Catholic members of Congress. And in any case, when retreat became necessary, it would not have been so ignominious had a more discreet position been taken earlier.

But was retreat really necessary, even under the Catholic pressures? Ribicoff's original analysis that the Administration had to depend on the representatives of the Eastern industrial states was true up to a point; but there were not enough of them to do the job. What was necessary was to attract support from a coalition of factions and sections, building upon such a power base as the industrial East. Some defections might be suffered from that power base if the Catholics were shut out; but it also included Catholics like Thompson who bitterly opposed the Church position. And if Catholic aid were included, what would be the hope of support from the Baptist South, the rigidly Protestant Middle West—precisely those areas where an education bill was difficult enough, in any case, to make appealing to conservative, entrenched legislators?

Thompson, for one, and other members of Congress who supported the education bill, as well as many officials then in the executive branch, believe that Kennedy should have remained adamantly on the course of aiding public schools only. They believe that the inclusion of aid to Catholics was the one thing that, in the climate of 1961, could have defeated the education package. Perhaps Abe Ribicoff had been right for the wrong reason; perhaps Kennedy should have remained silent on the Catholic question, not to invite Catholic inclusion, but so that the issue *might* not arise; and so that if it did, it could be thrashed out quietly rather than in an atmosphere of blaring headlines, intense Catholic pressures, and Presidential retreat.

The same day Kennedy laid down his new line, Ribicoff was the first witness as Senate hearings opened; he tried to counter still another developing threat to the school bill. The President, he said, was studying whether to issue an executive order barring the use of federal grants by school districts refusing to desegregate. But an amendment to the school bill barring aid to such schools, Ribicoff insisted "would definitely weaken chances for passage of this bill." The Administration, still with an eye to the Southerners, did not want to arouse them with anti-segregation legislation; but it sought to pacify restive liberals with promises of executive action.

It was an eventful day in the school debate. Monsignor Frederick G. Hochwalt, director of the department of education of the National Catholic Welfare Conference, disclosed the Church's specific plan in testimony to a Senate subcommittee headed by Morse. He proposed an amendment to the Kennedy bill, providing $350 million in long-term, low-interest loans—precisely the open loans as a part of the Administration bill that Kennedy had said he still could not accept.

Morse demurred. As had Mansfield, Powell and Thompson, he had quickly followed up the President's news conference by proposing a separate bill that would authorize certain kinds of loans to private schools; their aim was to keep the public school bill as clear of the religious controversy as possible. Mansfield said the private school loans idea "should stand on its own feet" but the loquacious Powell was franker about the pulling-and-hauling that had developed in the wake of the cardinals' thunderbolt and the President's retreat: "Unless this climate in some way is cleared up federal aid to education is dead now."

Powell even hinted that a separate, private school loan bill should go to the floor ahead of the general aid bill, just to show Protestant good faith to the Catholics.

Morse put the key question to Monsignor Hochwalt. Could the Church leaders accept as satisfying their interest a separate bill authorizing the desired loans?

"It wouldn't have much of a chance," Monsignor Hochwalt answered.

He knew enough about Congress to know that without all-out Administration support, a bill primarily designed to aid Roman Catholics would attract little backing outside heavily Catholic areas. Even Kennedy's new position seemed not to have cleared the way. Some liberal Catholic Democrats, like Senator Philip Hart of Michigan, were dubious anyway. He said he doubted if Congress would pass either an amendment or a separate bill to aid Catholics and that he could not support either if it was going to block general school aid. That was the position of a number of Catholic legislators and it lends support to the theory that the President should have continued to insist on aid to public schools alone, as a matter of the highest educational priority.

Monsignor Hochwalt must certainly have been aware of the public indignation and outcries of such decidedly Protestant leaders as the Rev. Dr. Daniel A. Poling, editor of the *Christian Herald*, and the Rev. C. Stanley Lowell, an assistant director of Protestants and Other Americans United for Separation of Church and State. Before Congressional committees, bitter opposition was expressed to the Catholic ambitions by the Baptist Joint Committee on Public Affairs, the American Jewish Congress and Protestants and Other Americans United. A National Council of Churches spokesman, Dr. Gerald E. Knoff, spoke out against grants for private schools. Robert E. Van Deusen of the National Lutheran Council delivered a particularly hard blow when he told the House subcommittee that Lutherans wanted no federal aid for their extensive parochial school system.

The protest obviously was not limited to sects or "fundamentalists." At Princeton Theological Seminary, 270 students and faculty members signed a document opposing private school aid "in any form." Nineteen well-known Jewish and Protestant clergymen issued a similar statement. How many sermons were preached on the subject, one may only guess.

Kennedy appeared even more conscious of the sudden dangers of the situation when he appeared at his next news conference on March 15.

> I am hopeful that when the smoke has cleared there will continue to be harmony among the various religious groups of the country. I am going to do everything that I can to make sure that the harmony exists because it reaches far beyond the question of education and goes in a very difficult time in the life of our country to an important ingredient of our national strength. So I am confident that the people who are involved outside the government, and members of Congress and the Administration, will attempt to conduct the discussion on this sensitive issue in such a way as to maintain the strength of the country and not divide it.

But it was too late.

The action continued until August 30. But after Kennedy opened the door he had himself nailed shut, there was more hope than prospect for a bill. Helen Fuller quotes a Democrat from that time: "A month ago, I was willing to die for the education bill. But there's been so much maneuvering and so much controversy that I don't care what happens."[9]

And another member of the House told *Newsweek* magazine: "You are wrong, whatever you do on a bill of this kind."

Ultimately, with John McCormack strangely in the role of a sort of floor leader for the hierarchy and the Catholic faction in Congress—a role he denied playing, to the delusion of no one—and Sam Rayburn and Thompson in the forefront for the Administration, an agreement of sorts was reached. The Administration bill would not be amended to provide aid to Catholic schools (Sam Rayburn's doubts about teacher pay were mollified by a "state's rights" amendment giving each state the right to decide what to do with its share of the federal loot); instead, an amendment to the separate National Defense Education Act would authorize a program of forty-year loans to parochial and private schools for such special purposes as building classrooms for math, science and foreign language courses, and building gymnasiums and eating facilities.

Meanwhile, in all the confusion and bitterness, organizations that opposed any kind of federal aid to education—for instance, the U.S. Chamber of Commerce—seized their opportunity to turn votes their way. So did Judge Howard Smith. He wrote a letter to more than one hundred Southern newspapers, declaring: "This is not a bill to aid education. It is a bill to aid the N.A.A.C.P. to complete the subjugation of the Southern states and control the direction and conditions under which our youth is to be educated."

On July ⁻8, the final blow fell—in, of all places, the House Committee on Rules, over which so much blood, sweat and tears had been shed in January.

The agent was a mild, sluggish, little-known Democratic Representative from a Catholic district in Queens, New York, James J. Delaney—known in the House less for the substance of his views than for a mulish streak, once his mind was made up. Usually a devoted supporter of the Administration, Delaney joined Judge Smith, Colmer of Mississippi and five con-

servative Republicans—all of whom opposed any federal aid
to education—in an eight to seven majority that refused to
send to the floor the Administration bill, the N.D.E.A. bill or
a third measure concerned with higher education.

Delaney's public position was that a single "non-discriminatory" bill was needed—"non-discriminatory" meaning a bill
that included aid to Catholic schools. In fact, his stand was
determined not only by his Catholic loyalties, which gave him
the firm conviction that the aid should go to parochial schools
as a matter of equity and right, but by the voting situation in
the committee.

Delaney knew that the N.D.E.A. bill, providing special aid
for Catholics, could not get out of the Rules Committee. Smith,
Colmer and the five Republicans would vote against it until
doomsday—and at least one and perhaps all of the other
Southern Democrats on the committee, who were usually loyal
to Kennedy (Trimble of Arkansas, Thornberry of Texas, and
Elliott of Alabama), would join them in voting against anything as repugnant to the South as aid to the Catholics. Delaney was determined that if there was to be no such aid, there
would be no school bill for anyone; he would not cast his vital
vote for the Administration bill until the N.D.E.A. bill was
approved, and the majority of the Committee on Rules would
see to it that that approval never came.

The seven-man bloc opposed to any school aid, therefore,
was delighted to join Delaney in taking a single vote on the
three bills together; and so they died together. When they did,
it is fair to say, John Kennedy had lost Congress. Nothing
could put his education package together again, although
Frank Thompson tried valiantly with a compromise plan that
the House killed under "Calendar Wednesday" rules on August 30. Nor would anything—until his death—restore in its
dazzling gloss January's idea of the conquering young hero in
the White House.

For what, again, had been the effect of all these events upon
men?

From March 8, 1961, when he yielded to pressure in his news conference statement on education, some members of Congress date the decline of Kennedy's ability to lead that body. Sixteen days later, the House, by one vote, defeated his minimum wage bill, despite his abandonment of the laundry women he had promised to help. And it was foul coincidence that a week after that, Kennedy reached the nadir of his overall leadership as fiasco unfolded at the Bay of Pigs.

This, too, had its disastrous effect on the mood of Congress, but that is another story. What had happened in the House, however, was there for all to see.

There had been too much concentration on the Southerners and too little to show for it; not again in his lifetime would Kennedy have the enthusiastic loyalty of liberals, just because he had talked their language and touted their programs in his campaign. He had not been able to deliver; nor had he bought any Southerners who would stay bought from vote to vote.

There had been the March 8 news conference statement on education. It was damaging, not just because it was a retreat, which is a familiar enough legislative tactic, nor even because in this case many members considered retreat unwise. It was that rare thing in politics—a matter of principle—that made the difference.

As we have seen, none of the concessions later made in the minimum wage fight reached the basic principle of the dollar-volume standard. But when the President conceded the possibility of aiding Catholic schools in his statement of March 8, it was an abandonment of just such a principle—one that *he himself* had insisted upon. It may have been conceived as a tactical move by Ribicoff and the White House; but it was viewed in Congress as desertion under pressure of one of the President's fundamental principles.

There was the messy minimum wage struggle. It had showed that Kennedy, having no more public support than his hairline election had disclosed, had no real majority in the House— that he could win only by logrolling and maneuver, and not even certainly with these tactics. After March 24, no one would believe that Kennedy in Congress was the machine-like collector of votes he had been at Los Angeles. And had it really been necessary to compromise so much? All along, the key to the minimum wage struggle had been to get a Kennedy-shaped Senate bill to conference with the House; the key had not been in the House vote at all, although the laundry women and all that they symbolized had been sacrificed for the sake of that vote.

There was the fact that Delaney had been allowed to sink the final knife into the single most important part of the new President's legislative program, and escape unscathed. Hard-bitten members of the House were amazed—even knowing Delaney's stubbornness—that the White House and the Democratic party had not somehow been able to bludgeon or wheedle that single vote in the Committee on Rules that would have made the difference in the education fight—especially after so many members had laid their necks on the line to give Kennedy and Rayburn a supposed majority of the committee. Nor, to anyone's knowledge, was Delaney ever punished. Here, then, was a President, for all his Irish Mafia, who apparently could be defied with impunity.

Thus, as Congress saw things, Kennedy had not only failed in his first big tests; he had botched the job. The minimum wage bill might have been passed at smaller political cost; the education bill might have been steered or slipped through if the President had not at first stood so firm, only to retreat so swiftly. The intellectual playboy was not, after all, another F.D.R.; it was not necessary to fear him and it might be risky to follow him. Since a leader requires, above all, the respect of his followers, in losing at the outset the essential respect of the Eighty-Seventh Congress, John Kennedy had lost whatever chance he had had to remake his country.

Could that chance ever have been recovered? Kennedy fought hard in the 1962 elections and prevented further Republican gains in the Eighty-Eighth Congress. By winning a re-election landslide in 1964, which he might have done with Barry Goldwater as his opponent, he might have brought into office the kind of liberal, responsive Eighty-Ninth Congress that Lyndon Johnson actually did have to work with in 1965. And it will never be known to a certainty whether the Kennedy tax and civil rights bills of 1963—ultimately passed under Johnson in 1964—would have been approved in Congress had Kennedy not been murdered when he was. These bills were widely believed to be bogged down and stalled on the day of his death, although the civil rights bill, in particular, probably could have been rescued in any case.

But in the time allotted him, Kennedy never was able to lead Congress effectively. I believe the reasons can be traced straight to the first months of 1961, when Mr. Sam's triumph over Judge Smith seemed to have opened the way to Hundred Days that never came.

And if the debacle of the education bill was the final blow to Kennedy's promised leadership, the irony becomes excruciating. For why had the Catholic hierarchy chosen 1961 to push their case so strongly, when they had scarcely been heard from, in so many years? Was it *because* there was a Catholic in the White House at last?

Perhaps that was at least a subconscious factor. But it could hardly have been dominant or decisive. The Catholic leaders showed themselves well aware of political realities. They could not have been unaware of Kennedy's campaign positions on church and state generally, or on aid to Catholic schools in particular; and they must have been able to see that his own Church connection was a handicap to them, not an asset.

The real answer may have been given by Monsignor Hochwalt to a House subcommittee when he said that the Church leaders ". . . have been in this a long time. We have always felt that if Federal aid came we would hope that some way would be found to include us."[10]

The reason, he seemed to be saying, was that there was a climate of such great hopefulness that 1961 was to be the year when federal aid to education at last would become a reality. John Kennedy had created that climate. It had infected the

Church leaders. The time was at hand, and they meant to participate in the fruits. The Church hierarchy would have been displaying a nobility and restraint uncommon in human affairs had its members not sought Catholic participation in benefits that seemed so tantalizingly at hand; by their own lights, they surely had a responsibility to do so.

By his convincing campaign and rhetoric, Kennedy had made aid to education seem just around the corner, created the climate in which it seemed possible; despite his repeated rejection of any thought of including aid to Catholic schools, the fact that he so effectively created that climate of hope brought into the struggle the Church leaders who ruined all prospects.

Thus, Kennedy was doubly trapped—first by the role he had assumed of strong, liberal President, of leader able by the vigorous use of power and personality to overcome all obstacles and move the country; second by his Catholicism, which in the education struggle imposed upon him still another outspoken political attitude, and another grievous limitation.

By August 20, 1961, when the last, hopeless effort had been made to pass some remnant of the education bill, Kennedy had suffered disaster at the Bay of Pigs. He was only recently returned from his "somber" confrontation with Khrushchev in Vienna. The Berlin crisis lay just ahead, in that cold winter the President had predicted the Soviet Premier would bring. So did the first great commitment of forces in South Vietnam, from which so much would follow that Kennedy would not live to see. It is perhaps not too much to suggest that the collapse of his education program ranked with Vienna and the Bay of Pigs in teaching John Kennedy what it really meant to be "alone, at the top."

Wilson may have been right that the President is "at liberty, both in law and conscience, to be as big a man as he can." But in the endless adventure, men and circumstance may not yield even to law and conscience, and the liberty of power has always to be won.

PART II

JOHNSON LOSES HIS CONSENSUS

*I have been through it all.
Rain don't always follow the
thunder.*—Uncle Joe Cannon.

10 *Dark Saturday*

While Lyndon Johnson was the Senate Leader of a Democratic party that had swept to a landslide victory in the off-year elections of 1958, he attended a meeting of legislative leaders and Eisenhower Administration officials in the Cabinet Room of the White House. President Eisenhower jovially indicated to Johnson the high-backed President's chair.

"You sit there," he said, the famous Eisenhower smile breaking across his face.

"Oh, no," Johnson replied. "That's your chair, Mister President."

Eisenhower looked at him ruefully. "It'll be yours someday," he said.

"No," Johnson replied. "I will never sit in that chair."

It is no wonder Lyndon Johnson thought that—and kept on thinking it, right through his ill-starred campaign against John F. Kennedy for the Democratic Presidential nomination in 1960 and his three years as Vice President. For, if no man ever came to the White House better acquainted with the ways of government and politics than Lyndon Johnson, few men ever came to that unique office with more handicaps, as well; few ever sat down in the famous oval room in the West Executive Wing so lacking in political or public enthusiasm for his arrival.

Lyndon Baines Johnson of Texas, fifty-five years old the day he was sworn in, a familiar figure in Washington for thirty-two years, was not a polished orator, a popular national personality, a powerful factional leader, a respected political theorist or the proponent of some attractive national program. So much less was he the generally recognized successor to the leadership of John F. Kennedy.

Johnson was, first, by blood and geography, a Southerner —although by nature, at least as much a Westerner. There had been no Southern-born President in the White House since Woodrow Wilson left it a broken man in 1921, and none elected to it from Southern residency since Zachary Taylor of Louisiana won on the last successful Whig ticket in 1848, thirteen years before the Civil War. Johnson's record, moreover, was not certifiably liberal or conservative and although he had been a New Dealer and had crept toward a progressive position on civil rights in his later career, his Southern background had amounted to a virtual blackball on his Presidential efforts, tentative in 1956 and vigorous in 1960.

"I don't think anybody from the South will be nominated in my lifetime," he had said in 1958. "If so, I don't think he'll be elected." Then, Johnson had regarded himself as having been as discriminated against in national politics as any Catholic, Jew or Negro; even today, he regularly includes "region" in the usual "race, creed or color" litany of those things one is supposed not to be prejudiced against if one is a good American.

Even after reaching the Vice Presidency, having been only the fifth man from a Southern state nominated on a national ticket since the Civil War, Johnson retained his doubts. In a television interview on March 26, 1963, he went so far as to disclaim having "reached" for the Presidency and added: "My friends put me in the race in 1960. They felt that they should have representation and my name should go before the convention. I doubted the advisability of that, and so stated . . . I didn't feel I was a candidate." Johnson must have been the only man at the Los Angeles convention and perhaps in the nation who had that impression.

By late 1963, Vice President Johnson's Southern heritage was far from his only handicap. His lengthy political career had been clouded by repeated charges of provincialism, servitude to the oil and gas interests of Texas, opportunism and "wheeling and dealing" in that state's Byzantine politics; by his controversial "one-man rule" as Majority Leader in the Senate; and by his disputed election to that body in 1948 with a suspiciously achieved margin of eighty-seven votes (a feat that had earned him the newspaper nickname of Landslide Lyndon).

At the time of his accession to the Presidency, he was embarrassed by the Senate investigation of the tangled business affairs of his protégé, Robert G. "Bobby" Baker, who had been Secretary to Senate Democrats and Johnson's right-hand man during much of his Senate leadership and his 1960 Presidential campaign.

Nine years earlier, Johnson had suffered a nearly fatal heart attack. In 1963, doctors said he was fully recovered, but the general populace does not believe that people ever "fully recover" from heart attacks. He was never to be farther from callous speculation about the likelihood that he would die in office than Dwight Eisenhower had been.

Johnson had had little or no experience in the conduct of foreign affairs, the overriding concern of post-World War II Presidents, despite the claims of apologists that his work in the Senate had taught him all he needed to know. His several trips abroad as Vice President had been largely ceremonial and, due to his informal and extroverted manner, not entirely successful. The quick impressions he had recorded on these tours would not always guide him well. Johnson was therefore an unknown figure in world politics, although the President of the United States was expected to lead the free world.

Because Johnson had long been personally familiar to people in Washington and Texas, there were many in both

places with doubts about the character of the man who had
so unexpectedly replaced the stylish Kennedy. Men said he
was flamboyant and a trickster; they called him an opportunist
political manipulator without ideas of his own. It was reported that he bullied his staff, and every reporter in Washington was familiar with stories of Johnson's personal vanity
and occasional pettiness toward those who crossed him. For
years, there had been reports that his influence had kept the
capital city of Texas (Austin—1960 population, 186,545)
from having more than one television station—the profitable
KTBC-TV, owned as a matter of record by his wife and daughters. Crudities and uncertainties of style and speech were part
of the extensive Johnson lore on file in Washington's ungener-
ous memory. The cruel capital cocktail-party circuit had
sniggered into its martinis, for instance, after Vice President
Johnson appeared for the riotous National Gallery showing of
the Mona Lisa in white tie and tails—while all the other men
present appeared in the prescribed black tie. It was widely
reported, too, that the intense Texan relied too much on the
Cutty Sark he liked in tall, watery highballs. Fits of flashing
anger, black despondence and almost overpowering ebullience
were known to be part of his mercurial temperament.

There was, as there always is, another side to the coin. As
the morning of November 23, 1963, dawned cold and grim
in Washington, with rain falling steadily upon the White
House and its black-draped façade, the single greatest public
asset of the new President of the United States was his long,
sometimes dazzling career in Congress and his reputation as
perhaps the ablest floor leader the Senate ever had seen.

Johnson's feats in the Senate were acknowledged to have
been substantial. It was he who had organized the perfectly
constituted hearing committee that had brought the ultimate
downfall of Senator Joseph R. McCarthy, a tumble to which
John F. Kennedy had contributed not even his vote or proxy.
It was Johnson who had put together the one-vote majority
that turned back a bill to negate the powers of the Supreme

Court, who had mustered the opposition against the Bricker Amendment that would have limited the President's treaty-making powers. It was Johnson's maneuvers, retreats, compromises and persuasion that had slipped the civil rights bills of 1957 and 1960 past the stout walls of Southern resistance. As Majority Leader, he had been consulted on, and usually supported, the major foreign policy moves of the Eisenhower Administration. It was Johnson's determination and leadership that had kept the Democratic Congressional majorities of the Eisenhower era moving usually in a responsible and productive direction (and it is not without significance that the public flow of criticism of Congressional inactivity and inefficiency did not reach flood tide until Johnson had left his Majority Leader's post for the Vice Presidency, nor recede until after he entered the White House).

But still—the public tended to think that it was Eisenhower, loftily ignoring both McCarthy and his victims, who had brought the Wisconsin demagogue to disaster. Neither the Supreme Court bill nor the Bricker Amendment had aroused the passions of the corner drugstore or the political backrooms. Johnson was almost as much condemned for compromising on the civil rights bills as praised for guiding them to passage; his party muttered peevishly about his bipartisan assistance to the Eisenhower foreign policy. His Congressional achievements might have been useful—but had they not been achieved by cloakroom manipulations, vote swapping, sacrifices of principle, and other shady machinations? Had not Democrats like Albert Gore of Tennessee and William Proxmire of Wisconsin lambasted his "one-man rule" and cried for more democracy among Senate Democrats?

Senator Harry F. Byrd of Virginia might confide to friends that Lyndon Johnson was the only man from whom he had never won an argument; other Senators might testify to his legislative skill, personal drive and political acumen; to most Americans Johnson remained "just a politician" and a Southern politician at that.

The events of 1960 did little to enhance Johnson's reputation—and his later claim that he had not really sought the Democratic nomination was merely derided by those who knew how hard he had run. But his ill-conceived and late-starting campaign for the Democratic Presidential nomination had disclosed not only his intrinsic weaknesses as a national candidate ("Can you imagine Lyndon campaigning in Harlem?" a lieutenant of John Kennedy once inquired) but his personal ignorance of national politics. Sometimes, that year, it had seemed that Johnson and his mentor, "Mr. Sam" Rayburn of Texas, believed the Presidency could be won by power in Congress rather than by power among the convention delegates. There is a story that Johnson considered Connecticut's delegates safely in his column, because he had the backing of the state's Democratic Senator, Thomas Dodd; in fact, State Chairman John M. Bailey had locked up all but Dodd for Kennedy months before.

That was at least the symbolic story of the Johnson campaign, however apocryphal, and when Kennedy rolled to his first ballot victory at Los Angeles, Johnson fell a hundred short of the total of five hundred delegates he had believed he commanded—a head-counting sin he would never have committed in the more familiar Senate. Kennedy's selection of him to run for Vice President nearly caused a party split, as liberals set up an outraged cry and as some Southerners labelled him a "traitor" for running on the liberal Kennedy platform. That he was simultaneously running to retain his Texas Senate seat seemed to confirm his reputation as a trickster and opportunist. His national campaign "from Austin to Boston" was waged fiercely and well, but it was all but lost in the hullabaloo over Kennedy and Richard Nixon. His contribution to the victory was substantial, especially in helping to win such anti-Kennedy states as Texas, South Carolina and Georgia; but others could make similar claims (New York state's Liberal Party, for instance) and most of the post-election analysis centered on the Catholic vote and alleged balloting frauds.

In his nearly three years as Vice President, Johnson had dropped from the national political limelight. He had hardly taken the oath of office when Democratic Senators rebelled against a proposal that he should continue to preside over their caucus. On July 4, 1963, just a few months before he became President, he made a remarkable civil rights speech at Gettysburg, Pennsylvania, and it went all but unnoticed in the press. He made headlines, if at all, when he whooped out loud in the Taj Mahal or brought a puzzled Pakistani camel driver, Bashir Ahmad, to the United States on a bizarre visit that moved Arthur Krock to a satire on the Arabian Nights in his column in *The New York Times:*

> And it is related that, in the end, when some hardhearted persons inquired how these shenanigans comported with the King's outline of and limitation of the Grand Wazir's mission, and gave it as their opinion that Bashir Ahmad's camel would wind up at the knacker's and his owner with an incurable case of maladjustment, they were saved from the headsman only by palace gossip that the same thoughts had been indicated by Kennedy the King.

These were scarcely advantageous notices; besides, in the excitement of the handsome era of Kennedy the King, who cared about the Vice President's travels or his great days in the Senate?

"This," said a White House Ivy Leaguer with relish and disdain, "is an Administration of men in their forties." Was not Lyndon Johnson in his fifties, a figure from an older, wearier time?

Nothing had changed his con man's reputation, either. The New Frontier chuckled at the story about Johnson, Kennedy and Secretary of State Dean Rusk being trapped in a boat drifting out to sea. Swamped with water, it could only support one man. Rusk, the story went, wanted to negotiate a solution; Kennedy began seeking delegate support; Johnson took a roll-call vote to see who would remain in the boat while the others jumped overboard—and it came out three to zero in his favor.

For all these reasons, right up to the moment of John Kennedy's murder, there had been widespread speculation that Johnson would be "dumped" from the 1964 ticket. On October 31, at a news conference, Kennedy denied it. Asked if he wanted "Lyndon Johnson on the ticket, and do you expect that he will be on the ticket?" the President replied, "Yes, to both of those questions. That is correct."

This did not still the rumors. Texas reporters, covering the fatal Kennedy-Johnson tour of their state, inquired of Washington colleagues if it could be true that Attorney General Robert Kennedy had inspired the Bobby Baker investigation as an opening maneuver in the "dumping" scheme. They were told that it was not true, but many of them would not be dissuaded. It was a measure of the general attitude toward Lyndon Johnson that the dumping rumor *sounded* true; and Johnson himself feared that it might be.

But the last words John Kennedy said to Johnson—as Johnson later recalled in a private conversation—were spoken in a room at the Texas Hotel in Fort Worth, not much more than an hour before shots rang out near the Triple Underpass in Dallas. "Lyndon," he said, "there are two states I know we're going to carry next year—Massachusetts and Texas."

But on the morning of November 23, 1963, the vigorous young life of John Kennedy was gone forever; he would never carry another state. Only in death would he receive the big majority for which he had hoped and worked. So on that gray, rainy morning, John Kennedy's body had been returned to the White House and all that day the great men of the nation would file past his bier, some of them weeping openly. All across the land that Kennedy had traveled for four years in search of the delegates to whom Lyndon Johnson had paid so little heed, men and women who had never seen the young President wept, too. For the President stands at the epicenter of the national life and Americans want to believe he is somehow immune to life's wounds and ephemerality. But Kennedy had not been, as no man is, and James Reston spoke for us all in the *Times:* "Somehow," he wrote, "the worst in the nation had prevailed over the best." People were unbelieving, afraid. Many were bitter. All were desperately unsure of what would happen next. The world, it seemed, was a dark and malignant place; the chill of the unknown shivered across the nation. And no one yet could look to Lyndon Johnson; hardly anyone thought of him.

In his sprawling brick house, The Elms, in the Spring Valley section of Northwest Washington, an establishment he had bought from Perle Mesta, just as he had done for three years past, Johnson arose, dressed, had his breakfast. At 8:40 A.M. he went off to work, as usual. That day, his long black car had to nose past a knot of television and news photographers outside the gates. The cameramen could see him in the rear seat, grim and hunched. The spectre of such a morning, while it had occurred to few others, had been raised in Lyndon Johnson's mind at least once, and at the outset. On July 14, 1960, in Los Angeles, when Kennedy asked him to be his running mate, Kennedy had said that he believed Johnson "should be the one who would succeed if anything happened to him."[1]

Now the dread possibility had come to pass; and although a young assistant, Bill D. Moyers, rode with the new President, it occurred to some who saw them leave The Elms that already there had closed around Lyndon Johnson that terrible loneliness to which all Presidents have testified: that loneliness born of the reluctance of ordinary men to believe that the President, too, is human and one of them.

Yet, he is just that, and therefore there is not only grandeur but appalling risk of mortal fallibility in the fact that a President, in Kennedy's phrase, is "alone, at the top." When all the advisers have advised and all the analysts have analyzed, a President must decide, and even if he dodges that necessity he still will have decided; if he causes nothing whatever to happen, he still will have acted.

This extraordinary exposure to risk as well as to power added dimension to the difficulty of the position Johnson found himself in that morning as he drove to his first full day in the Presidency. Only if all his original handicaps and challenges are seen, and seen in the human light of the Presidency's unique pressures, is it possible to give him appropriate credit for what he accomplished in so short a time, and for the astonishing height of power and prestige he soon would scale. In turn, only if this original achievement is credited and understood can the magnitude of the ultimate collapse of Lyndon Johnson's consensus be appreciated.

The full detail of his rise and fall must be considered if his part of the endless adventure is to have its due measure of splendor and ignominy. That is beyond the scope of this essay, which is designed rather to show how his character and personality meshed with circumstance to dictate his course at crucial moments. But we need not worry that such a summary will be made. In time, men might even see him as the tragic figure so rarely to be found in politics; or only as a vain posturer; or as one who merely did the best he could and was found wanting. But history, long removed from the clash and cries of his contemporaries, and of his and their petty, momentary indictments, will never ignore Lyndon Johnson; his story is too full of humanity, its majesty and failure, its victories and deceits, for chroniclers to overlook.

11 *The First Priority*

Johnson turned, that grim first morning, directly to what he later called "the first priority." It was "to try to display to the world that we could have continuity and transition, that the program of President Kennedy would be carried on, that there was no need for them to be disturbed and fearful that our Constitutional system had been endangered. To demonstrate to the people of this country that although their leader had fallen, and we had a new President, that we must have unity and we must close ranks, and we must work together for the good of all America and the world."

Johnson was not thinking only of the American people and their friends. The world to whose leadership he had so suddenly fallen heir was not everywhere a friendly place, and to most Americans—including the new President—that dismal morning, it seemed more threatening than usual. It was still not certain (it may never be) that the assassin had acted alone.

Johnson wanted any potential enemy, any nation or leader who might attempt to seize advantage of what they took to be a shocked and rudderless country, to know "that we were sure and we were confident, that we were united, that we had closed ranks, and not to tread on us."[2] But in that hour, the American people actually were 190,000,000 dazed individuals; he had to give them that unity and confidence; he had to represent it to the world.

"Nobody," Johnson said later, in privately discussing his actions on the day of Kennedy's assassination, "was going to say that Lyndon Johnson was in a hurry to grab power."

But he had to be in a hurry to exercise it. In the confused hours after the murder, Johnson feared that, even while aloft on the way to Washington, he might have to confront a fearful challenge from some foreign enemy; who knew, then, who had pulled the trigger or ordered the shots? Lee Harvey Oswald had only just been arrested.

Even if such a threat did not materialize, if the "first priority" was to be fulfilled, it would have to be done at the outset. There would be no time for recovery. A seasoned leader's mind, such as Kennedy's had been and Johnson's is, must recognize the moment for action; when the moment comes, that mind must react instinctively and send out its orders, wrong or right, good or bad. Otherwise, it is not the mind of leadership.

Nor could Johnson's reaction be altogether altruistic. He had been delivered in a flash from the political wilderness. That office he had thought he could never have was his, and that power for which he had worked and maneuvered all his life, at the last moment, with hope for it all but dead, miraculously was within his reach. But to such a practiced political creature, it would have been instantly apparent that his personal position still was precarious—Presidency or no Presidency. He was acceding to the White House later in a term than any Vice President in history; he would have less than a year in which to impose himself upon the office, prepare for an election, and win it.

He knew he had been John Kennedy's personal choice for the Vice Presidency, not that of Kennedy's political supporters. He had no vestige of a national political organization of his own. Labor and the liberals of the Democratic Left were suspicious of him, if not downright hostile; they had shown that at the 1960 convention. The Negroes who had voted so strongly for Kennedy would fear his Southern origins. Johnson personally could no more afford than could the country an impression of floundering, or a mass departure of the Kennedy Administration, or a developing lack of confidence in his own ability and character.

In many ways, his hardest problem was with those who had been closest to Kennedy. Johnson had no time to conduct an effective "transition," that peculiarly American fruit-basket-turn-over of officials that has had to be accomplished by most newly elected Presidents; he could not substitute a new Administration for the old. Even if he could have, an exodus of Kennedy's aides would have been equal to an exodus of Democratic party confidence in Lyndon Johnson, as well as of public confidence in the government. And a shift away from him of the political loyalties that had flowed so strongly to Kennedy and his family would amount to the creation of a powerful opposition within Johnson's own party; for Robert Kennedy was a natural and appealing symbol to which those loyalties, once set free, might instantly attach themselves.

Few Kennedy men—certainly not Lyndon Johnson—had forgotten the heat and rancor of the 1960 pre-convention battle. The memory of Johnson's hoarse voice shouting, on various political occasions, "Do you think we should have sent regrets to Khrushchev?" (as Kennedy had suggested in the wake of the U-2 incident) was all too green. So was the memory of a Johnson—whether he thought he was a candidate or not—whose aides had questioned Kennedy's health, and who in the most desperate stages of the 1960 convention had said himself: "I never was any Chamberlain umbrella policy man. I never thought Hitler was right . . . When Joe McCarthy was on the march in this country, and someone had to stand up and be counted, I was a voting liberal . . . I was not contributing comfort to his thinking or contributions to his campaign." These allusions to Joseph P. Kennedy, who had supported Chamberlain in the 1930's and Joe McCarthy in the 1950's, and to John Kennedy's failure to vote on the McCarthy censure motion, would long rankle in Kennedy breasts. Johnson was under no illusion that his loyal years in the Vice Presidency had erased these memories.

Therefore, the first step toward the first priority was plain; both to renew the national spirit and to underpin his personal political outlook, Johnson had to cover himself with the mantle of Kennedy as quickly and as fully as possible. He had to retain the Kennedy staff and Cabinet—a task at which he was largely successful, for as long as he needed to be. He had to reassure the world that the flow of policy was unbroken, and he was able to set about this both in a series of cables to other nations and in an exhausting chain of meetings with those national leaders who had come in such numbers for the Kennedy funeral.

Nevertheless, when Johnson drove out of the White House grounds at 12:07 P.M., Wednesday, November 27, he was still no more than President *pro tem*—the man who was legally replacing Kennedy. His most important task, the climax of the first priority, lay ahead. He had preserved the old but he also had to offer something new and acceptable—himself. And for this, not only tradition but Johnson's deepest instincts decreed a return to Congress—that comfortable home in which he had grown up to power, which he knew so well and confidently, to the bosom of which he would often turn in the months ahead.

As he rode with Pierre Salinger, Lawrence F. O'Brien and Ted Sorensen, only sparse crowds stood along Seventeenth Street N.W. to watch the black limousine with its six preceding motorcycles; at the Agriculture Department's sprawling complex on Independence Avenue, the government workers had been released to the sidewalks and made a braver show of applause and interest. Policemen holding rifles could be seen atop the buildings lining the route of the nine-car motorcade. In the car just behind the President's rode Rear Admiral George Burkley, the White House physician; his motorcade location had been sensibly upgraded since the assassination of John Kennedy five days before. But there seemed to be little danger to Lyndon Johnson; even in the East Plaza of the Capitol, as he got out of his car, only a few people watched and applauded.

In the huge chamber of the House of Representatives a hundred feet away, however, there was excitement and anticipation. At 12:17 P.M., sepulchral John McCormack, the Speaker of the House and the nearest thing there was to a Vice President, called the House to order. William E. "Fishbait" Miller, the House doorkeeper, ludicrously bearing his ceremonial mace, and in a voice honed on grits and redeye gravy, was announcing distinguished arrivals ("membahs of the Cabinet" . . . "ambassaduhs and charjay da-fairs"). Cabinet members took their seats, in temporary chairs placed at the front row to the right of Speaker McCormack. Robert Kennedy stared with ravaged eyes at the floor; he was flanked by McNamara and the crewcut Stewart Udall, Secretary of the Interior, an old Kennedy lieutenant who had purloined a number of Southwestern state delegates from under Lyndon Johnson's nose in 1960. Somewhere in the group of Senators that had marched in with stately tread to occupy the best seats, Ted Kennedy also was present. Ancient, skeletal Carl Hayden of Arizona, President *pro tem* of the Senate, and now second in line to the Presidency, mounted the rostrum and sat by John McCormack—two men past seventy, either or both of whom might yet become President, by no more remote a fate than the one that had obliterated John Kennedy's life.

From the packed gallery, where even the aisles were jammed with onlookers, television lights sent down their peculiarly searching glare. A group of still and newsreel photographers shoved each other in a gallery box and clicked their shutters in purposeful confusion. In the press gallery, above the Speaker's head, it was a "card day"—admission by ticket only, with seats assigned; every one was taken. White House reporters who had ridden down in the Presidential motorcade stood on the floor of the House, behind the diplomatic section to the left of the Speaker.

Above their heads, a box was reserved for the new First Lady; when she entered with her two statuesque daughters, those on the floor stood up for a standing ovation that lasted a minute and twenty seconds. The three women received it unsmiling; it was not a time for levity and they well understood that the applause was not only for them but represented things more profound—the respect of a nation for its established institutions, the expectations of a people that those who embodied those institutions would be worthy of them.

When the applause died and the audience sat down, those who continued to peer at Mrs. Johnson's box could see the first Presidential fruit of Lyndon Johnson's genius for balancing a ticket, a committee or an investigating group—that genius exemplified years before in the finely contrived panel of respectables that had heard the Senate's charges against Joseph R. McCarthy, and doomed him. That day in the House gallery, the First Lady was surrounded by Mayor Robert Wagner of New York and Mayor Richard Daley of Chicago—urban liberalism and Democratic city machines personified; former Governor David Lawrence of Pennsylvania—from an older generation, like Mayor Wagner a Catholic, and an example of Democratic influence in the big industrial states; Governor Carl Sanders of Georgia—a youthful exponent of Southern moderation but a representative nonetheless of the old "solid South" and of a state that never had voted Republican, not even against Al Smith or for Dwight Eisenhower; Arthur M. Schlesinger, Jr., whose standing among Democratic intellectuals had forced Johnson to talk him out of a sudden resignation from the White House staff; Sargent Shriver, Kennedy's brother-in-law; Abe Fortas and Leonard Marks, old-line Democrats from Johnson's own close circle of friends. The party was completed by Mr. and Mrs. Sammy Wright, family retainers, and by close personal friends and relations.

At 12:30 P.M., the chamber was bustling with activity, rumbling with chatter, fiercely lit by the television lights. The great doors leading to the long central corridor of the Capitol swung open and Fishbait Miller appeared with mace:

"Mistah Speakaah—the Pres-dent of the U-nited States!"

A momentary hush fell before an outburst of applause. Johnson entered, wearing a sober blue suit and a blue tie with a white shirt. He was followed by a committee of Senators and Representatives appointed by McCormack and Hayden to accompany him to the rostrum. Applause, even a few cheers and whistles, continued to roll through the House as everyone present rose. There were few men in that chamber who did not know Johnson personally; most had worked with him in his Congressional years; a good many counted themselves personal friends and not a few were old enemies and critics. Some applauded because they knew him; others because he was President; all—even those who disliked or mistrusted Lyndon Johnson—because it was to him, now, that the nation had to look for leadership in what Kennedy so often had called "difficult times." Slowly he came down the aisle, shaking hands here and there, unsmiling; in the gallery, Lady Bird Johnson fought to hold back tears as she watched her husband go down that gauntlet of applauding men, to that rostrum above them all. Perhaps she sensed he would never be quite the same man again. No man could be; for, as he walked, all the solitude and responsibility of the world's loneliest eminence—and thus, its grandest—closed about him. Never again could their mark leave him.

He waited momentarily on the rostrum, and Speaker McCormack's gavel fell.

"I have the high privilege and personal honor," the old man said, in his sharp Boston Irish accent, "of presenting to you our former colleague, the President of the United States."

Once again, applause shattered the stillness of the Chamber, and men rose to their feet in tribute, not so much to the man as to the history he would continue. It was a spectacle that comes as near as anything ever does in the United States to pageantry—the appearance of a President in a single chamber with his Cabinet, with Congress, with the black-robed Justices of the Court, with the diplomatic representatives of other nations; even the court-jester interludes of Fishbait Miller were appropriate, in that people's gathering. Here were the people's representatives, the people's government, and it was right, it was reassuring, that there should be no gaudy uniforms of privilege, no coats of arms, no prancing horses or ceremonial troops—only these grave men in their drab suits, only the single flag on the rostrum, over it only the carved and star-flanked motto: "In God We Trust."

As the applause rose and fell, Lyndon Johnson stood silently, unsmiling. Johnson and his aides had been at work on his speech since Saturday, through all the demands of the ornate Kennedy funeral and the first days of a Presidency. The speech had precipitated a serious dissent from Ted Sorensen, who felt his original draft—consisting largely of tributes to John Kennedy—had been ruined. The night before, in the quiet of The Elms, Johnson and Abe Fortas had worked out the final draft, while Lynda Bird Johnson sat at a typewriter and put their words on paper. Johnson felt that never again would he make a more important speech, and now he was at the first moment of what he believed would be "the most critical hour" of his life.

Johnson began in a voice almost inaudible at the rear of the chamber—a low-key beginning for what has to be one of the remarkable performances of modern American politics:

"Mr. Speaker, Mr. President, Members of the House, Members of the Senate, my fellow Americans—all I have, I would have given gladly not to be standing here today."

It was exactly the right statement, delivered in exactly the right tone. Six miles away, a Washington reporter's wife, watching Johnson on television, felt that nothing said in the sad, foregoing days had more perfectly expressed the nation's feeling of loss; it was to be the one thing from Johnson's speech that she would remember word for word.

But there were to be other, greater moments in an address that surprised even Johnson's admirers with its force, its eloquence, its mood of quiet confidence—an address that moved many of those in the chamber of the House to tears. The obvious meaning of the speech was that the new President planned to continue the policies and maintain the spirit of the old. But there were deeper and more important meanings.

The greatest of these came, with a force no less stunning because it had been expected, when the first Southerner to become President since Woodrow Wilson said slowly and with immensely dramatic effect:

"No memorial oration or eulogy could more eloquently honor President Kennedy's memory than the earliest possible passage of the civil rights bill for which he fought."

Those in the House broke into a storm of applause, although Southern members like Russell of Georgia sat silently. Johnson waited with patient timing for the applause to lapse, then continued—as slowly but without hesitation.

"We have talked long enough in this country about equal rights. We have talked for one hundred years or more. It is time now to write the next chapter—and to write it in the books of law."

Again there was applause. Not in the history of the Republic had such words been heard in a Southern accent, from such a forum, such an office. Since the beginnings of the slavery controversy, the South had maintained its long, tenacious resistance to Negro equality; that resistance had become once again, in the contemporary atmosphere of the Negro revolution, the cornerstone of the region's politics. Now one of the South's own was in the White House, but what he was saying, in words as slow as the tolling of a bell, meant—could mean nothing else—the ultimate death of the lingering Southern dissent in American politics.

Johnson proceeded to leave no doubt of his meaning, and of his personal stand:

I urge you again, as I did in 1957 and again in 1960 [a reference to the Senate debates on civil rights of those years, in which Johnson had played a leading role], to enact a civil rights law so that we can move forward to eliminate from this nation every trace of discrimination and oppression that is based upon race or color. There could be no greater source of strength to this nation both at home and abroad.

But if Russell and the other senators had been listening carefully, they had heard, too, what was to be the political theme of Johnson's Presidency—one which, as a Southerner, he was peculiarly equipped to make believable in the case of civil rights. And although the civil rights issue is not otherwise germane to this study, it is worth examining Johnson's position on the matter at this point. It was the first real display of the theme of consensus he would sound so repeatedly, so successfully—and which would bring him both triumph and disaster. Johnson held out to the South that day, what no politician but a Southerner in the White House could have offered with such sincerity—the hope of reconciliation, the suggestion of a future in which Southern states and Southern men would no longer have to stand together against all the rest.

We will serve all of the nation [Johnson said]—not one section or one sector or one group—but all Americans. These are the United States—a united people with a united purpose. Our American unity does not depend upon unanimity. We have differences. But now, as in the past, we can derive from these differences strength, not weakness; wisdom, not despair. Both as a people and a government, we can unite upon a program, a program which is wise, just, enlightened and constructive.

For a century, the South had been isolated and defensive, feeling its back against the wall and a knife at its throat. Its institutions, if outmoded, had been genuinely rooted in old necessities, and such solid constructions fall slowly if at all. Only a century before Johnson spoke there, Atlanta had lain in ashes beneath Sherman's boots. Redemption, from the chaos of manipulated Negro and Carpetbagger governments was only ninety years in the past—just yesterday, in the Southern sense of time. Generations of American politicians had waved the bloody shirt at the South, denounced its customs, held up to scorn its people, and steadily derived in their own regions what the South saw as blatant political benefit from so doing. For the same generations, American businessmen had exploited the Southern farmer, the Southern merchant, the Southern family, never lifting a finger to help its Negroes, its laborers, its worn and dying soil; and even when industrialization came to the South, it was to exploit cheap labor, not to bring the blessings of abundance.

Now the President of the United States, a Southerner, speaking in the unmistakable accents of their own region, was saying to Southern men that *they were not outlaws*. They were not immoralists or degenerates or colonial subjects but men who had lost a struggle. He held out promise, not a threat. He was proposing to meet them halfway, as Lincoln always, even in the devastation of war, had hoped to do a century before; he would bury the bloody shirt in the same unmarked grave with the Klansman's sheet. The future could belong to the whole nation, and the price was only to go forward together to "the dream of *equal rights* for all Americans, whatever their race or color." Magnanimity, not righteousness, was being offered at last to the South, by a man who shared its heritage of defeat, and who had suffered for it in his own way.

It would be idle to suggest that all non-Southerners in the chamber agreed with Johnson, or that men from the Old Confederacy—even the more intelligent Southern leaders—welcomed his overtures. It would be an obvious misstatement to say what Johnson himself would not have expected, that even if they had recognized his meaning, the response could have been immediate, that it could even have been rapid. Events were to show that many Southerners, including the embittered Russell, saw Johnson only in that long line of politicians who had taken up the Negro cause to win Northern votes.

They were not, of course, entirely wrong. Political leaders

move always in a political context; and the fact was that Johnson had no political choice whatever but to commit himself to
the civil rights bill Kennedy had sent to Congress. In the first
place, the only program of action that it was possible to present
in five days was the Kennedy program. In the second place,
it was still the Kennedy family and political apparatus that
dominated not only the organization but the spirit of the
Democratic party; by the mere act of taking the oath of office,
Johnson had by no means assumed the title "President" in all
its meaning. That would have to be won, and it would not be
won by casting aside the cardinal points of the Kennedy
program. In the third place, there remained the social necessity
that had driven Kennedy reluctantly to present the most sweeping civil rights legislation in history; American Negroes were
in the streets, in the heat of what was only tenuously a "peaceful" rebellion against second-class status, personal humiliation
and degradation, last place in the job lines, rat-infested homes,
ramshackle schools, and the back seat of the bus. No American President, in the summer and fall of 1963, could have held
back from action to alleviate these grievances, to maintain
internal order, and to bring one-tenth or more of the population more nearly into the national abundance. Legislation, if
it was not the only or even the best response, was the symbolic
necessity; unless the government had shown some willingness
to act, there is hardly the slightest doubt that the bloodshed
that did occur in 1964 and after would have been increased a
hundredfold.

Finally—justifying the suspicions of the Southerners—the
cause of Negro rights had come to be a rallying point of that
urban "liberalism" which was not so much historic or philo-
sophical liberalism as it was the program of the dominant
interest groups that controlled the big-population states and
thus the Presidential elections. The Democratic party had become the instrument of that dominant-interest program, and it
was committed to its pursuit. It was the party of the big states,
and the balance of power in those states—New York and

Michigan, for instance—was crucially affected by the bloc votes of the millions of Negroes who had migrated to them from the South in a vain, tragic search for a place of equality and opportunity. Neither John Kennedy nor Lyndon Johnson could conceivably have won the election of 1964, nor could the Democratic party have maintained its contemporary shape, had either alienated the Negroes and the urban "liberal" interests by a refusal to support civil rights legislation in 1963.

Johnson had an additional problem. As a Southerner, as a man who had cast votes against earlier civil rights proposals than those of 1957 and 1960, he had the necessity of convincing Negroes and liberals—the heft of his own party in the most important states—that he was acceptable on the issue; that he was fully in support of the civil rights cause; that as President, he could rise above the sectionalism of the South to a national outlook, even though that outlook itself was not so much a true consensus as it was the program of the dominant interest of the Twentieth Century—urban industrialism with its concomitant labor organizations.

Always, Johnson had wanted to be a *national* leader, not just a sectional representative. For years, his efforts had been toward achieving that goal, and his guidance of two civil rights bills to passage in the Senate had been a direct result. It was the civil rights issue that had made sectionalists out of men like Russell and so many others; it was the civil rights issue upon which Lyndon Johnson would win recognition that he was a truly national figure.

Thus, it was unquestionably true that Johnson was politically motivated that day in the House chamber; there never had been any possibility that he would accede to his old friend and mentor, Russell, who already had passionately told him that the one thing he must not do, as President, was to press on with a civil rights measure that Russell regarded as unconstitutional and sectionally divisive. Johnson was committed to the civil rights bill by causes outside himself and outside his control, as so many Presidents have been committed to historic measures—as for instance Abraham Lincoln had been committed, in the master political exercise of Presidential history, the timing, issuance and form of the Emancipation Proclamation as a weapon of war, of party and national unity, and of social reconstruction.

That is not to say that Johnson's motivation was cynical, for it was not aimed merely at personal political benefit; the national interest dictated his course as well as his own predicament. It is at least likely, moreover, that Johnson was as personally committed to it as the fine words of his joint-session speech suggested. He had never been truly a part of the Southern resistance; if his deepest political roots were Populist, he had come to his political maturity in the West more than a half-century after Populism in the South had foundered on its adherence to white supremacy. He had lived in a different time, a different place. Negroes had not been a large part of the society of his native Texas hill country. He had campaigned nationally, been part of a national government; even in the Senate, as its Majority Leader, his attitude had had of necessity to transcend state or regional limitations. In his travels for Kennedy, he had seen the world revolution of blacks, and he could speak with the crude power of revelation of the abject miseries and splendid determination he had seen in the huts of Africa and the slums of Asia. As Vice President, he had been in charge of the Kennedy Administration's efforts to achieve equality of job opportunity among government contractors, and he had been impressed and alarmed at the extent of the disaffection he had discovered among Negroes.

Months after he became President, he told a group of reporters in the White House:

The fact that I had impressed on me more than anything else the three years that I was Vice President was how had the leadership of the Negro communities been able to contain them as long as they had with the feeling that I saw demonstrated in their meetings with me. Even though they tried to be nice and polite and cordial to a Vice President who was trying to provide leadership in jobs, you could see a deep bitterness that I would feel if I had been forced to sit at the second table or go into the basement and be denied a job and be denied a school for my child and be denied a place to live, making me live in a part of town where it took me forty minutes .nore to get to Andrews Field [near Washington] than it would if I lived out there—all of those things. There was a pent-up feeling that was very obvious to me, and I pointed this out to President Kennedy many, many times. . . .[3]

The essential difference in Johnson's civil rights approach, however, was in the overtures he was able to make to the South *at the same time*. Kennedy could not have done that, nor Nelson Rockefeller, and perhaps not even Dwight Eisenhower; certainly not Barry Goldwater.

Lyndon Johnson could do it because he was a Southerner cast into the White House by accident. Southerners knew he had shared their bitter alienation; among other things, it had helped lose him the Democratic nomination they and he thought he deserved in 1960—just as it had cost the able Richard Russell his chance at the Presidency in 1952. Johnson might play politics in the North, but he did not come to the South with vindictiveness in his heart; there might be a little Scalawag in him but a Carpetbagger he could never be. He was one of the South's own; he had a sympathy for their outlook that many Southerners could believe was genuine. He understood them, and they him.

Yet, even Johnson's approaches to the South were not free from the ubiquitous influence of political necessity. *As a Southerner,* he had much greater opportunity to win the Southern states in 1964 than Kennedy, whose name had become synonymous with civil rights, would have had. He was, *as a Southerner,* less sure of victory in the big northern states than Kennedy would have been; strength in the South was more of a political necessity for him. Moreover, *as a Southerner,* Johnson desperately wanted to carry the South. No triumph is as sweet as those scored among the home folks. Finally, *as a Southerner,* Lyndon Johnson was better placed than any man to recognize that full national unity and sweeping national progress, on civil rights or any other questions, was not possible until the South had somehow been brought back into the Union. A further embittered South, defiant and implacable, would be a dead weight on the Democratic party, on the nation, on the so-called "great society" that Johnson was to make his political goal. And if a bloody year of racial violence did lie ahead, as a result of Southern intransigence, its effects upon Johnson's re-election prospects could hardly be helpful to him.

It is in such complex and sometimes unseen ways that political pressures always have their impact upon men and events —and that character and attitude have their effect upon the same men, the same events. *I claim not to have controlled events,* Lincoln said, *but confess plainly that events have controlled me.* Yet, the nature of Lincoln's response to events was as inevitably influenced by what he was, where he had come from, what he had seen, as by those events itself. That is why "men of principle," however they may be revered, so rarely succeed in the great art of political leadership. Richard Russell may be honored for the profound respect for principle that prevented him from moving an inch on the civil rights question, but such a man could never be President. For principle, if clung to through all events and influences, does not react or respond at all; and politics is always a thing of response. What is important in politics is not so much *principle* as *character,* and character can have no more effective weapon than a sensitive awareness of the way things are, the way things happen, the way things go. Only with such an awareness can character express itself, expand itself, have its influence in any necessary direction.

And so Lyndon Johnson responded as Russell never could

have, that November noon in the old chamber of the House, to events as *he* saw them, to men as *he* knew them, to influences as *he* felt them. It was as natural to him as breathing. All his political life—in the sanguinary Texas politics he had mastered, later in the limited wars of the Senate—Johnson had walked carefully and softly among factions, reaching out to all, throwing in completely with one or another only when he had to. "There comes a time in poker and politics," Cactus Jack Garner had told him, as Johnson would frequently recall, "when a man has to shove in all his stack." Before Lyndon Johnson would do that, he wanted to be as sure as a man could be that he held a winning hand. Always he had sought the middle ground, the consensus, the central place upon which to assemble the necessary majority—whether for his own re-election in Texas, or for the passage of some controversial bill in the Senate. He had always been willing to accept an opponent on one day as a supporter on another, and in his first Presidential address he was signalling plainly that, in the White House, too, he meant to hold the middle ground and reach out to all around him. It was his dominant political characteristic coming to the fore.

"I pledge," he said, for instance, "that the expenditures of your government will be administered with the utmost thrift and frugality." This evoked whoops and cheers, as such remarks always do in Congress, and they came again when Johnson said his Administration would "set an example of prudence and economy."

This is standard rhetoric in Washington; American politicians never run on spendthrift platforms, or at least never get elected on them. But Johnson had a little more in mind than this bow to the greatest shibboleth in American politics. He quickly followed his obeisance to economy with a bow to the liberal left wing of the Democratic party. "This does not mean [he said] that we will not meet our unfilled needs or that we will not honor our commitments. We will do both."

Johnson, as events were to show, aimed to keep both

pledges, or at least to give the appearance of doing so. He began at that moment the work that led to perhaps his most striking achievement—the consolidation of business interests behind a liberal Democratic President, who meant to spend taxpayers' money for social purposes.

Then the new President reached in two directions again, this time with Congress itself in mind, a Congress that had so reacted against executive leadership in John Kennedy's time that even students of government were beginning to despair of the system of divided powers and to suggest far-reaching change in the majestic system that had functioned for nearly two centuries. Johnson meant to find common ground here, too. "For thirty-two years, Capitol Hill has been my home. I have shared many moments of pride with you, pride in the ability of the Congress of the United States to act, to meet any crisis, to distill from our differences strong programs of national action."

Ruffled Congressional feathers could almost be seen settling, for members of Congress had shown signs of extreme sensitivity to the charges of indifferences, inefficiency, localism, even of senility, that had been made against them. But Johnson quickly laid on the lash as well as the honey:

> As one who has long served in both Houses of the Congress, I firmly believe in the independence and the integrity of the Legislative Branch. And I promise you that I shall always respect this. It is deep in the marrow of my bones. With equal firmness, I believe in the capacity and I believe in the ability of the Congress, despite the divisions of opinion which characterize our nation, to act—to act wisely, to act vigorously, to act speedily when the need arises. The need is here. The need is now. I ask your help.

Thus, Lyndon Johnson began to build his Consensus. It has to be recognized how quickly and instinctively he set about it because only then can it be understood how much it was a part of his nature to do so. Almost never in his Presidency would he *knowingly* burn bridges behind him; his doors would remain ajar to all factions and interests as long as he could keep them so; and in order to maintain these openings, he would have to offer some measure of satisfaction and attraction to all of them. This was to be an integral cause of his success, and then of the downfall that that success only made the more resounding.

So, too, would be his pursuit of "continuity," another major theme of his address. Recalling that Kennedy's inaugural challenge had been "let us begin," Johnson built upon it dramatically: "Today, in this moment of new resolve, I would say to all my fellow Americans—let us continue."

He called for quick action on tax reduction and virtually every other point of the legislation pending in Congress when Kennedy had been killed—education, youth employment, medical care for the aged. He rededicated the Administration to the support of the United Nations, to its commitments to its allies, to the search for peace but also to the maintenance of a military strength "second to none," to the stability of the dollar and to continued foreign aid programs.

These things, too, were political necessities, although none of them were necessarily antithetical to Johnson's own preferences. Nevertheless, the cardinal fact was that he had then little political support and no solid base of his own. Circumstances forced Johnson, and even had he desired he could not have disputed that fact, to build upon what Kennedy had bequeathed him—much of which Roosevelt and Truman and Eisenhower had bequeathed Kennedy.

Despite the importance of all these matters, and the manner —not then so visible—in which Johnson's first words were setting him inevitably upon a course that would prove difficult to change, the longest and loudest applause came when he spoke what was in the minds and hearts of millions of Americans, that day.

"John Kennedy's death commands what his life conveyed— that America must move forward," he said, to strong applause.

"The time has come for Americans of all races and creeds and political beliefs to understand and to respect one another." Again, applause rang through the chamber, in the moment of sorrow and shame and resolution that had fallen upon a nation.

"Let us put an end," Lyndon Johnson said, slowly and quietly, "to the teaching and the preaching of hate and evil . . ." His head snapped forward suddenly, and his voice rang through the House. ". . . and violence!"

And now the applause was not just long and loud; it was heartfelt, emotional. Perhaps not until another shattering tragedy had laid bare, for a moment, the beast that lurks beneath the surface; perhaps not until in horror's recoil men were forced again to reflect upon the nobility also submerged in the human spirit, would applause like that be heard again in America—for anyone, for any words.

Johnson took a sip of water. Now he was at the end of his speech, and those who were following its text, who knew his reputation for flamboyance and "corniness," prepared themselves anxiously for the undoing of all he had done.

"Let us here highly resolve that John Fitzgerald Kennedy did not live or die in vain," Johnson said. Robert Kennedy applauded, for the first time more than perfunctorily. "And on this Thanksgiving Eve, as we gather together to ask the Lord's blessing, and give Him our thanks, let us unite in those familiar and cherished words:

> *America, America*
> *God shed His grace on thee,*
> *And crown thy good*
> *With brotherhood*
> *From sea to shining sea.*

John Kennedy would never have spoken such a blatant sentiment; but Lyndon Johnson's instinct had been sure. The almost forgotten training of his mother, an elocution teacher, perhaps served him well; his voice, that voice native to an America rolling, as in the line of the song, from sea to sea, for once rang as clear and true as children singing. Banal it may have been; sentimental it surely was. But it was also just right —that day, in that place, from that man.

So Lyndon Johnson went back to the President's oval office in the West Executive Wing of the White House, where he now was entitled to sit. He had not failed at his most critical moment. He had married himself to the Kennedy program, the Kennedy political legacy, and placed his own emphasis upon it—the theme of consensus. He had met his political necessities. And the evidence of editorials and public opinion polls and every other gauge was to show that he had made the American people believe in him as their leader.

To many of those who knew him so well—particularly to those who feared for him, questioned in their hearts his capability and readiness—he had offered a particular reassurance.

It was in the way he had spoken, in the dramatic force of his delivery, the seemingly sure grasp of word and emotion. At a time of deep sentiment and national sorrow, Johnson had sensitively, surely, shaped his sentences and used his voice to capitalize upon the mood and the moment. Several times, his voice had dropped almost to a whisper; at other times, it had sung out challengingly. Throughout his speech, his only gesture was an occasional forward snap of his head to emphasize his points. This was not the sweating stump speaker who had ranged the hinterlands in 1960 with careless and evangelistic fervor; nor the cloakroom persuader; nor the insensitive boor of Taj Mahal. This was not, in short, the vain, imperious, crude Johnson of Washington legend.

For Lyndon Johnson had become President and that is not an ordinary event. If he had brought something of himself to the office of Lincoln and Roosevelt, it also had imposed itself on him. For a time, the Presidency would be a particular thing —a combination of enduring office and temporary occupant, a blend of institution and man, a vector of law and personality. What Johnson would do and believe in that office would be influenced by the institution, but the man would also shape and mold the office and its works by what he was and could be.

He had already started to build the remarkable instrument that would become known as the Consensus. He had taken the necessary grip on the Democratic Left, he had conciliated the Kennedy loyalists, he had reached out, as had no President since Lincoln, to the segregationist South. He had suggested that he could become the first liberal Democratic President to win the support of the immensely important business community and the conservative legislators who looked to it, servilely or with conviction. And he had begun the necessary reconciliation of President and Congress.

In five days, Johnson had met the "first priority" of achieving continuity and restoring confidence; and he had set in motion something of his own, from the deepest recesses of his character, his experience and his political sensitivity—the Consensus that would carry him to the greatest election victory and to a period of perhaps the greatest political power in American history.

But the moment of that power would be brief, because it is one of the excruciating ironies of the endless adventure that in the same five days Lyndon Johnson also had started down the long road to the ultimate collapse of the Consensus he had scarcely begun to build. He had accepted his predecessor's pledges and commandeered his predecessor's men, and on Sunday, November 24, he had met with Ambassador Henry Cabot Lodge and committed himself to the war in Vietnam.

12 *Commitment*

Lodge, the patrician Republican who had lost to John Kennedy for the Senate in 1952 and to Lyndon Johnson for the Vice Presidency in 1960, had been sent to Saigon a few months earlier in an obvious effort to give a bipartisan cast to the American effort there, which in 1963 was first becoming a national concern. He had reached his station just in time for the overthrow of Ngo Dinh Diem, and it was through Lodge that the Kennedy Administration's acquiescence in the coup had been passed to the dissident generals who would effect it—and who, to Lodge's lasting dismay, would murder Diem and his brother.

Following this upheaval, which came just three weeks before Kennedy's assassination in Dallas, Lodge was ordered home for consultations. He was to have had lunch with the President at Kennedy's new Virginia country place on Rattlesnake Mountain, and Kennedy had planned to return from Texas—after spending the night of November 23 at Vice President Johnson's LBJ Ranch—on Sunday in time for the luncheon.

Lodge was at the St. Francis Hotel in San Francisco when he heard the news of Kennedy's assassination. Even in the excitement and panic of that weekend, however, he was told to come on to Washington since the new President would be even more in need of consultations than the old—a sensible

instruction that Lodge recalls as having come from the
self-possessed McGeorge Bundy.

Lodge arrived on Saturday, visited the East Room of the
White House where Kennedy's body lay in state, and early on
Sunday afternoon met with the new President and other officials
in Johnson's high-ceilinged and roomy old Vice Presidential
suite in the Executive Office Building.

It was not a propitious time for high-policy discussions.
Johnson had just returned from accompanying Kennedy's body
in the formal procession to the Rotunda of the Capitol. Just before the procession had started from the White House, Jack
Ruby further shocked an already dismayed nation by murder-
ing Lee Harvey Oswald in the basement of the Dallas police
station, with television cameras watching. E. W. Kenworthy,
posted at the White House by *The New York Times* that day,
wrote that on Johnson's return from the Capitol, where he had
placed a wreath at Kennedy's bier and listened to the dolorous
eulogies, "his face was drawn, and tears welled in his eyes."

But Johnson, as he would make plain in his Congressional
address three days later, had made continuity the first order
of business; that day, Pierre Salinger announced from the
White House news office that the new President had asked all
members of the Kennedy staff to remain at their posts, as he
had already requested of Cabinet members. The ugly situation in Vietnam might be unwelcome but continuity and necessity required that it be faced as soon as possible.

Secretaries Rusk and McNamara, Bundy, John McCone, the
C.I.A. director, and George Ball, the Undersecretary of State,
met with Johnson and Lodge. Rusk, McNamara, Lodge
and Bundy all had taken part a few days earlier—before the
assassination—in a general political-military review of Vietnam
that had been held in Honolulu.

Lodge's report was bleak, although he made no specific
requests for Johnson to decide upon. In the wake of Diem's
removal, the Ambassador said, the new government of South
Vietnam was shaky and ineffective, political rivalries were

sprouting in and out of it, and the various forces set free by the end of Diem's repression were threatening political chaos. The Viet Cong, already powerful enough, seemed to be redoubling their efforts to take military advantage of what amounted to a divided and leaderless nation. The South Vietnamese Army had managed the coup but otherwise it was corrupt and inefficient and lacked a real will to fight as well as the leadership to succeed in such battles as it could not avoid.

In short, Lodge—an old friend of Johnson's from their Senate days, whom Johnson once had recommended to Eisenhowever for Secretary of Defense, and who was thus close enough to the new President to speak his mind (Lodge is not a man to mince words, anyway)—told the emotionally drained Texan that if Vietnam was to be saved, hard decisions would have to be made.

"Unfortunately, Mr. President," Lodge said, "you will have to make them."

This was, in essence, what Lodge would have told John Kennedy, had Kennedy lived to take his Sunday lunch at Rattlesnake Mountain. What Kennedy might have replied can never be known to a certainty. It is clear and important, however, that had Kennedy been able to listen to Lodge he would have been a President in vastly different circumstances from those that surrounded President Lyndon B. Johnson on November 24, 1963; and it must never be forgotten, in any case, that Kennedy and Johnson, whatever their circumstances, were different men—in background, experience, outlook, personality.

This is not to suggest that Kennedy would have met the growing crisis in Vietnam differently than Johnson met it; there is ample testimony from Kennedy's close associates to suggest that he probably would have done just about what Johnson, in fact, did do. It is interesting, nonetheless, to study the differences in what his circumstances would have been and what Johnson's circumstances actually were; such a study suggests that Kennedy *could* have had an alternative, while Johnson had none whatever.

Throughout 1963, the cost and the political pressures of the war had been mounting (there were nearly twenty-five thousand American military men in South Vietnam by the time Lodge reported to Johnson), and consequently there had been a growing division of opinion within the Kennedy Administration. Officials in the Defense Department and the military—particularly the disastrous General Paul D. Harkins, then commanding in Vietnam—viewed the situation as a mere war, to be fought as a war, and believed that to insist on its political nature, or more particularly on the need for political reforms by the mandarin regime of Diem, was only to hamper the military effort.

In the State Department and in Kennedy's personal circle, on the other hand, some influential men believed that political reforms, notably an end to the persecution of the Buddhists by the Roman Catholic Diem and his brother, Ngo Dinh Nhu, were necessary; not only to mobilize South Vietnamese public support for the war effort but to make South Vietnam into the sort of progressive nation that could win the loyalty of its people and maintain its political and territorial integrity, especially in some dim future when the present insurgency might have been repulsed and American assistance might be rendered only at arm's length. (It is not clear that Secretary Rusk shared this view but in the late stages of the Kennedy Administration he was by no means the influential voice he was to become under Johnson.)

This conflict between the military and political views of the war was to remain, in greater or lesser degree, part of the official American attitude toward Vietnam. But in late 1963, there were suggestions that the "nation-builders," with their political ideas, had caught Kennedy's ear.

In a television interview with Walter Cronkite on September 2, he had said he did not think "the war can be won unless the people support the effort, and in my opinion, in the last two months, the government [of Diem] has gotten out of touch with the people . . . In the final analysis, it is their war.

They are the ones who have to win it or lose it. We can help them, we can give them equipment, we can send our men out there as advisers but they have to win it, the people of Vietnam against the Communists." He did not, obviously, see the situation as one requiring purely military action from whatever source.

On October 2, McNamara and General Maxwell D. Taylor, then Chairman of the Joint Chiefs of Staff, predicted after a jaunt to Saigon that the United States could withdraw most of its troops from Vietnam by the end of 1965, and would be able to pull perhaps a thousand men out by the end of 1963.

No doubt this statement was only partly sincere and was mostly an effort to put a better domestic political face on an increasingly controversial war; what it clearly did *not* suggest was any high Administration inclination whatsoever to increase the American role, to plunge American troops (then in training, technical and advisory capacities) directly into the fighting, or otherwise to expand the war.

While there is no evidence that the McNamara announcement was intended in any way as a signal to the Viet Cong or to their backers in Hanoi, it is possible that it might have been read as such by them; the mere presence of American troops in South Vietnam led the Viet Cong to label them aggressors and imperialists, and a publicly stated American intention to withdraw these troops gradually by the end of 1965—if followed by action to suit the words—might have been used later to move toward some form of political negotiations to end the insurgency, if military victory proved elusive.

It is true that, so far from showing any desire for such negotiations, the Kennedy Administration's pressures on Diem, which brought about his downfall and murder and the accession to power of the generals' junta headed by Duong Van Minh, were caused, first, by disaffection in Washington with Diem and his repressive tactics, under which enthusiastic South Vietnamese public support for the war obviously could not be generated; and, second, by Washington's apprehension that

Diem's unstable brother, Nhu, was trying to make a "neutralist" settlement with the Viet Cong and North Vietnam through French intermediaries.

In fact, *The New York Times* reported from Washington on November 2, immediately after the fall of Diem, that the Kennedy Administration not only believed it "had created the atmosphere that made the coup possible" but that it was "confident of greater progress now in the war against the Communist guerrillas."

Nevertheless, after the fall of Diem there were visible signs in South Vietnam of a growing "neutralist" sentiment, and the fact was that the generals who had come to power were probably in the best position of any government before or since to make a political arrangement with the Viet Cong, and through them, with Hanoi. There were several reasons for this, and the first was the obvious fact that these generals had overthrown and done away with the hated Diem and his brother, against whose dictatorship at least the nationalist, Southern, non-Communist elements of the National Liberation Front had gone to war in the first place. The South Vietnamese Army was certainly not a choice successor, but undeniably the new junta was not composed of Catholic Mandarins, and its leader and the nearest thing to a South Vietnamese national hero, "Big" Minh, was a Buddhist peasant from the South. These changes must have represented immense gains for many who had fled Diem and entered the N.L.F.

Controversy continues even now as to whether the N.L.F. is a genuinely indigenous Southern resistance group, to which North Vietnam has been extending more and more aid over the years; or whether it is a front formed specifically by and for the aggressive purposes of Hanoi. In late 1963, however, the N.L.F. certainly contained strong Southern Nationalist elements and a number of non-Communist groups; given the extreme rivalry and suspicion between Tonkinese (Northerners) and Cochin Chinese (Southerners), which is one of the deepest and most significant elements of Vietnamese politics, and what then appeared to be the rising tide of Buddhist political power, Southern nationalist non-Communists within the N.L.F. must surely have welcomed (or at least preferred to Diem) the Southern Buddhist peasant, "Big" Minh. At first, they might also have been impressed with his considerable popularity among the people—something with which Diem had never been able to threaten them.

Bernard Fall also has pointed out that for years "the main drawing card" of the N.L.F. had been its *My-Diem* ("American Diemist") propaganda line. The Front could attract the support of peasants with double-barrelled blasts at "a hated mandarins' regime backed by the United States"—a puppet dictatorship propped up by the white imperialists and colonialists (as they described them) who had come to take the place of the French. With Diem dead and disavowed by the Americans, the N.L.F. had lost its "main drawing card."[4]

For all these reasons, and no doubt for its own purposes, on November 8, 1963, the N.L.F. broadcast statements on its clandestine radio which seem clearly to have raised the possibility of negotiations with Saigon. Jean Lacouture, the French journalist, reports that the broadcast called for "a regime with a broad and democratic base" and for "negotiations between interested groups in South Vietnam, in order to arrive at a cease-fire and a solution to the great problems of the country."[5]

The FBIS Daily Report, which summarizes foreign broadcasts for circulation within the government in Washington, does not contain this statement—for which Lacouture gives no authority—but in its issue of November 13, 1963, reports another by the N.L.F. radio which said the Minh junta could have "a future which will be brilliant, which will have no more nightmares," if it separated itself from the United States, worked for national independence and brought "freedom and democracy to the people."

The latter version, at least, was surely known to Kennedy, the assiduous reader and foreign-policy buff, since it was available in Washington nine days before his assassination—twelve days after the death of Diem.

Big Minh himself, in November, 1963, does not appear to

have been a "neutralist." To Lacouture, at that time, he said: "In the present situation, such men [neutralists] can only prepare the way for communism."[6] But some members of his junta showed interest in the neutralizing proposals of General de Gaulle (notably Le Van Kim and Nguyen Van Vy), and when General Nguyen Khan overthrew the junta and established his own regime on January 31, 1964, he said in a proclamation that he had acted because some members of Minh's government had "a tendency to advocate neutrality, thereby paving the way for the Communists to enslave our country."

It is entirely possible, then, and it may even be likely, that the overthrow of Diem and the accession of Big Minh—no matter for what purpose the Kennedy Administration had sponsored these developments, and regardless of Minh's personal view—had created one of those rare moments in the troubled history of the Second Indochinese War when a negotiated peace, arising out of some form of reconciliation between the Saigon junta and the National Liberation Front, was genuinely possible.

It will be argued at once that, even so, such a settlement—when the Viet Cong were in a clear ascendancy and Saigon was just beginning to wake groggily from the long night of Diemist oppression—would have been disastrous both for South Vietnam and for American interests in Southeast Asia; in short, that it would have led inevitably to a "Communist takeover" through the quick domination by the N.L.F. of a coalition government; and perhaps, even to reunification with the North. That well may be. What has to be weighed against such an argument is whether even such a Communist takeover would have been so damaging to either South Vietnam or the United States as the costly, expanded, bloody, dangerous war that, instead, was to come (aside from the question whether an N.L.F. takeover in 1963 and 1964 would have been quite the same as a Communist takeover, let alone a North Vietnamese takeover).

The purpose here is not to make that judgment but to point out that, had the luncheon at Rattlesnake Mountain taken place, John Kennedy conceivably might have replied to Lodge's blunt description of a deteriorating situation in a different manner from Lyndon Johnson; that, at least, he would have had the opportunity to have done so, because he would have been a different man in different circumstances.

Kennedy, it must be remembered, had consistently labelled the war as one that had to be won or lost by the South Vietnamese—with American help to be sure, but not with Americans doing the fighting. His September statements and the fact that he assented to the overthrow of Diem demonstrate that he believed in the need for political reform in Saigon, if the Viet Cong were to be overcome. In Lodge's discouraging report, therefore, he might have seen evidence that the necessary political reform, even with Diem out of the way, would be a long time in arriving and that Saigon's victory was only the faintest of hopes, one which would be of untold cost to achieve.

Moreover, Kennedy had told Arthur Krock two years earlier that he had grave doubts about the so-called "domino theory,"[6] which held that if South Vietnam collapsed so would Thailand and the rest of Southeast Asia, perhaps including the Philippines, and that therefore American vital interests were engaged in South Vietnam. His insistence that the war was Saigon's to win or to lose supports his remark to Krock; for if American vital interests really were so fully at stake in South Vietnam as the domino theory asserts, then it would be up to any American President to see that they were protected, no matter what Saigon did or did not do, political reforms or no political reforms, civil war or no civil war. Arthur Schlesinger's assertion that Kennedy "had never really given [Vietnam] his full attention"[7] also raises the question whether Kennedy really considered it a question of vital American interest.

It is true that in a television interview with David Brinkley and Chet Huntley on September 9, 1963, long after his con-

versation with Krock, Kennedy said that he did believe in the
domino theory because "China is so large, looms so high . . .
that if South Vietnam went, it would not only give them an
improved geographic position for a guerrilla assault on Malaya,
but would also give the impression that the wave of the future
in Southeast Asia was China and the Communists."

But this statement has to be weighed against the Cronkite
interview, already mentioned, which Kennedy had granted a
week earlier. Then, Kennedy had said of the South Vietnamese: "In the final analysis, it is their war. They're the ones
who have to win it or lose it . . . the people of Vietnam against
the Communists."

The earlier remarks, suggesting, as they did, the possible
abandonment of Diem, had caused a sensation in Saigon; it
is conjectural to what extent Kennedy might have tried in the
second interview to soften his position. What seems clear, however, is that in September, 1963, Kennedy considered a Communist rebuff in South Vietnam as an important American
goal; but he was not yet speaking of it in terms of a *vital
American interest,* which could hardly be left in the uncertain
hands of a Saigon government that, he had told Cronkite,
had to make "changes in policy and perhaps with personnel"
if it was to win its war.

The United States, he also told Cronkite, had "to participate
—we may not like it—in the defense of Asia," as it had participated in the defense of Europe; but to Huntley and Brinkley
he described the trouble plainly: "We can't expect these countries to do everything the way we want to do them . . . We
can't make the world over, but we can influence the world."

The only hard evidence to suggest that Kennedy thought
of South Vietnam in terms of vital American interest is that,
in December, 1961, he ordered a sharp increase in American
personnel in South Vietnam, to about 16,000 men—one of
the key steps toward the enormous engagement that was to
follow. But by late 1961, Kennedy already had suffered disaster at the Bay of Pigs; he had been bullied by Khrushchev

at Vienna; the Berlin Wall had gone up in his face; he had agreed to a coalition government, including Communists, in Laos; and he was under fire at home and under suspicion abroad as to his will to maintain the American position in the world. Undoubtedly, at the time he ordered the expansion of his forces in Vietnam, he was under a strong compulsion to make a show of strength and determination somewhere in the world. He gave James Reston the impression that this might have been his primary motivation for sending additional forces to Vietnam, rather than the situation in Vietnam itself.[8]

In December, 1961, moreover, the Sino-Soviet ideological split was not yet fully recognized in the West. There is a strong likelihood that Kennedy's momentous decision of that month was directed at least as much at Khrushchev as at those Chinese Communists he cited to Huntley and Brinkley two years later.

If Kennedy might have been discouraged by Lodge about the prospect of a victory for Saigon, even with its new government, and if he was not totally committed to the "domino" idea of American vital interest in Vietnam, he would also have had a suggestion before him for a negotiated settlement. In November, 1963, Secretary General U Thant of the United Nations presented Washington with a plan for a neutralist coalition government in South Vietnam that would have included some of the Vietnamese exiles living in Paris. According to a later report, it was the failure of these exiles to embrace the plan that caused it to flounder.[9]

With the FBIS report also available, suggesting a bargaining mood in the N.L.F., Kennedy could have seen the moment as one when the conference table might have become preferable to the battlefield, even though Saigon was obviously in a weak bargaining position. He had, after all, suffered his Bay of Pigs, with its lasting effects. "What is prestige?" he had demanded, after that debacle. "Is it the shadow of power or the substance of power? We are going to work on the substance of power."[10]

He had already made one agreement to a coalition government, in Laos, and had managed to live with it both at home
and in the world. Just a year before, in October, 1962, he had
gained the immense prestige and the position of strength he
had needed, when he forced the Soviet Union (and Khrushchev, for all his bullying at Vienna) to withdraw its missiles
from Cuba.

Above all, in the summer of 1963 he had concluded the
nuclear test ban treaty with Moscow. Since the disaster of his
first Cuban adventure, Kennedy had offered little deference
to generals. The Laotian agreement had avoided the very sort
of war that Vietnam now was threatening. And in the second
Cuban episode, he had stockpiled all the diplomatic and political credit he needed to deal with the inevitable cries at home
that he had "sold out Southeast Asia" and to dispel worries
abroad about other American commitments. His steadfastness,
after Cuba, could hardly be questioned.

On his last swing around the country before going to Texas,
Kennedy had experimented with political speeches extolling
the test ban treaty, and everywhere the crowd response had
been gratifying. Knowledgeable members of his staff confided
to the press that the treaty would underpin a major peace
theme in Kennedy's developing 1964 campaign. At that time,
it appeared ever more likely that the belligerent Barry Goldwater, with his alarming notions about nuclear weapons and
Cold Warmanship, would be the Republican candidate. This
would offer a natural opening for Kennedy to sound a peace
theme that could be greatly amplified if a settlement in Vietnam also allowed some or all of the 25,000 American troops
there to come home in an election year.

All this, unquestionably, is mere speculation—primarily in-
formative because it was *not* John Kennedy who replied to
Lodge that grim Sunday afternoon of November 24, 1963,
in the Executive Office Building. It is not intended to suggest
that Kennedy would have at that point extricated the nation
from the Vietnamese involvement, or even that he would some-

how have avoided the war that actually followed. It is intended
to show a relative flexibility and freedom of action that was
by no means available to the far different man, immersed in
far different circumstances, who would actually respond to
Lodge.

To take the man first—the new President was, perhaps
above all, something of a throwback to another time. He was
a decade older than Kennedy—just enough older to identify
him with an earlier generation and its somewhat different view
of the world. He was not a product of the Ivy League and the
East; he had not come under much influence from the liberal
intellectuals who had surrounded Kennedy; unlike them, he
had not chafed on the sidelines during the Cold War years
of the Eisenhower Administration. But it was these liberal intellectuals who had come to power in 1961, while Johnson's
obscurity in the Vice Presidency had kept him out of the main
channels of Kennedy Administration talk, thought and outlook. His view of the world had been shaped neither academi-
cally nor in Kennedy's service, but while he was the Senate
Majority Leader in the Fifties, in the full chill of the Cold
War, when he would be frequently summoned to the White
House for briefings by Eisenhower and Foster Dulles, and
when in "responsible" bipartisan fashion he generally supported their foreign policy objectives in Congress (much to the
dismay of those liberals and intellectuals on the Democratic
Advisory Committee he and Sam Rayburn had disdained to
join, and some of whom in the past three years had been the
men around Kennedy).

Johnson was a middle-aged man of smalltown America,
both a Westerner and a Southerner, and except where politics
had demonstrably forced his growth—as on the question of
civil rights—he functioned like most men, as a product of his
background. There is little to suggest that at this time he saw
the world moving away from the stereotype he had accepted
in the Fifties—the notion of the "Communist bloc" monolith-
ically seeking to bury "the free world." Like any Rotarian or

state legislator and many members of Congress, he saw this world conflict in terms of good and evil and if he was by no means a right-winger who spied a Communist under every bed and believed in holy war against them, he still was at the time of his accession to the Presidency one of those millions of Americans who were nationalist almost to the point of nativism; impressed by the lesson of World War II that aggression unchecked was aggression unleashed, and whose years of greatest activity had coincided with the frustrations and passions of the Cold War. Thus his kind of "internationalism" was in many ways only the reverse coin of the old isolationism of the Thirties; both were based on a self-righteous sense of American superiority, on a sort of "higher morality" that derived from pride in democracy, free enterprise and material success. And in Johnson's case it would never be entirely free from the attitudes of the hard-scrabble Texas hill country in which he had grown up, amid dust, poverty and struggle.

"I know these Latin Americans," he remarked privately, to a group of reporters not long after becoming President. "I grew up with Mexicans. They'll come right into your yard and take it over if you let them. And the next day they'll be right up on your porch, barefoot and weighing one hundred and thirty pounds and they'll take that too. But if you say to 'em right at the start, 'hold on, just wait a minute,' they'll know they're dealing with somebody who'll stand up. And after that you can get along fine."

If there was a suggestion here that despite his genuine concern for the poor and downtrodden, Johnson thought somewhat in terms of a "white man's burden" to do something useful for other races without yielding much to them, he was more explicit, early in 1964, about his attitude toward Communists.

He didn't agree, he said in another private conversation, with the liberals who thought that "fat Communists" were better than lean and hungry ones. Communists were all alike, he went on, and he believed in keeping them off balance and worried. "The more trouble they have the better for us," he said.

It was not, then, a President with "sophisticated" or adventurous views about coexistence and "taking the chill out of the Cold War" to whom Lodge gave his blunt description of the situation in Vietnam that November day in 1963. Nor was Johnson, at that time, a man who had learned the hard way, as Kennedy had had to do, the limitations of American power or the deficiencies of the apparatus with which he had to work.

Johnson had not presided over disaster at the Bay of Pigs, nor necessarily drawn Kennedy's conclusions about the dangers of relying upon so-called "experts" rather than upon his own judgment or that of men he knew to be sound and trustworthy, whether or not "expert." He had not personally suffered the frustrations, anguish and political dangers of that debacle, nor undergone the "sombre" experience of Khrushchev's polemics at Vienna, nor found himself and his government unprepared and embarrassed by the Berlin Wall. With the military, Johnson's primary experience had been in Congressional committees and then more as an ally against the traditional enemy, the executive branch politicians, than as a critic or judge. When Curtis LeMay was Chief of Staff for the Air Force in the early months of Johnson's Presidency, Johnson liked to tell privately how LeMay used to slip him notes at Senatorial hearings suggesting questions that ought to be asked. As President, Johnson said, he had exacted a pledge from LeMay not to do this with some other senator, at the Johnson Administration's expense. Apparently, he believed, therefore, that LeMay would not.

Significantly, Johnson came into office with considerable confidence in Secretary Rusk, who had been of declining influence in the Kennedy Administration, and in Secretary McNamara—although in McNamara's case he was wary, at first, of the Secretary's close relationship with Robert Kennedy. This was quickly overcome by McNamara's cooperation and loyalty. Rusk had been the official deputed by Kennedy to keep the touchy Vice President Johnson informed on world affairs; with his bureaucrat's scrupulous attention to detail and possibility, Rusk had carried out the assignment generously, and Johnson took to the White House with him no little gratitude as well as the impression that the Secretary was a man who appreciated him and with whom he could work. In fact, Johnson considered Rusk to have been, like Johnson himself, an "outcast" from the Kennedy inner circle; having shared a mutual trial, he was convinced, they now could share a mutual faith in each other. Since in more influential circumstances than the Kennedy Administration had accorded him, Rusk would reveal himself as the hardest of the "hard-liners" on Asian Communism, this relationship was of profound importance for the future. Of McNamara, with whom he had at that time no such special relationship, Johnson was nonetheless admiring. Following the first meeting of the Kennedy Cabinet in 1961, Johnson once related, he had, with characteristic imagery, told the journalist William S. White (a close friend), that "that man with the Sta-Comb in his hair is the best of the lot." A month after becoming President, Johnson said flatly: "I think McNamara is the ablest man I ever met."

Johnson, for sound political and diplomatic reasons, had chosen "continuity" as the theme of his new Administration; on November 27, he would say to Congress: "Let us continue." Already, he had asked Kennedy's Cabinet and staff to stay with him. It was easier for him to make this decision and make his request to the officials meaningful because he had high regard for Rusk and McNamara, the top men in the Cabinet (with some others, Johnson had little rapport and Interior Secretary Stewart Udall, at least, had actively worked against Johnson as a Kennedy lieutenant in the pre-convention stages of 1960). Johnson's personal belief in the Secretaries of State and Defense also meant that continuity in foreign policy was not likely to be a quick pose for political effect but a fact for some time to come. Because he respected them, and men like McGeorge Bundy, and because he needed desperately to win the confidence and keep the services of these links to the Kennedy Administration, Johnson was unusually deferential to these men and to their views in the first months of his Presidency.

Rusk, McNamara and Bundy were closely identified with the Kennedy Administration's policy in Vietnam. They had a vested interest in its success, on which largely depended their own reputations. They were not likely to recommend its abandonment or fundamental alteration and as long as Johnson needed them in his service and retained his own real admiration for them, continuity in Vietnam—more of the same—was very nearly certain. And Kennedy, at his death, was not moving openly toward ending the war.

A good deal, moreover, is known of Johnson's own views on Southeast Asia at the time of his accession to the Presidency. In May, 1961, under instructions from Kennedy, he had visited Southeast Asia on an official mission, stopping in South Vietnam, Taiwan, the Philippines, Thailand, India and Pakistan. Among other things, Johnson reached an agreement with Ngo Dinh Diem—whom he incautiously called "the Churchill of today"—for increased American military assistance. According to news reports of the Johnson tour, he also discussed the possible stationing of American troops in both Thailand and South Vietnam.

Carroll Kilpatrick, a reliable reporter for the *Washington Post*, accompanied Johnson on that trip. Years later, as president of the Washington chapter of the Overseas Writers Club, Kilpatrick introduced Graham Martin, then the U.S. Ambassador to Thailand, who was to address the club. Kilpatrick said he had always believed that Johnson's fundamental Southeast Asian policy had been heavily influenced by Thailand's attitude during Johnson's 1961 visit.

Kilpatrick expanded on this idea in a note to me:

I remember that those of us on the trip were greatly surprised by how bluntly people in the Philippines, Thai-

land and Pakistan criticized the U.S. for failure to give
more support to Laos [in early 1961]. This was especially true in Thailand, which wanted a tougher anti-
Communist policy in all of Southeast Asia by the U.S.

Johnson also effected an increased military assistance agreement with Thailand. In South Vietnam, he laid heavy stress
on combating "Communism's allies"—the poverty and misery
he saw in the native villages. Upon his return to Washington,
his public statements were concentrated on this aspect of his
finding—the need for the United States to do its part in the
economic and social development of Southeast Asia as a
major means of keeping that area in "the free world."

At a news conference immediately after his return, however, Johnson was asked about the need for sending American
troops to the countries he had visited. There was no plan or
need for such a step at that time, he replied, and no promises
had been given. But he added: "I would not want to forever
foreclose the possibility of America *protecting her interests*
wherever it might be." [Italics added]

And, he said, he had been "disturbed" that "so many Asian
leaders should express doubt as to United States intentions."

Johnson's private report to Kennedy stressed the need for
economic and social development but bore down much more
heavily on the military problem than the Vice President had
done in his public remarks:

> Our mission arrested the decline of confidence in the
> United States. It did not—in my judgment—restore any
> confidence already lost . . .
> I cannot stress too strongly the extreme importance of
> following up this mission with other measures, other ac-
> tions, and other efforts . . .

The report presented an almost classic statement of the
so-called "domino theory":

> The battle against Communism must be joined in South-
> east Asia with strength and determination to achieve

success there—or the United States, inevitably, must surrender the Pacific and take up our defenses on our own shores. Asian Communism is compromised and contained by the maintenance of free nations on the subcontinent. Without this inhibitory influence, the island outposts—Philippines, Japan, Taiwan—have no security and the vast Pacific becomes a Red Sea.

The "key to what is done by Asians in defense of Southeast Asian freedom," Johnson wrote the President, "is confidence in the United States. There is no alternative to United States leadership in Southeast Asia . . . SEATO is not now and probably never will be the answer because of British and French unwillingness to support decisive action."

Of course, "these nations cannot be saved by United States help alone." They had to help themselves, particularly in fighting ignorance, poverty and disease. Nevertheless:

We must decide whether to help these countries to the best of our ability or throw in the towel in the area and pull back our defenses to San Francisco and a "Fortress America" concept. More important, we would say to the world in this case that we don't live up to treaties and don't stand by our friends . . . I recommend that we move forward promptly with a major effort to help these countries defend themselves.

But this would not be an easy program, Johnson continued.

This decision must be made in a full realization of the very heavy and continuing costs involved in terms of money, of effort and of United States prestige. It must be made with the knowledge that at some point we may be faced with the further decision of whether we commit major United States forces to the area or cut our losses and withdraw should our other efforts fail. We must remain master of this decision.[11]

This is an important Johnsonian document. It shows, first, a full acceptance of the Eisenhower-Dulles "domino theory," which in itself is an expression of an *American interest:* maintaining the frontier in Asia, keeping the battle away from American shores, and holding the "vast Pacific" as part of the "free world" rather than seeing it become a "Red Sea." Johnson's report, moreover, is couched throughout in terms of American interest—enlightened interest, it may be, but American nonetheless; and that is the context in which he spoke to the press about the possible use of American troops in Southeast Asia.

By May, 1961, when there were only a few hundred American advisers and technicians in South Vietnam, Johnson—so seeing the American interest—laid down to Kennedy what was to become a blueprint of the policy he himself would follow in years to come, *including the risk of committing "major United States forces to the area."* Since the term "major" is an imprecise catchall, it is debatable whether Kennedy ever went that far; at his death, U.S. forces in South Vietnam numbered only about 25,000, which no one could have believed was sufficient for the purpose of which Johnson had written. Johnson ultimately raised this number to about a half-million, and there is no doubt that this makes up a "major" force.

This was a significant switch by the Vice President—had it been generally known—because in 1954, during the Dienbienphu campaign, Johnson and Senator Richard Russell of Georgia—the Democratic leader in the Senate and the chairman of the Armed Forces Committee—had been the loudest and strongest opponents of the Eisenhower Administration's tentative plan to go to the aid of the French; both argued strongly the lesson of the Korean War, that the United States never again should become "bogged down" in a land war on the Asian mainland, with its teeming millions, its human waves of soldiers. By early 1961, however, Johnson, who by then could become President in the blink of an eye, could already think of putting "major United States forces" into

Southeast Asia in pursuit of the *American interest* as expressed in the "domino theory." No doubt this reflects to some extent Kilpatrick's observation of the powerful effect on Johnson of his conversations in Thailand, the Philippines and Saigon in 1961.

This preoccupation with the American interest in Vietnam is a significantly different attitude from any that Kennedy had displayed in dealing with Vietnam. This fact alone probably would have dictated his answer to Lodge, even had it not been for the circumstances in which he found himself that November afternoon. Even the most immediate and personal of these may have been significant.

Despite all that has been disclosed since to suggest that the generally good Johnson-Kennedy relationship had been ruffled by frequent disagreement, even on the last trip to Texas, those who know Johnson well have never doubted that he was genuinely stricken by the young President's horrible death; the peak of emotion in his Congressional address on November 27 came when he discussed it. And the likelihood is that he also was humbled by the enormity of the responsibility that had fallen so unexpectedly upon him. He would be super-human if he were not daunted by it. And Lyndon Johnson is not superhuman but immensely human.

As he talked with Lodge, Johnson had just returned from the moving ceremony of eulogy for Kennedy in the Great Rotunda of the Capitol; he had come back to work with the evidence of weeping on his face and if it was not the best time for high-policy making, it was even less a time when so sentimental and sensitive a man as Lyndon Johnson was likely to make a sweeping reversal or fundamental alteration of his predecessor's works.

More demonstrably, he would have had great difficulty in doing so; already he had chosen continuity for his theme. Already he had asked the very men most responsible for policy in Southeast Asia to stay on with other high officials, and as earnest of his intentions he had made it clear that he con-templated no fundamental changes in what they had been doing. One peculiarly Johnsonian quality was involved here. He believed there was a close relationship between the Kennedy family and "claque" and political columnists like Joseph Alsop; he was exceptionally eager to avoid action that would cause these columnists to write that he was ignoring or going against the advice of McNamara, Bundy, Taylor, Lodge and others who had been appointed by Kennedy.

Johnson, in his unique position as a part of, yet not *in*, the Kennedy Administration, probably had little knowledge of the developing controversy in that Administration as to whether the military emphasis in South Vietnam was well placed or promising. He had called Diem the "Churchill of today" and I believe that, if asked, he would have been against Kennedy's decision to let the mandarin ruler be overthrown; it was in his nature to believe that a tough, known, anti-Communist leader, even if he dragged his feet on social reform, was a better risk than the unknown and perhaps unreliable forces that might replace him. And, indeed, to the extent that he viewed the Vietnamese war as a military contest, with American interest at stake, he may have been right; no South Vietnamese government since Diem has been much of an improvement in those terms.

In November, 1963, McNamara had made the statement that troops would soon be coming home and that the American task could be completed by the end of 1965. Lodge's report might be grim and McNamara had spoken before the fall of Diem, but the situation was obviously not hopeless if "the ablest man" in the Administration had been willing to make such a forecast. And its suggestion, whatever Johnson might have said he was willing to risk in the 1961 report to Kennedy, was that there might never be a question of having to commit "major forces" to South Vietnam.

Even had he known of it—which is unlikely for a Vice President with little interest in foreign affairs, who had spent part of that November touring the Benelux countries and the rest of it preoccupied with Texas political troubles—the N.L.F.

gesture toward negotiations recorded in the FBIS Daily Report for November 13, 1963, probably would not have overcome these considerations in Johnson's mind; even, moreover, had the statement struck him as a political opportunity perhaps worth the alienation of Rusk and McNamara and the unsettling of "continuity," Johnson's belief in the stereotypes of anti-Communism and the "domino theory" probably would have inhibited him from seizing it.

But it was another, and probably the major circumstance of that day, outweighing even his own predilection, that made Johnson's position inevitable. So Lodge concluded his presentation and gave the President his opinion that hard decisions would be necessary to save South Vietnam.

"Unfortunately, Mr. President," the Ambassador said, "you will have to make them."

The new President, as recalled by one who was present, scarcely hesitated.

"I am not going to lose Vietnam," he said. "I am not going to be the President who saw Southeast Asia go the way China went."

"What kind of political support will you have?" Lodge, the experienced politician, asked his old friend and Vice Presidential opponent.

"I don't think Congress wants us to let the Communists take over South Vietnam," Johnson said.

His instructions to Lodge were firm. The ambassador was to return to Saigon and inform the new government there that the new government in Washington intended to stand by previous commitments and continue its help against the Communists. In effect, he told Lodge to assure Big Minh that Saigon "can count on us." That was a pledge.

So the tragedy of Lyndon Johnson—for it may well be that—was set in motion, barely forty-eight hours after he had taken the oath on the plane at Dallas. The moment, if it was there at all, would pass—that moment when with Diem gone, there might have been the faint possibility of some initial reconciliation between Saigon and the National Liberation Front, and the history of the 1960's might have been changed. All that would follow—the bombing of the North, the half-million young Americans trudging the roads and hills and through the jungles of Vietnam, the huge expenditures, the political divisions at home, the decline abroad, the sapping of a Great Society then unborn, the collapse of the Consensus yet to be contructed—had been determined in that hour of political decision in the old Executive Office Building, while Kennedy lay mourned in the Rotunda and Lee Harvey Oswald gasped away his miserable life in Parkland Hospital.

It *was* a political decision, made by a political man, in political circumstances that left him no real choice. For the first, but not the last, time Lyndon Johnson's cherished "options" were foreclosed; and even if he had been a different person of different experience, even if he had not chosen continuity and clung to Kennedy's men, even then he could have said nothing else nor could he have given Lodge less binding and fateful instructions.

Because he was, after all and above all, a new President; he was virtually unknown; he was not universally trusted and he was even less understood. Six months in the future the Democrats would choose or reject him; and if, as was likely, he survived that hurdle, it was less than a year before the nation itself would pass upon his leadership. Throughout the Kennedy years, the people had been narrowly divided; nothing in American politics then was certain—nothing but that a President who failed to pursue a strong line against "Communists" would be vulnerable to political opponents at home and to ambitious adversaries abroad. Even Kennedy, in 1960, had been forced to abandon his "soft" line on such unimportant matters as Quemoy and Matsu; his willingness to apologize to Khrushchev for the U-2 incident had been a major liability—exploited in pre-convention days by none other than Lyndon B. Johnson.

Adversaries at home and abroad were watching the new

man. Both would measure his responses, his politics, his attitudes, probing for any weaknesses. Above all other things, that dreary and unpromising November Sunday, Lyndon Johnson had to be strong—which is to say that, at the minimum, he had to *appear* to be strong; in his own words, he, no less than the nation he now must lead, had to convince the world "not to tread on us." In this case, Johnson also had to convince Saigon that it could count on its ally if it continued the struggle.

It is a necessity any new President feels, and not merely as an ambitious politician. That a nation should be respected for its strength as well as its purpose and its past is essential for its security and its ideals, let alone for international leadership.

To show strength may well be argued that the greatest respect of mankind should flow to moral rather than military strength, and it is certainly true that there are times when retreat is more to be admired than attack, and when the frank confession of error is more courageous than persistence in it. It ought even to be true that, in Wilson's phrase, there is such a thing as a nation being too proud to fight—or even too moral.

Unfortunately, it cannot be true because in the world of men, that strength which unerringly gains the most respect is armed strength; and if might does not truly make right, who can say that it does not rule most of the affairs of men? "How many divisions has the Pope?" Stalin inquired, and although he undoubtedly did find out in Heaven, this made little difference to Eastern Europe, which well knows where the earthly power lies. Thus, political leaders, no matter how beneficial their purposes, tend always to gird up their good intentions with ample armament. "We arm to parley," Churchill said, and in the very first State of the Union message, George Washington advised the nation that "to be prepared for war is one of the most effectual means of preserving peace." Almost two centuries later in his inaugural address President Kennedy declared ringingly: "Only when our arms are sufficient beyond doubt can we be certain beyond doubt that they will never be employed."

This instinct may be regrettable but it is based on a sure knowledge of man, a predatory animal who does not in practice often turn the other cheek. Thus, armed strength and the willingness to use it are the first requisites of international power and if this fact is sometimes blamed on political leaders, the righteous who make the charge should ask themselves which came first—men or politicians?

After the Bay of Pigs and after the Khrushchev confrontation, as an example, John Kennedy was in something near despair because he sensed that Khrushchev thought he was inexperienced and weak; James Reston saw Kennedy before he left Vienna and Kennedy told him he feared that he could never negotiate or deal with the Soviet leader as an equal until he had shown strength and convinced the world of his steadfastness.[12] It is instructive that it was not until the Cuban crisis over a year later, when he threatened to use nuclear weapons on Moscow, that Kennedy finally achieved that goal.

In the meantime, one of the actions he took in pursuit of it may have been his fateful first escalation of the American commitment in Vietnam during the fall of 1961. Now, Lyndon Johnson, under the same pressing necessity, for much the same reason, had taken the second step that would lead to so great a war that none of the distinguished men in the room with him could possibly have imagined it. *"I am not going to be the President who saw Southeast Asia go the way China went."*

A whole lifetime of political and human experience was distilled in that sentence; the deepest meaning of the endless adventure is to be found in the circumstances that impelled it. Still, it is doubtful that anyone that day, even Johnson himself, thought about the confidential report he had written in 1961 on his return from Southeast Asia. Nor is there anything to suggest that even in the harsh echoes of Lodge's summary anyone foresaw that terrible decision of which the new President once had written "we must remain the master."

13 *'One Great Democratic Tent'*

In the musty, cavernous old municipal auditorium of Minneapolis, the faithful of the Democratic-Farmer-Labor party that Hubert Humphrey had been nursing for twenty years gathered on the night of June 27, 1964, to hear President Lyndon B. Johnson on what turned out to be a rather symbolic occasion. To a state party that was in itself a powerful coalition of once opposed forces, Johnson defined the Consensus that he was building.

"As long as I am your President," he cried in the hoarse, harshly accented voice with which the whole country was at last familiar, "this government will not set one group against another. We will build a creative partnership between business and labor, between farm areas and urban centers, between consumers and producers. This is what I mean when I choose to be President of all the people."

The nation, he shouted, drew its strength from a system of government "that is the envy of men around the globe; a system where the capitalist can put in his capital and have a reasonable expectancy to get it back with a fair return and without fear of going to bed tonight to wake up and see it confiscated or burned the next morning."

The crowd was cheering and Johnson, as is his nature, was exhilarated by its response and by his power to move it; the flow of his language was hurried, the Texas idiom and the homely similes in which he communicates best were welling up in him. It was a system he cried, in which

> The manager of that capital can get up at daylight and work to midnight, developing stomach ulcers trying to manage money and men and bring them together, but he still has the hope of retiring at sixty-five and sharing in the profits that he helped to create. And finally we have the producers, the men, the horny-handed sons who get out and produce a better mouse trap at less cost than can be produced anywhere in the world. And capital and management and labor divide the fruits of their joint effort.

No "regimented slave labor" could ever outproduce the United States, Johnson declared, but "our job is to let our own people know that we not only never had it so good—we got to make it better . . . we have to move [the nation and its economy] further in the next two centuries than it has moved in the last two, and that is saying something, isn't it?"

And how would the nation and the system be moved so far, so fast?

> Not by eating on ourselves, not by blaming each other, not by dividing up in harassing groups that can find something wrong with what their fellow man does. We are going to build it by uniting our people, by bringing our capital and our management and our labor and our farmers all under one great Democratic tent, and saying to all of them, 'contribute your part, do your share, and you will share in the fruits that are ours.'

That was, perhaps, the politician Johnson at his best in the 1964 campaign—the Year of the Consensus. It was the same politician Johnson who had, for instance, at San Francisco, eight days before the Minneapolis speech, stated his case in equally hortatory terms:

So let us resolve tonight to stand together for the programs that will give America more action and more progress for four more years. Let us resolve here tonight that in California and in the nation the Democratic party will be the party that worked for the people, will be the party that stood with the people, will be the party that believed in the people, will be the party that journeyed with the people across the new frontiers toward a richer and a better life for all human beings.

And tonight I appeal to all Americans, regardless of policy, who believe in the people, who want them to have a richer and better life, to join us in our march, because we are marching. We have not come here to condemn or confuse, or to even criticize. We have come here to ask all good Americans to unite under one great tent to give every American a better tomorrow than yesterday, a richer and better life for himself and for his children, and his grandchildren.

This was the central theme of the 1964 campaign—the "great Democratic tent" under which could shelter all who loved their country, all who wanted to share in its fruits, all who wanted their fellow men and their children to prosper, all who wanted no jeopardy for peace and prosperity. Business, labor, farmers, housewives, intellectuals—all were summoned to the tent by the rough, evangelical voice from the pulpit.

It was a unique appeal—not non-partisan, not really devoid of issues (Johnson was, after all, proclaiming and pledging to continue the unlimited virtues of every Democratic Administration since Roosevelt's), and not really idealistic, either. It represented a strategy made inviting by the nomination of Barry Goldwater on the Republican ticket, even if it also was entirely congenial to the President who formulated it.

Goldwater was a radical; he was barely on the edge of that broad center in which American politics necessarily functions. He was a factional leader with ideological notions that, if put into practice, might have brought sharp angles and turns to the twentieth-century curve of American history, and he proclaimed his radicalism boldly and bluntly. His inarticulateness compounded the fears he thus aroused; when he stumbled through a confusing series of contradictions about the United Nations, nuclear weapons, and Social Security, it was possible to believe that he would do whatever one feared most in these areas. It was not possible to pin him down precisely on Social Security, for instance, but President Kennedy, informed shortly before his death that President Eisenhower felt himself "unclear" about Goldwater's ideas, probably spoke for millions of Americans when he said at a news conference: "I don't think Senator Goldwater has ever been particularly deceptive. I think he has made very clear what he is opposed to, what he is for. I have gotten the idea. I think that President Eisenhower will, as time goes on."

A great many Americans shared, in other words, a common fear that Goldwater would cast aside the known and stride off into the unknown. And, as Kennedy pointed out, the Senator never even tried to hide his radical views.

Thus, he was only the second Presidential challenger in American history (the Bryan of 1896 was the first) who became *the* issue; the campaign turned on the question whether Goldwater should be President or not—not whether Johnson should be elected to his own term. This opened to Lyndon Johnson the golden political opportunity of the Twentieth Century. He became the safe candidate, the respectable candidate, the candidate of the known and the established, the man who would lead, but only down visible and well-marked paths.

Goldwater was nothing less than a godsend to Johnson, at least for campaign purposes. Of tenuous popularity himself (his support, Johnson once remarked, with his gift for simile, was like a Western river—wide but shallow), with a con man's reputation that made him widely distrusted, and a personal manner that attracted few Americans, Johnson, even as a President in office, could not have been the respectable, responsible candidate against almost any other Republican available in 1964—Rockefeller, Lodge, Scranton. Each of impeccable lineage, established reputation, demonstrable moderation, each with roots deep in the Eastern Establishment, each supposedly knowledgeable in world affairs, any one of them would have placed Johnson himself in something like the position of William Jennings Bryan—the Western wild man, uninformed, undignified, provincial, above all radical, an untrustworthy and flamboyant political parvenu. But Barry Goldwater played that role to the hilt; he became the first Republican Presidential candidate of the twentieth century who was not politically respectable, and Lyndon Johnson embraced the opportunity in a Texas bear hug.

It is not clear when Johnson decided privately that Goldwater would be his opponent. In the summer of 1963 he told friends that Kennedy would be running against Goldwater, and that "we'll hold Texas even against the man they [the Right] worship."

At his Clear Creek ranch house on the shore of Lake Johnson in Texas, on January 3, 1964, he watched Goldwater's announcement of his candidacy on television. Mrs. Johnson passed bits of cheese and deer-meat sausage impaled on toothpicks as the President stared impassively at the screen; only when Rockefeller came on just after Goldwater to challenge the Arizonan to a debate did Johnson allow himself a derisive chuckle—at whom, it was not clear. At that time, the new President would talk freely about almost anything but politics.

As early as March 30, 1964, however, only twenty days after Goldwater's defeat by Lodge in the New Hampshire primary, when the chances of a Goldwater nomination were no longer taken seriously by most politicians, Johnson made it clear, in a private conversation, that he considered Goldwater his most likely opponent. He offered the opinion that Rockefeller could not defeat Goldwater in the California primary in June, and added that if Goldwater won the California delegates to go with those he surely would get in Illinois, the South and the other Western states, "he'll be close to that ring" (a shorthand reference, apparently, to "the brass ring").

Goldwater created opportunity for Johnson but the building of the Consensus was well under way before it could possibly have been settled in Johnson's mind that Goldwater would be his opponent. Consensus had been his method in Texas, where he had fought always to prevent the emergence of a dominant machine or faction—say, of the state's large cities. Instead, he had sought to keep the Texas Democratic party Balkanized so that in years when he was running for office, or was supporting some other candidate, he could pull it together on whatever ground then seemed expedient, rather than having to accept its dictates and its partisan limits. Even in his first campaign for the House, when all the numerous other candidates had been castigating Franklin Roosevelt's Supreme Court packing plan, Johnson had recognized that Roosevelt was still a magic name in his district, a rallying point around which all factions could unite; so he became the only candidate to declare unlimited support for F.D.R., and won an upset while the other candidates split the anti-court packing vote.

In the Senate, too, consensus had been his method—the search for the irreducible minimum, the lowest common denominator, the ground on which enough senators of either party could stand to produce the necessary majority. His political aim was not to drive people away but to bring them in; it is inconceivable that Johnson ever could have said, as Goldwater did at San Francisco, that "those who do not care for our cause, we don't expect to enter our ranks in any case." To Johnson, a vote was something to be obtained and its party label had nothing to do with it; what you had to do to get that vote mattered less than the fact that ultimately it could be yours—*any* vote.

At the Democratic National Convention in 1964, for instance, the fiery and eloquent Senator John O. Pastore of Rhode Island had the party faithful cheering and stomping during his keynote speech, a blistering and derisive attack on Goldwater in particular and Republicans in general. But conventions are now televised and, across the country, presumably millions of Republicans as well as Democrats were tuned in. Johnson, as carefully commanding the proceedings from his White House television screen as any stage director presenting a Broadway musical, promptly ordered an end to such broadsides. Attack Goldwater as a defector from the great Republican party, he ordered other convention speakers; but since many Republicans were themselves believed ready to defect to Johnson, make no more attacks on the party generally. Nothing was to be done to alienate any Republican who might otherwise find Goldwater too strong for his stomach and prefer even a Democrat.

There are those who view such hunger by Johnson—and others—for votes as a cynical lust for power. They fail to grasp the nature of American politics, particularly Presidential politics, in which to win is the first requirement. Here, truly, there is no substitute for victory. Our political parties exist for no other reason than to win power; they are not ideological debating societies designed to present a particular political philosophy and to persuade voters to accept it. Philosophy and program come later, when a party is in power and has the means not only to present them but to effect them—as for instance, the New Deal was a slogan, not a program, until Franklin Roosevelt won the White House on a bland, cautious platform which promised little but unspecified "action" and committed the new President to virtually nothing else that he subsequently did. Thus, Johnson's instinct in 1964—to win—was not only sound but in the best tradition of American politics; and those who would have it otherwise may contemplate Goldwater's fate.

In any case, to a man with Johnson's view of politics, an opponent like Goldwater was almost too good to be true; Goldwater, who could advocate the sale of T.V.A. in Tennessee (Johnson, in his best Dixieland form, quickly seized

on this to recapture Southern Democrats tempted to defect for
racial reasons: "The time will come in your lifetime," he said
in a speech in Tennessee, "when these men of little faith and
great fear who are marching around under another banner not
of their forefathers, the blush of shame will come to their
cheeks and they will hang their heads when they are told by
their children that they supported a party that wanted to sell
the T.V.A."); Goldwater, who could criticize Social Security
before the old folks in St. Petersburg; Goldwater, who was
made to be exploited by a real politician. Lyndon Johnson
was just the man for the job.

Nor can it even be said that Goldwater, however unwise,
was the more courageous of the two. It was not a timid politician who, late one night at a rally in racially conscious New
Orleans, shouted an anecdote about an oldtime Democratic
senator from the South who had said:

> I would like to go back there and make 'em one more
> Democratic speech. I just feel like I've got one more in
> me. Poor old state, they haven't heard a Democratic
> speech in thirty years. All they ever hear at election time
> is nigger, nigger, nigger!

It was not a timid politician; it was Lyndon Johnson, and
he added that the kind of Democratic speech politicians ought
to be making in the South would be "about the economy and
what a great future we could have in the South if we just
meet our economic problems, if we could just look at the resources of the South and develop them."

Thus, in his old style Johnson reached out to all, while
Goldwater merely preached to his followers. It was a golden
opportunity—but on the issue of Vietnam, the President's
passion for Consensus would lead him into an excess that
would come back to haunt him.

It is difficult now, with all that has happened, to recall that,
although Johnson did picture himself as a "man of prudence"
on Vietnam, in contrast to what the Democrats depicted as
Goldwater's warmongering, the war was *not* the central issue;

in fact, Johnson never delivered a prepared campaign speech about it after the conventions, and the remarks for which he has been justly criticized were mostly extemporaneous and uttered in the personal excitements of the campaign.

The real issue of war and peace between the two candidates was Goldwater's rather obscure, but ominous, views about the proper controls for nuclear weapons. Although both he and Nelson Rockefeller (the latter in the primary campaigns) had advocated the bombing of North Vietnam, this never became a central issue. Johnson's assurances that he did not plan to "go North" were generalized statements, in keeping with his position as the candidate of responsibility and safety, rather than specific pledges in a specific debate on a specific proposal. But what counts is that he made them.

Nor is it entirely true that Johnson's campaign altogether misrepresented his real views on the war, that, as an old joke has it, the public "voted against Goldwater and got him anyway." Just as Johnson had foreshadowed in his public statement in May, 1961, the views he ultimately would bring to the Presidency, ("I would not want to forever foreclose the possibility of America protecting her interests wherever it might be"), so he suggested in 1964 what the future might hold. But other words he uttered rang more dramatically in the public ear.

The first significant public statement Johnson made about Vietnam, as President, came on February 21, 1964. He was so new to office that he actually was keeping an appointment made by President Kennedy when, at Charter Day observances at the University of California at Los Angeles, he said:

> The contest in which South Vietnam is now engaged is first and foremost a contest to be won by the government and the people of that country for themselves. [But] those engaged in external direction and supply [of the war in Vietnam] would do well to be reminded and to remember that this type of aggression is a deeply dangerous game.

It may be, as we shall see, that the first of these sentences was the most significant in the long run. At the time, however, both the President and the public were more interested in the second sentence.

There is no doubt that Johnson intended this passage as a warning to the North Vietnamese and perhaps to the Chinese that the armed intervention he had been willing to think about in May, 1961, was still a possibility in his own mind. Just to dispel any doubt, Pierre Salinger, the White House Press Secretary, saw to it that White House reporters traveling with the President understood how important Johnson considered the statement. Philip Potter, the irascible and long-experienced correspondent of the *Baltimore Sun,* happened to consider a passage about China more significant. He told off Salinger, to the cheers of his colleagues, for trying to "dictate my lead."

Those who not only disagree with Johnson's policy in Vietnam, as it has developed, but who also feel that he duped them during the campaign and later betrayed their hopes, may be right on the facts, but it is a little too much to allow them to have it both ways. In fact, the protests of domestic "doves," following the Los Angeles speech, were so great that Secretary Rusk called a news conference and denied any implication that the United States was planning to escalate the war. Even so, he carefully repeated that external support of the Viet Cong was a "serious business," but insisted: "Whatever happens in the north, there is a large problem in South Vietnam to be dealt with . . . No miracle in the north is going to suddenly transform or eliminate the problem in South Vietnam."

Johnson himself let the impression get around that he did not understand how the press could have interpreted the U.C.L.A. speech as a threat to escalate. I spent an hour with him in his office four days after the speech and asked specifically for the President's own interpretation, and here are the notes taken on the response:

Asked him [LBJ] for his version of meaning of passage in UCLA speech. Never got it in so many words but did get long lecture on Vietnam. LBJ started by saying if Gen. Eisenhower had tried to invade Normandy the way we have tried to run the Vietnamese war, the Nazis would be in Paris today. Describes our situation in Vietnam as "new" because Lodge now has new general, new chief of mission, new CIA man, complete authority from LBJ. McN [McNamara] to look into new Lodge request, for more pay for the [Vietnamese] troops. So in position to get something done. The policy there is to train Vietnamese troops to win their own war. Notes we already pulled out 1,000 men no longer needed. Says more can be pulled out as more Vietnamese get training. Praised Kanh [the latest general to have taken over in Saigon, Nguyen Kanh] as young, vigorous. Used analogy of somebody coming into my yard, burning my trees, killing my mother. Wouldn't that be a "deeply dangerous game?" But no suggestion in itself of expanding the war or enlarging American commitment. Implied criticism of Kennedy because we have mess on our hands over there.

The political situation in which Johnson found himself in February, 1964, was clearly not conducive to frank talk about a wider war in Vietnam. Even then, Goldwater was "pooping around" snow-covered New Hampshire, beginning the process of making himself an open and irresistible target for a "prudent" candidate, while horrifying much of the old-line Republican party. Whatever Johnson may have been thinking privately, whatever the actual situation in Vietnam, the demands of politics—which is to say, the demands of men and circumstance—dictated that Johnson disclaim the intention, if not the possibility, of "going north." Just as Goldwater's campaign was being shaped in New Hampshire, so was Johnson's, in the response to his Los Angeles speech.

On June 28, however, Johnson gingerly warned again of the possibility of escalation. As more than fifty thousand people attending the *Svenskarnas Dag* (Swedes' Day) picnic listened in Minnehaha Park in Minneapolis, he said the United States, "when necessary," would not hesitate to "risk war" to preserve peace. This was a last-minute alteration of a prepared text which had declared that the United States "would use the force necessary" to maintain South Vietnam's freedom; some reporters already had filed stories based on the first text and all called attention to the change. The altered wording showed how politically delicate the matter was, but also that Johnson had not fundamentally changed the views he brought home from Southeast Asia in 1961.

The nation was "strong enough to protect ourselves and our allies," Johnson said, but it also was committed to "restraint in the use of power." It would never intervene in "honest clashes of belief or goals." But, he warned, "we seek neither dominion or conquest but where it exists we must work to dispel it." Both the Kennedy and Johnson Administrations had portrayed the war in Vietnam as, at least partially, an effort at "dominion or conquest" from the north, and thus the *Svenskarnas Dag* speech was essentially a repetition of the U.C.L.A. warning.

Up to this point, a nice ambiguity had been achieved about Vietnam; Johnson had promised to support Saigon but had not made clear how far he was prepared to go militarily. But in August, with Goldwater nominated and campaigning against what he called the Administration's "no win" policy, with Johnson ready for his own anointment at Atlantic City, a startling development caused the President to make his attitude even clearer.

North Vietnamese gunboats attacked an American destroyer in the Gulf of Tonkin on August 2, without success. Johnson ordered American ships to destroy such attackers in the future. On August 4, new gunboat attacks were reported in the Gulf and the President went even further. He ordered retaliatory air raids directly against North Vietnam.

Explaining this action in a late night television appearance on August 4, Johnson called the air raids a "positive reply" but said "we still seek no wider war." The next day, in a speech at Syracuse University, he added:

> To any who may be tempted to support or to widen the present aggression, I say this: there is no threat to any peaceful power from the United States of America. But there can be no peace by aggression and *no immunity from reply*. And that is what is meant by the actions that we took yesterday. [italics added]

Whether there would be no immunity for whatever Johnson defined as aggression, or just for attacks directly on the American flag, like those in the Tonkin Gulf, the President did not make clear—which, with Hanoi presumably listening, he could hardly have been expected to do. But the operative words— *no immunity*—were still another way of saying the same thing that had been said at Los Angeles and Minneapolis.

Johnson also seized the moment of the Tonkin crisis to send substantial new forces to Southeast Asia; these were primarily air and sea units and their presence in the area was to play a large role in the future. Finally, he also used the episode to drive through Congress the celebrated resolution that gave him Congressional authorization "to take all necessary measures to repel any armed attack against the forces of the United States and *to prevent future aggression*."[13] [italics added]

The story of this resolution is one of the most controversial of the war. Looking back on it at a news conference on February 26, 1966, Johnson himself said:

> I did not feel that it was essential that the President have a resolution in order to take the action that was taken. As a matter of fact, in the Tonkin Gulf, I took the action before the resolution . . . I have no desire to operate without authority, although if the resolution is repealed I think I could still carry out our commitments [in Vietnam].

If that was the case, why did Johnson send up the resolution at all? He was obviously right that, under the Constitution, the

Commander in Chief needed no Congressional authorization
to "repel any armed attack against the forces of the United
States." Congress knew that well enough; Johnson had, in
fact, already repelled the attacks in question; and as opinion in
Congress and out of it in August, 1964, made plain, any Commander in Chief who had failed to do so would not be long in
favor—or in office, if he was seeking re-election. But what
about "to prevent future aggression?" Against whom, or what?
Here was the nub of the matter, the fourth statement of what
Johnson thought might become necessary, the reiteration of
the theme of Los Angeles, Minneapolis, Syracuse; and this
time he was asking Congress to join him in it.

Three years after the passage of the resolution, on August
17, 1967, Undersecretary of State Nicholas deB. Katzenbach
gave to the Senate Foreign Relations Committee the official
description of why Johnson had asked for it. Congress already
had approved the Southeast Asia Treaty Organization, he said,
expressing "the security concerns, the general obligation of the
United States in accordance with its constitutional process to
attempt to preserve order and peace and defense against
aggression in Southeast Asia."

As the "situation there deteriorated" to the point of the
Tonkin Gulf attacks, Katzenbach said:

> The President of the United States came back to Congress
> to seek the views of Congress with respect to what should
> be done in that area and with respect to the use of the
> military of the United States in that area, and on those
> resolutions Congress had the opportunity to participate
> and did participate. The combination of the two [SEATO
> and the Tonkin Gulf resolution], it seems to me, fully ful-
> fills the obligation of the executive in a situation of this
> kind to participate with the Congress, to give the Con-
> gress a full and effective voice, the functional equivalent,
> the constitutional obligation expressed in the provision
> of the Constitution with respect to declaring war.

But *had* the Executive "fully fulfilled" its obligation to Congress, as Katzenbach insisted it had? Had Congress been made fully aware of the President's views, of what the situation in Southeast Asia might portend? After all, as Katzenbach inquired rather angrily:

Didn't that resolution authorize the President to use the armed forces of the United States in whatever way was necessary? Didn't it? What could a declaration of war have done that would have given the President more authority and a clearer voice of the Congress of the United States than that did?

Not much, obviously. What bothered members of Congress was the difference between what Katzenbach said they had done, three years after the event, and what at least some of them had thought they were doing at the time. J. W. Fulbright of Arkansas, who in 1964 had acted as the Administration spokesman on behalf of the resolution, had specifically resisted an amendment that would have recorded Congress against any "extension of the present conflict" and would have sharply limited the President's freedom to act with Congressional support. Fulbright told the Senate that the amendment, offered by Gaylord Nelson of Wisconsin, was "an accurate reflection of what I believe is the President's policy," and therefore was not needed.

Fulbright told Katzenbach in 1967 that he had "misinterpreted" the resolution in 1964 and that Congress had acted "wrongly, precipitously, without due consideration" in passing it; in 1964, he had believed, he said, that the repeated statements of both John Kennedy and Lyndon Johnson had made it clear that "in Vietnam, it was not the policy of this country to use American forces, that we were there only to help them. It wasn't our war."

Fulbright's rejection of the Nelson amendment prevented a Congressional *foreclosure* of a "wider war"; and the Tonkin resolution, as approved, allowed Johnson to claim advance

Congressional approval for whatever strong action he might think necessary in the future. The ambiguity of his policy was maintained for the purposes of the electoral Consensus he was building, and the flexibility he sought for the future was guaranteed.

Katzenbach, in 1967, no doubt put the issue in proper perspective, bitter as his words may have seemed to Fulbright.

> Mr. Chairman [Katzenbach said], whether a resolution of that kind is or is not, does or does not perform the functions similar to a declaration of war must indeed depend upon what the language of that resolution is and what it says. Now the language of that resolution, Mr. Chairman, is a very broad language.

Indeed, it is; it said plainly that Johnson was prepared to take strong action if necessary, and believed it well might become necessary. That was implicit in the Tonkin Gulf Resolution, and it was not long before Fulbright publicly accepted blame for not have realized it.

But there was another side to the matter that the Katzenbach testimony did not touch upon. Congress, in fact, had but little choice in the election year of 1964 and in the public atmosphere created by a reported attack on American ships, after the President already had taken military action in response and after he had gone on national television to defend that action and to ask for the Congressional resolution. Congress *had* to approve the resolution, whatever the fears of some members.

In the world of men, governments believe they cannot afford to show anything less than resolution at such a time; even less can legislators afford to impair the leadership of a President or a Prime Minister by rejecting his executive actions, handicapping his responses as a commander, or embarrassing him before the world; and still less than that does the politician in an election year care to appear anything but zealous in his patriotism and desire to protect "American boys."

Johnson's timing of the resolution was, therefore, perfect for his purposes; a few weeks later, a White House official in a position to know confided to me that the President had been carrying around the text of the resolution "in his pocket" long before the Tonkin episode gave him the right opportunity to lay it before Congress.

A somewhat different perspective on this was given by William P. Bundy, the Assistant Secretary of State for Far Eastern Affairs, in secret testimony to the Foreign Relations Committee on September 20, 1966. His testimony, released by the committee on December 21, 1967, was that the Administration "had contingent drafts which, however, did not very closely resemble the [actual] draft, for some time prior" to August, 1964.

Calling this a matter of "normal contingency planning" to which "no serious thought had been given . . . prior to the Gulf of Tonkin," William Bundy added:

> We had always anticipated, and as a matter of common prudence, I think, should have anticipated the possibility that things might take a more drastic turn at any time and that it would be wise to seek an affirmation of the desires of and intent of the Congress. But that is normal planning. I am not sure that my drafts were even known to others.

Bundy's contention that no real thought had been given to seeking Congressional support before the gunboat attacks lends plausibility to the view that I obtained privately from still a third official involved in the events of the Tonkin crisis. Speaking more than two years after the episode, he said that nothing like the gunboat attacks had been expected by the President and that the actual resolution, as passed by Congress, was hastily written in the Executive Branch, "in anticipation of more Tonkins," rather than as the legal groundwork for a big escalation. This official, by no means a Johnson apologist, believed that the President did not trick Congress or mislead it but by the inclusion in the resolution of a "lot of governmentese" fortuitously was voted authority that he then found useful in justifying other actions he later decided upon.

In any case, when the opportunity arose, Johnson was ready to capitalize upon it. It might have been tidier, of course, even more conventionally ethical, if Johnson had sent the text to Congress in some moment of non-crisis—if one could have been found—when it could have been debated and explored soberly and on its merits alone, aside from public and diplomatic pressures; but it would have been bad politics and Johnson was President in order to provide the United States with the political leadership that he thought it needed. He acted as any astute politician might have, in seeking Congressional support —as Eisenhower had done, for instance, in earlier crises over Formosa and the Middle East—and even if the fact that Congress, as a result, almost literally had no choice but to acquiesce gives some of us Constitutional qualms, it is not grounds for impeachment that a President acted politically while occupying a political office. It may be grounds for other penalties, as we shall see.

Certainly, it was a contemporary political triumph for Lyndon Johnson. No matter how easy, even mandatory, public opinion made it for him to do so, he had *acted* during the Tonkin Gulf crisis to give credibility both to his restraint *and* to his strength. At the time, at least from the political point of view, it seemed almost as if Hanoi must have wanted Johnson's election; the foolhardy gunboat attack on American ships had given him a heaven-sent opportunity to show strength and restraint at the price of little, if any, domestic criticism. The air attacks launched in response struck a body blow at Goldwater's contention that the Democratic Administration was too "soft," if not too Communistic, to protect American interests abroad. But, shrewdly, Johnson also demonstrated that "restraint in the use of power" that he had pledged to the doves. Assiduous Administration leaks pointed out how "limited" and "fitting" a response the single wave of bombing raids had been; Hanoi could not misread the episode as "escalation." The President, the leaks confided, had personally ruled out one strike that would have threatened too many helpless North Vietnamese civilians.

In one stroke, Johnson had been able both to flex his muscles and prudently to limit what could have been a war-provoking crisis. One of his aides said later that one of the President's purposes had been "to win Republicans and conservatives with a responsible show of force. He already had the Left."

But the cost was high because in the endless adventure of governing men, the ironic is almost the norm; today's triumph is tomorrow's burden but disaster may also be a blessing in disguise. The caterpillar yields the butterfly; the kitten turns to alley cat. The Tonkin crisis, however it seemed at the time, ultimately produced for Johnson two of his major difficulties. No doubt, he handled it superbly; yet it would return again and again to haunt him because the circumstances that apply one day may be—usually will be—entirely different on another. And particularly in politics, what one does to achieve success may prove more important and lasting than the success itself.

With the resolution that the President maneuvered through Congress, and with the deception or guile—whatever description one chooses—that he used to keep it intact and his freedom of action unhampered, the most astute Congressional strategist of our time planted the seeds of distrust and suspicion in that body. He alienated not just Fulbright; in both houses, an undetermined but significant number of members came to look back upon the episode of the Tonkin Resolution as a ruthless power play and a betrayal of the Congressional-Executive trust.[14] A year later, when Senator Wayne Morse of Oregon sought to repeal the resolution, competent reporters could ascertain that very nearly a majority of the Senate would have supported Morse had it not been that to do so would have destroyed Johnson's leadership at a time when, under the Constitution, there could have been no legal alternative to it for nearly four years. Once done, the Tonkin Gulf resolution could not be undone, in more ways than one, for all parties to it.

But all of that, and the concomitant bitterness and suspicion that would radiate through Congress and affect all of Johnson's future efforts, was somewhere in the future in late August of 1964, as the Texan and Barry Goldwater got down to the grueling months of the formal Presidential campaign. And in those months, the success of his response in the Tonkin Gulf would guide Johnson straight into an even more damaging mistake than his Congressional tactics on behalf of the resolution. For the fact was that, having shown his strength, having diminished Goldwater's ability to charge him with a "no win" policy and with soft-headedness toward Communism, having established his own "restraint," Johnson seemed free to do what came so naturally to so political a creature. With every rattle of the Goldwater sword, every reference to the use of nuclear weapons by the Air Force General on the Republican ticket, every provocative remark about bombing the North from the avid jet pilot who was his opponent, Johnson was lured by politics into the profitably contrasting position of deploring— even forbidding—war, escalation, and nuclear brinkmanship. The Tonkin Gulf was the background against which he seemed able to do so safely; in the long run, it was the birthplace of the credibility gap.

Every political indicator of the day confirmed the President in his instinctive course. Polls never failed to support Johnson's general position against Goldwater's; neither did professional political operators and reporters; neither did most astute Republican professionals. "Prudence" about Vietnam fitted beautifully into the general Johnson campaign theme that, however much he might advocate action and advance and even spending, he still was the safe and responsible candidate— for business, for the minorities, for the old folks, for labor, for the intellectuals, for all those who wanted peace, not war. The mere presence of Goldwater in the race made this theme entirely credible; for as his campaign developed, the Republicans' remarkable nominee seemed to become a threat to all of these people.

A deeper and greater man than Johnson might still have avoided the pitfall. Lincoln, in 1860, did not yield to the temptation of picking up a quick political profit either by urging abolition or tempering his view against the extension of slavery to the territories; he knew that to do so might have assured the dissolution of the Union which it was his fixed determination to preserve. Roosevelt, promising bold action in 1932, never described what he would do so specifically as to alienate the conservatives who believed some change was necessary, but who would not have supported the kind of changes that ultimately came. But Lyndon Johnson did not have the greatness of Abraham Lincoln; and Franklin Roosevelt did not have the insatiable political hunger of Lyndon Johnson.

All the evidence visible at the time, and much testimony gathered since, suggests that, in 1964, Johnson was not deeply concerned about Vietnam. He was learning his job, weighing his men, getting Congress on the move again, waging his campaign —indulging, for instance, in untold man-hours of speculation, conversation and maneuvering on the question of whom he should choose for Vice President. The war was not going all *that* badly; the excellent Rusk and McNamara, as well as Lodge's competent "new team," were on hand to handle it and anyway, the "issue polls" Johnson studied with as much care as he gave to C.I.A. reports showed that Vietnam, then, was the major concern of only a small proportion of the voters. There was no real fear in the White House that the war would become the central issue of the years ahead, that every word spoken now would have its later impact, and not always the one intended.

But if the war was not a matter of night-and-day care, the election was. A few months before, in the terrible hours of Kennedy's assassination, Lyndon Johnson had found himself reprieved from political oblivion. At the peak of his powers and experience, he was out of power in the Vice Presidency and without hope of a political future, when the opportunity suddenly had come from the blue to show the world his worth and to use that power he had coveted for so many years, that he had seen others wield so much less effectively than he believed he could do. His whole life, in a sense, had been resurrected and Johnson meant to make the most of it.

"He wants to carry all fifty states, Latin America, Greece and Turkey," a White House correspondent quipped, late in 1964. And as the opening created and widened every day by Goldwater began to yawn before him, the accidental President was as irresistibly drawn toward it as a lemming to the sea.

Frustrated and angered throughout 1964 because his genuine achievements as Kennedy's successor had not made him loved, because at every hand he still found himself compared unfavorably to his glamorous predecessor (usually on unfair grounds), constantly seeking a scapegoat for this state of affairs in an unfair press, his Southern origins, or the machinations of Robert Kennedy and "the intellectuals," Johnson had told James Reston privately in the summer of 1964 that he might not even run in November. The country was "not far enough from Appomattox" to accept him, he said mournfully. Reston recognized this as self-pity and told Johnson to forget it—advice which probably was not needed. Feeling so, nevertheless, Johnson provided one of the phenomena of 1964 by his response to the crowds that came out to see him. An energetic stump campaigner anyway, he reacted to the jammed streets and cheering mobs as if to several good shots of Cutty Sark. By mid-Autumn, he could scarcely be kept in the White House; as Goldwater's campaign sagged, Johnson's rocketed; and with every point-climb in the polls, every new sea of faces gazing up at him from airports, city plazas and jammed auditoriums, Johnson's ebullience grew. He would take reporters by the arm and pull them to the rostrum and point out at the people. "What do you think of that?" he would shout. "What about that crowd?"

Police reported a summertime crowd in San Francisco at five hundred thousand people. Such estimates are only guesses, and I reduced the figure to three hundred fifty thousand (still an amazing turnout) in my report to *The New York Times*. Six months later, reviewing the year in a White House backgrounder, Johnson mentioned the San Francisco crowd.

"*The New York Times* said it was three hundred fifty thousand," he said, "but it was really half a million."

Not only was his personal hunger for popular favor being satisfied at last; he also wanted to win a landslide for eminently practical political reasons. Believing as he did in his Populist, politician's heart that the best politics was to deliver "something for the folks," with his Great Society program already being drawn up, Johnson recognized that he had the chance to break the decade-long deadlock of American politics; he could win the overwhelming mandate Kennedy had never had, swing Congress decisively as Eisenhower had never done, and deal with the backlog of urgent domestic business that had been piling up since the Fifties. Then, like his idol Roosevelt, he could go on to break new ground.

Goldwater, in short, offered almost unlimited opportunity to a politician who had proved his skill in domestic affairs (the Kennedy tax and civil rights bills had been moved, the long-threatening railroad strike had been settled) and demonstrated both his strength and his restraint abroad; few men, certainly not hungry, mercurial Lyndon Johnson, could have resisted the openings offered, with Vietnam and peace in many ways the greatest of them. The President knew he had Goldwater on the ropes, knew he could be champion—perhaps the greatest of champions—when for so many years it had seemed impossible; and it was just not in him to stop punching or to pace his attack carefully.

Thus, on September 25, at Eufala, Oklahoma, Johnson declared:

We don't want our American boys to do the fighting for Asian boys. We don't want to get involved in a nation with 700 million people and get tied down in a land war in Asia.

And on September 28, with enthusiasm rising, he said in a speech at Manchester, New Hampshire:

We are not going north and drop bombs at this stage of the game, and we are not going south and run out . . . We

are going . . . to try to get them to save their own freedom with their own men . . .

And on October 21, at Akron University, with Goldwater
clearly in mind, he was caution itself:

> Sometimes our folks get a little impatient. Sometimes they
> rattle their rockets some, and they bluff about their bombs.
> But we are not about to send American boys nine or ten
> thousand miles away from home to do what Asian boys
> ought to be doing for themselves . . . There is only one
> road to peace and that is to work at it patiently, deliber-
> ately, wisely, step by step, year by year, never to become
> reckless, never to become weary of the journey and irri-
> tated with folks who may not agree with you the first
> time you talk to them.

It was marvelous campaigning, in that year, against that
candidate. But it was not Consensus. For if the idea of Consensus is to keep one's doors open to all factions, and if that
can be done only by holding out some promise to each of them,
it follows that, at some point, one will have to deliver something against each promise. Consensus politics is a cyclical
thing—in order to accumulate power, one must dispose of it,
and as one disposes of it, one must accumulate more power to
replace it. In financial terms, a dollar must be spent to make a
dollar—or two, if things go well.

In the fall of 1964, Lyndon Johnson may or may not have
known that he was not going to deliver on his promises that he
would not "go North." He told the reliable Charles Roberts of
Newsweek that he had decided to bomb North Vietnam as early
as October, 1964.[15] He told me in 1965 that as early as
October, 1964, the targets had been chosen for attack, if
bombing was ever decided upon. Given Johnson's obfuscation
of his own motives and actions, and his occasional bombast,
he may have been saying the same thing to both of us, in different ways. Contingency plans for bombing the North had been

in existence for years; planes were readily available, as the Gulf of Tonkin had demonstrated; as early as 1961, Walt W. Rostow had been an ardent advocate of bombing and his proposals and justifications had been brought to Johnson's attention. General Taylor, who had succeeded Lodge as Ambassador to Saigon in 1965, advocated bombing strikes in October, 1964, after earlier opposition.

During the campaign, however it may have diverted his attention, Johnson—or any President—could not have failed to know that the situation in Vietnam was deteriorating. Nothing anywhere suggests that Johnson himself had fundamentally changed the view he had expressed in 1961—that a "free" South Vietnam was vital to American interests and that, if necessary, "major American forces" would have to be committed to keep it "free." Given everything, it is fair to say that if he did not know that he could not keep his promises not to "go north," he certainly did not know that he *could* keep them.

In his search for personal vindication, for Consensus, and for the power Consensus would bring him, therefore, he had gone a step too far. He had transgressed the acceptable limits of his political reach. If he had not actually made up his mind what to do in South Vietnam, he had no way of knowing what might be required of a President who believed protecting it so vital to American interests. Yet, he could say in the Manchester speech: "As far as I am concerned, I want to be very cautious and careful, and use it only as a last resort, when I start dropping bombs around that are likely to involve American boys in a war in Asia with seven hundred million Chinese."

But he was not that "cautious and careful" in what he said in his campaign, or in how he said it. And this would be what was remembered—not Los Angeles, *Svenskarnas Dag* or the Tonkin Gulf Resolution.

The drama of the confrontation with Goldwater, the monstrous outpouring of crowds, the posturing television images, the insistent words, the ever-mounting ebullience of Lyndon Johnson, the souring, vaguely ominous tone of his opponent—

all these combined to produce an enormous impact on the public, as a Presidential campaign usually does. In that impact, the earlier warnings, the carefully maintained ambiguity of policy for the sake of Consensus, the clear suggestions of what might have to be done, all were forgotten by President and public alike. Lyndon Johnson was promising peace and Barry Goldwater was promising war; the President had shoved in all his stack; that was the effect on men, and in the endless adventure it is not the fact, so much as the impression, that controls.

"It seems," Lyndon Johnson told reporters on election night at the LBJ Ranch, near where he had grown up in the dust and poverty of the hill country, "that I have spent my life getting ready for this moment." And as the returns poured in, state after state falling into his column, the electoral total mounting, the great sweep developing, governors, senators, congressmen, members of legislatures riding in on his coattails, that long wait seemed eminently worthwhile. Everything seemed justified because it was the greatest election victory in history. The deadlock was smashed; the Consensus was built; the Great Society was on the way; and Lyndon Johnson, the accidental President, would belong to the ages.

For months to come, it would still seem true. Well-prepared legislation rolled in waves across Capitol Hill—notably to provide federal aid for education for the first time, to provide medical care for the aged, votes for Southern Negroes, money for the cities, the arts, the environment, the poor.

In the early months of 1965, it could fairly be said that no President—save possibly F.D.R. in 1933, in vastly different circumstances—had disposed of so much sheer political power, or faced such a limitless future of achievement, as did Lyndon Johnson of Texas. The great tent was crowded with more Americans of more varieties than had followed any other American at any time. The President's beloved polls reflected his astronomical scores in public favor—for instance, seventy-one per cent in the Harris poll for February, 1965. It even seemed that Johnson might really achieve the goal of which he had spoken frequently, but most movingly to the graduating class of the University of Texas on the rainy night of May 30, 1964, when he still was in his hour of testing and no one had heard of the Gulf of Tonkin or could know how thoroughly Goldwater would be smashed.

During his travels to every part of the country, he told the two thousand robed seniors and the fourteen thousand others in Austin's civic auditorium, he had come to believe that:

> The farmer in Iowa, the fisherman in Massachusetts, the worker in Seattle, the rancher in Texas, have the same hopes and harbor the same fears. They want education for their children and an improving life for their families. They want to protect liberty and pursue peace. They expect justice for themselves and they are willing to grant it to others.

> This is the real voice of America. It is one of the great tasks of political leadership to make our people aware of this voice, aware that they share a fundamental unity of interest, purpose and belief.

He was "going to try and do this," he said—ungrammatically, but with genuine emotion.

> I intend to try and achieve a broad national consensus which can end obstruction and paralysis and liberate the energies of the nation for the work of the future.

But history played a demonic joke upon Lyndon Johnson and, therefore, upon us all. Once, in 1964, he had told some reporters he had invited for lunch that he did not intend to make the mistake that he believed had ruined Franklin Roosevelt's second term. "Roosevelt was never President after 1937 until the war came along," he said. Lyndon Johnson would not forget the limits of power; he would not carelessly throw away the fruits of his great victory for some unattainable goal, as Roosevelt had done in trying to pack the Supreme Court.

But he did.

14 *The Ebullience of Power*

Hanoi and Saigon, of course, had heard the campaign oratory, too. By the time the election was over, South Vietnam was in deep political and military trouble and its American advisers were nearing despair. A succession of coups in Saigon had resulted neither in political progress toward needed reforms and stability, nor in military advances. Diem had been followed by chaos. Neither the Viet Cong nor the North Vietnamese had failed to take advantage of this situation.

Militarily, the Viet Cong were mounting ever bigger and more successful battles, and the evidence suggested that they were getting more and more help from North Vietnam. Deliveries of weapons and supplies apparently had increased, although there are no reliable figures to suggest by how much. So, apparently, had the infiltration of North Vietnamese fighting men, although here again the figures are fuzzy. On July 0, 1967, the Defense Department gave the following infiltration figures for the period.

November 1964	800
December 1964	800
Total 1964	12,500
January 1965	2,000
Total 1965	26,000

Whether or not these figures are precise, there is little reason to doubt that they give a fairly accurate picture of increasing infiltration, which was getting to be a serious matter by the beginning of 1965. The United States itself had put in an additional five to six thousand troops in August, 1964, though not ostensibly for purposes of combat, and as the war seemed to be moving toward a showdown, the North Vietnamese would have had every reason to increase the military pressure in the South, and the N.L.F. to welcome the assistance.

By the end of 1964, according to General Maxwell D. Taylor,

> . . . we were finding in the ranks of the Vietcong not just South Vietnamese who had been "regrouped" north, trained there, and then infiltrated back south, but also pure ethnic North Vietnamese who were members of the armed forces of North Vietnam who had never before been in the South . . . the leaders in Hanoi had decided not only to introduce individual North Vietnamese soldiers but to throw in complete units of the armed forces of North Vietnam to reinforce the Vietcong guerrillas in the South.[16]

General Taylor attributed this new effort to the possibilities of victory open to the Communists after the death of the "determined anti-Communist patriot," Diem, and in the political chaos that followed in Saigon. He did not mention the virtual certainty that they also had been influenced by the political campaign in the United States.

Johnson had warned in February, 1964, that those who supported the Viet Cong were playing a "deeply dangerous game." In the same speech, however, and preceding this remark, he had said plainly: "The contest in which South Vietnam is now engaged is first and foremost a contest to be won by the government and the people of that country for themselves."

In the days following, as a sharp "dove" reaction developed to the "deeply dangerous game" remark (the other was scarcely noticed), both Johnson and Rusk had been at pains to deny any intention of American military escalation. All of this represented Johnson's first major pronouncement on Vietnam, and it is likely that Hanoi read this episode as evidence that the United States would talk harshly but would not intervene and that Johnson would have little domestic political backing if he did; Johnson himself came to believe that this statement was a major error on his part, in that it misled Hanoi about his willingness to intervene.

Again, the Tonkin Gulf response was deliberately designed *not* to be taken by Hanoi as an escalation—which was the last thing the President wanted to order or be accused of in the middle of the campaign against Goldwater. It was specifically described in Washington as a responsible, restrained "retaliation" (an incident in exchange for an incident), it was confined to one wave of attacks and when in late September new gunboat forays against American ships were reported in the Gulf of Tonkin, the Administration not only did not retaliate, it would not even confirm that such attacks had taken place (and they probably did not; Johnson once told me he thought a nervous American Navy might have been "shooting at whales").

Two days before the American election, Viet Cong mortars had destroyed six B-57 bombers and killed five Americans in a surprise attack on the South Vietnamese air base at Bien Hoa. Lyndon Johnson had done nothing—not surprisingly, from an American point of view, because as the campaign had developed it might have been a bad risk for him to have launched even limited reprisal air raids that close to Election Day; his image as a "man of prudence" might have been shaken and although the election surely could not have been lost, Johnson was by then in no mood to jeopardize even one vote. He wanted them all.

But it is also not surprising if Hanoi and the N.L.F., which harbor few American political experts, drew their own conclusions. Bien Hoa was a more costly attack than the one in the Tonkin Gulf—a Communist victory, in fact, resulting in dismaying American losses. Since it was generally believed that the American bombers were at Bien Hoa to impress the North Vietnamese with the potential of American air power, and since they had been placed there as part of the response to the Tonkin Gulf crisis, the mortar attack could have been nothing but a direct challenge to the United States— the sort of thing Johnson had said would be accorded "no immunity." American men were killed and that made it surely the kind of attack on American forces that the Tonkin Resolution had authorized him to "take all necessary steps" to repel. But he did not act.

These events, taken with the general tone of Johnson's campaigning in the final months against Goldwater, can have had no other effect in Hanoi except to convince Ho Chi Minh's government that it could step up the level of its military effort to a final push in 1965 without danger of major American intervention. A mortar attack directly on an American billet in Saigon just before Christmas also drew no American response; Johnson is reported to have been reluctant to shatter the Christmas season with warlike acts, or to dispel the general good feelings of his pre-inaugural period; but again, the North Vietnamese were unlikely to take such considerations into account. It is no wonder that in January, according to the figures quoted above, the first big increase in infiltration into the South could be counted, or that General Taylor's intelligence agents had detected whole North Vietnamese units gathering for the kill. Hanoi had decided it had the green light.

This interpretation is supported by events in Saigon and elsewhere. As 1964 turned to 1965, seldom if ever had there been such unrest and turmoil in that unhappy capital. It is not part of this narrative to trace the bewildering successions of governments, uprisings, riots, resignations, statements and outside influences at work, but in sum, a powerful anti-American, neutralist sentiment was visible, with Buddhist street mobs its most dramatic instrument; a strong South Vietnamese anti-Communist military bloc opposed it; and insofar as the outside world could judge, there seemed to be a climactic power struggle between these elements. Some Americans in Saigon actively feared the emergence of a Buddhist-neutralist government that would seek peace with the N.L.F.

In the world at large, both de Gaulle of France and U Thant of the United Nations were seeking negotiated peace, and it even appeared to some that the Soviet Union was in the same mood; *Izvestia* called for a Johnson-Kosygin meeting, and Peking was alarmed enough to accuse the new Soviet leaders of practicing "Khrushchevism without Khrushchev." Both in Saigon and elsewhere, it was apparently believed that Johnson—as he had seemed to say in the campaign—would countenance no "wider war" and that peace, therefore, was the realistic alternative.

At home, too, involvement in Vietnam was not popular. The Gallup Poll for November 29, 1964, reported that fifty per cent of the respondents believed the United States had handled Vietnam badly; in January, Lou Harris showed that twenty-three per cent wanted to "negotiate and get out," and another forty per cent were willing to do no more than "hold the line." A few respected Senate voices—Mike Monroney of Oklahoma and John Sherman Cooper of Kentucky, for instance—were expressing public doubts.

On its face, it might therefore seem that here was a second moment, somewhat comparable to that following the fall of Diem, when peace could have been had in Vietnam; and so it might have been, had policy been made in a vacuum, or by some computer spewing out its printed answers, rather than by flesh-and-blood men into whose calculations went all their prejudices, interests, fears, ambitions, fallibilities, and the pressures to which they were subject. But the endless adventure is an account of men and circumstances, and in that context peace was far away indeed.

Johnson, it well may be, could have found a reasonable

excuse for disengagement. He could have pointed out that there was evidently in Saigon neither sufficient will to win the war nor anything resembling the free government and free people for whose benefit both he and Kennedy had maintained the war was being fought. Following the theme Kennedy had insisted upon, and which Johnson had sounded fervently in the closing stages of his campaign, he could have said that it was a war for Asian boys to win; that the United States was willing to lend technical and material support; but since the Asian boys and their leaders displayed too little concern whether they won or not, the United States thought it the better part of good policy not to send good money—much less men—after bad. It is even possible, considering the state of things in Saigon and how the United States had influenced events at the time of the Diem overthrow, that a government could have been nudged into power that would have announced peace aims and made further United States participation a moot question.

Johnson not only had this on-scene situation within which to operate, in the weeks following his election; he also had a solid domestic position to cover any retreat. He could have extricated himself from the war with less difficulty, probably, than de Gaulle had had during the Algerian disengagement. The Texan had won the most enormous political victory any President ever had; his mandate was unchallenged. He had spared the country Goldwater, and the collective sigh of relief was as audible as any political sentiment of this century. The response to Johnson's "peace" statements on Vietnam during the campaign, while not universal, were as near an expression of solid public support as most Presidents ever get. The Republicans and the Southern Democrats—the only conceivable organized political powers that could have objected—had been shattered in the one case and badly shaken in the other. Never again would Lyndon Johnson have anything approaching the "free hand" that the 1964 elections gave him in foreign and domestic policy in the opening months of 1965.

In his State of the Union Message that January, Johnson himself made it clear where he wanted to go. He propounded a sweeping program of domestic reform and, as he later would do in his Inaugural, called for rapprochement and a pooling of energies with the Soviet Union for peaceful purposes. A major war in Vietnam could do little to advance—it would actively pervert—both his domestic and his international purposes, particularly his desire to end the Cold War and co-operate with the Soviets. Given the activities of U Thant, France and the Soviet Union, it is likely that a strong Johnson move toward a negotiated settlement would have met some international cooperation that might have borne fruit; U Thant, for one, is convinced that it would have. That mythical policy-making computer might well have called for a settlement of the war, basing its judgment on Secretary McNamara's fabled "cost-analysis" system of determining whether an action would be worth its price.

The machine might have been right, too. More than two years after the crucial decisions of that winter, one of Johnson's most astute and loyal assistants looked back on the period with a hard political eye; setting aside personal judgments on the necessity and value of the war, he concluded that it would have been better domestic politics had Johnson opted in January, 1965, for a "Laos-type settlement"—a coalition between the Saigon government and the N.L.F.

This might well have resulted in the domination or absorption of South Vietnam by Ho Chi Minh, and it would certainly have left Johnson open to ferocious Republican attack on the theme of "Who sold out Southeast Asia?" Nevertheless, the Johnson aide clung to his belief. Johnson had won enough prestige and political power in his landslide election, he believed, to have ridden out such a storm, particularly if he had obscured it with the kind of major domestic program he, in fact, did achieve in 1965.

Undoubtedly, the aide conceded, the Democrats would have been hurt in the 1966 elections, but the in-party is almost al-

ways the loser in any non-Presidential election; and as it happened, even without compromising their way out of the war,
the Democrats lost heavily in 1966, as they were bound to do
after the 1964 landslide. But a compromise in 1965, the
Johnson man believed, would have made Vietnam a dead
political issue by 1968. Above all, the President would not have
been saddled with the damaging "credibility gap" which his
campaign pledges of 1964 and his subsequent war policy
did so much to create. Johnson could have run for re-election
on the strength of his domestic achievements and as a peace-
maker, with the classic slogan of "peace and prosperity" as his
strongest supporter.

But that is hindsight. That mythical computer of 1965
would have operated on data, the only input it could accept;
it could not have comprehended and reacted to the infinite
variety of pressures and influences that modified, in men's
brains and hearts, the cold conclusions data might otherwise
compel. How could a computer have accounted, as one ex
ample, for the insistence of Lyndon B. Johnson that his 1965
State of the Union Message should contain this passage:

> In our relations with the world we shall follow the ex-
> ample of Andrew Jackson who said: "I intend to ask for
> nothing that is not clearly right and to submit to nothing
> that is wrong." And he promised that "the honor of my
> country shall never be stained by an apology from me for
> the statement of truth or for the performance of duty."

Quoting the pomposities of famous men is a ritual of
politics; but in an age of ghostwriters, drafts "for my signature,"
and texts rewritten until the original is unrecognizable, what
did it mean that Lyndon Johnson was adamant, as he was
upon no other words, about the inclusion of that bellicose
passage from the proud and rigid Jackson, a man accustomed
to fighting duels over abstract points of "honor"?

Enough can never be known about such matters. What
pressures were at work upon the intricate mind and personality

of Lyndon Johnson, that triumphant winter of 1964-65, prob-ably no one will ever know to a certainty—least of all Johnson himself, with his minute capacity for personal objectivity. But we know enough about Lyndon Johnson, about that winter's circumstances, and about the endless adventure itself to make the reasonable conjecture that their conjunction left little pos-sibility of peace, regardless of what the computer said—even of what Hanoi said.

There probably had been no other point in the Vietnamese involvement, as we have seen, when the American effort seemed so near to abject failure. Political chaos in Saigon; apathy toward the war evident among the South Vietnamese populace; corruption everywhere; an aggressive Viet Cong pushing its sanguinary efforts in the countryside; tough North Vietnamese units and replacements arriving in force to help the insurgents; and the South Vietnamese army badly, if not criminally, led by an inept, closed and politically divided officer corps—these facts meant that a major defeat was at hand unless something was done, soon, and in Washington. And more than a year earlier, one grim November afternoon in the Executive Office Building, Lyndon Johnson had told Cabot Lodge, *"I am not going to be the President who saw Southeast Asia go the way China went."*

Lyndon Johnson was personally and politically committed, and therefore, in his shrewd and involuted mind, the moment looked entirely different from what it might have on computer tape. The political power derived from the landslide he had just won could not provide, in his view, an opportunity to liquidate and get out from under a war he had not started; rather, it offered a chance to turn that war around and start, at last, on the road to victory. For more than a year, he had hedged and retreated and chided Goldwater for belligerence, while just hanging on in Vietnam ("keeping it quiet," as one of his aides later described the war policy of 1964) as the situation there steadily declined. Now he could get down to business, the election past, four years in office assured him.

Only by some abstract standard might it have been a moment to cut losses and get out. In fact, a human being named Lyndon Johnson—steeped in and shaped by the Cold War era of American history, a devout believer in the "domino theory" and the evil intentions of Communism—was in charge and he was not looking for a way out; he was looking for a way to win, or at least to get the terms he believed were necessary.

The important thing, therefore, was that Johnson had no bargaining position whatever in Vietnam. In early 1965, he was on the edge of defeat, and toppling over, and Ho Chi Minh knew it as well as he did. Given a little more strength, a little better field position, it might have been possible even for sincere anti-Communists like Johnson and Rusk to have made a pragmatic settlement, as the best of a bad bargain, on which the face of victory might have been painted. But the only way Lyndon Johnson or any other President could have negotiated his way out of Vietnam early in 1965 was by the virtual surrender of the anti-Communist government in Saigon and the abandonment of the American commitment to it.

Political negotiations, after all, do not create new situations; they only ratify power relationships that already exist. A negotiated settlement of any controversy is a ratification of the status quo (unless one side or the other foolishly gives away its position). In early 1965, the power relationship that existed was that North Vietnam and the N.L.F. had all but won their war; they were in general control of South Vietnam outside Saigon, and any conceivable negotiation would inevitably give that status quo a legal as well as de facto standing. Lyndon Johnson not only knew that better than anyone; he believed that to permit such a conclusion to the Vietnamese affair would be disastrous abroad and politically explosive at home.

Johnson was confronting the new Soviet regime of Brezhnev and Kosygin and he wanted them to be under no illusions about the strength and determination of the man in the White House—just as Kennedy, after Vienna, had desperately wanted to prove his steadfastness and nerve to Khrushchev. This concern on the part of Johnson was neither idle nor vain. To the extent that power is a determining force in the affairs of men —and who would deny that that is a great extent?—one of the essential ingredients of power is its credibility. Power has no meaning if it will not or cannot be used, and not all of America's might would have impressed the Soviet leaders had they believed Johnson feared, or had not the political ability, to use it.

After the long campaign of 1964, with Johnson in the role of peace candidate, there might well have been a question in Moscow on that point. It was sound diplomacy, as Johnson saw it, to remove any doubt about his willingness to stand fast when challenged. Moreover, it was characteristic of his whole experience in politics that, having established in his campaign a position of moderation and restraint on the war, he then faced the other way and set about proving his readiness and ability to use his power when he had to.

But Johnson was not concerned merely with his own position, important as that was in the world, and particularly in the eyes of his Soviet counterparts. On October 16, 1964, as he and Goldwater drew near the end of their one-sided contest, the Chinese Communists had exploded a nuclear device in the interior of Asia; the increased power and prestige that immediately accrued to Peking was a new factor in the balance of forces in Asia. Believing, as Johnson did, in the threat of Asian or any kind of Communism, he could only have seen an American withdrawal from, or compromise in, Vietnam as a further, and unacceptable, gain for the Chinese.

As he had in 1961, he saw the containment of Communist expansion and influence in Southeast Asia as a necessity of American national security, and he saw South Vietnam also as the key "domino," not only in Asia, but in the whole string of American commitments upon the credibility of which—so Johnson and Dean Rusk believed—world peace depended. If he pulled out of Vietnam, he believed, Communism, seen almost as a mystic force rather than as a policy of national states, would in swift progression outflank Thailand, menace the Malaysian peninsula and Indonesia, surround India and throw the American line of influence—perhaps even defense —back somewhere into the Pacific. Wars of liberation, vindicated as a technique, would spring up like bonfires throughout the underdeveloped world. Even Europe might be in difficulties because the American commitment to defend it, and particularly West Berlin, was a key factor in its security; and Johnson believed that if he pulled out of Vietnam ignominiously, no one—least of all Brezhnev and Kosygin—would believe that he would honor a commitment anywhere.

Johnson had absorbed that kind of Cold War thinking, and reinforcement for the sincere, moralistic anti-Communism which was, in any case, congenial to the Texas background upon which it was based, from Foster Dulles during the Eisenhower Administration, when Johnson was the powerful leader of the Senate opposition whose support was vital to the White House (just as Everett McKinley Dirksen was to become the centerpiece of Johnson's support in the Senate a decade later), and from Dulles' disciple, Dean Rusk, during the Kennedy Administration, when the meticulous Secretary of State saw to it that the obscure Vice President got his foreign policy briefings. The resulting Johnsonian view of a world divided into Communist and non-Communist blocs necessarily influenced his domestic political approach, too.

Johnson was keenly aware of how quickly the great political power of Franklin Roosevelt had evaporated after he had won it in the landslide victory over Alfred M. Landon in 1936. Ever alert to the potential threat of Robert Kennedy, who had become, with Johnson's help, the Senator from New York, and with his sharp sense of the flux of power, how it was won and how it was lost, Johnson had no intention, as he had made plain to friends during his campaign, of making F.D.R.'s mistake and throwing his victory away in some impossible effort like the court-packing scheme of 1937. Lyndon Johnson would play it safe, as a lifetime in politics had taught him to see

safety; he would not jeopardize everything he had won, everything he wanted to do, by showing what he saw as a politically
fatal weakness in Vietnam—"turning tail," he was likely to
say—and opening himself and his party to the grave charges
of being soft on Communism and of losing another part of
Asia to it. The year 1952 and the McCarthy era were not
easily forgotten by those who had lived through them, and if
anti-Communism was the bedrock of Lyndon Johnson's view
of the world, it was also, in his mind, the obvious shield against
the kind of domestic political savagery McCarthyism had
loosed on America, and which might come again.[17]

There was at work here a crucial, if ironic, generational
difference between Johnson and Kennedy. The latter had suffered McCarthy in silence, to say the least. Yet, a decade later,
he had sponsored the test-ban treaty with the Soviet Union.
Opposing nuclear tests had been widely regarded as madness,
if not treason, in the Fifties, and proposing a ban on them
probably cost Adlai Stevenson any chance to win the 1956
election. Lyndon Johnson had been instrumental in destroying
Joe McCarthy; yet, in the Sixties, he was just far enough removed in time from Kennedy's "new generation of Americans"
to share the old political attitudes and fears of the Eisenhower
era rather than the less militant, less ideological, less fearful
sentiments set loose and exploited by John Kennedy.

Johnson was playing it safe all down the line, as he began
his full term. His theme still was continuity; both in pursuit of
it and because he sincerely admired most of the Cabinet members he had inherited from Kennedy (and knew he was unlikely to "trade up" in replacing them), Johnson still planned
no real transition from a quasi-Kennedy Administration to a
Johnson-picked Administration. He had been elected President
but it was John Kennedy who was being canonized throughout
the world; it was the Kennedy family who posed the only real
threat within the Democratic party; and it was the Kennedy
mantle Johnson most wanted, both because of its political
value and because Kennedy somehow had managed to win the

love and admiration that Lyndon Johnson coveted above even the power that could not bring them to him.

So there would be as little break with the Kennedy image as possible. That meant not only that the "commitment" of Eisenhower and Kennedy to South Vietnam had to be honored—one might find a way to escape that kind of entanglement—but it meant also that Rusk and McNamara and Bundy and Maxwell Taylor and ultimately, even Cabot Lodge, would still be there. The architects of the Vietnamese involvement would be Johnson's advisers in the new circumstances created by his landslide, just as they had been Kennedy's in the fall of 1961 and Johnson's in November, 1963.

Johnson had inherited those men with the war. Their reputations were, in many ways, staked on its success, and they were both personally, and in principle, committed to its continuance and even more to its intrinsic rightness. The war could hardly be liquidated or compromised without a corresponding repudiation of at least some of these men (Rusk surely), none of whom showed any inclination whatever to declare the war a lost cause, or one not worth the cost and effort.

Among Johnson's high-level advisers, only Undersecretary of State George Ball, a European specialist and a professional devil's advocate who could argue any proposition with skill, if not fervor, openly took the negative on Vietnam. In October, 1964, he had sent the President a hundred-page memorandum advocating a withdrawal from the "gluepot" of Indochina; or, if that could not be done, at least a concentration upon the ground war in South Vietnam itself rather than "going north" with air power. Ball's memo thus confirms the fact that even before the election, while Johnson was still assuring the voters that he did not want to "start dropping bombs around" in an Asian war, an air attack against North Vietnam was considered likely enough by a sub-Cabinet officer to get up a major argument against it.

But Ball was only one among many, and Johnson's decision

to retain the Kennedy Cabinet deprived him, practically speaking, of much of the political freedom a landslide election in his own right had provided. He might talk to reporters about "keeping his options open" but he already had limited them severely for the sake of political continuity. The men with the greatest vested interest in winning the war, and in demonstrating its rightness, would continue to be his principal advisers—advocates as well as judges, fact-finders as well as fact-weighers —on war policy.

Several officials who were close to Johnson at that time also recall the sheer ebullience of the moment. One of them had also served Kennedy and remembers the same sense of omnipotence in the White House in early 1961. "Everything had always worked out for us," he said. "The primaries, the convention, the debates with Nixon, the confrontation with the Houston ministers, the election itself. We thought we had the golden touch. It was just like that with Johnson after sixty-four."

In Kennedy's case, the sense of the golden touch vanished at the Bay of Pigs, never really to return. But by January, 1965, Lyndon Johnson had even more reason for sheer confidence in his ability to make things come right. He had maintained the government in an hour of crisis, taken over the Democratic party from the Kennedys, pushed through the legislation John Kennedy couldn't (as Johnson saw it), crushed Goldwater, and won the White House with the biggest vote margin in history.

People who have known Johnson the longest maintain without exception that he is at his best when the going is toughest —as, for instance, when he had a Democratic majority of only one Senator in 1957, or just after he succeeded Kennedy in the White House. Richard Nixon put it another way during the campaign of 1964. He was working as hard for Goldwater as he could, he said privately, because as a political realist he was most afraid of a Johnson landslide. He had observed Johnson over many years in the Senate, and he agreed with

Johnson's friends. When the going was hardest, when there were practical restraints on him, Johnson was an exceptionally able leader; but when he was powerful enough to have a free hand, Johnson lost his otherwise sure touch and his vanity and mercurial temperament were likely to take charge of him.

If Johnson nevertheless maintained most of his habitual political caution as 1965 opened, that had little to do with his attitude on military operations in Vietnam. He might worry about Republicans being able to charge him with softness, but he had no fear that Americans would condemn a fight against Communism, or that their soldiers could not win a war.

It would be too much to suggest, in the light of the Korean War and of the French experience in Indochina (not to mention the American experience to that point in South Vietnam), that Johnson or his advisers thought the war could be easily or quickly won by an American intervention. But the history of the war, one of these men has said in retrospect, is "a search for the quick fix." It has been one effort after another to force a quick end to a situation that cannot even be sharply defined, much less circumscribed. Men in Washington now understand, a great deal more clearly than they did in early 1965, that the war in Vietnam is neither as simple as a rebellion or as clear as an aggression. It is an immensely complicated struggle, with historical and social as well as political and economic roots, a terribly total, but curiously limited, war in which military power is only one of the weapons needed. Even in its strictly military aspects, it is not necessarily a war in which firepower and sophisticated equipment and tons of supplies (in all of which twentieth-century American armies specialize) can be decisive.

But how could Lyndon Johnson, in his moment of triumph, with his sense of the golden touch, doubt that his superbly equipped forces, representing all the technological and industrial genius of America, organized by the incomparable McNamara with his modern administrator's skills, trained and led by the impressive generals and admirals with whom John-

son had conspired politically in his Congressional days, backed
by the most powerful industrial capacity and the most impressive economy in history—how could he doubt that this jugger-
naut could deal with a few ill-clad guerrillas, if necessary with
the old-fashioned Chinese-style infantry divisions of Vo
Nguyen Giap, with an enemy who had to steal his weapons,
bring in his supplies on bicycles and the backs of old women,
and whose soldiers were regimented Communist slaves without
the incentives of freedom and democracy to make them fight
well?

As for the political aspect of the thing, was not Lyndon
Johnson the man who had brought the R.E.A. to Texas? He
knew how to deliver the political goods to the people. And
once America brought its famous know-how to the task of
raising the Vietnamese standard of living, the Saigon government ought to have no more difficulty winning the loyalties
of the people than L.B.J. had had in getting elected to Congress down in the hill country.

And there is something else, too, something that must be
discussed delicately, but discussed nevertheless. Lyndon Johnson was not then, and is not now, a racist, or even an imperialist. He was and is, however, a fervently nativist American
who still, in the White House, could remember and recite his
childhood oration from George Frisbie Hoare, the famous
encomium to the colors that includes the phrase ". . . the fair-
est vision on which these eyes ever looked was the flag of my
country in a foreign land . . ." and whose patriotism and
conviction of his country's superior virtues were passionate
and instinctive.

He was and is a man of the South in whom the heritage of
Ol' Massa had been overcome but not forgotten, as it never
can be by any Southerner. He was and is a child, too, of Texas
and Colonel Colt, influences just as powerful. He was and is
a man, therefore, of power and pride, and the latter will not
brook much hindrance of the former, particularly from men
who, though not perhaps inferior, still have to be reminded
from time to time of the realities of things:

They'll come right into your yard and take it over if you let them. And the next day they'll be right up on your porch, barefoot and weighing one hundred and thirty pounds and they'll take that too. But if you say to 'em right at the start, 'hold on, just wait a minute,' they'll know they're dealing with somebody who'll stand up. And after that you can get along fine.

The enemy in Vietnam was barefoot and weighed one hundred and thirty pounds. He was the kind of man who might be fine in his place, who could be a useful citizen and a good friend if he let you train him right and help him a little, but who would take over your front porch if you didn't stand up to him. Lyndon Johnson was not about to let little brown men who skulked in the jungle do that to him and to the United States of America, and he was not capable of believing that the barefoot guerrillas might try to take the front porch anyway, even if told to "hold on, just wait a minute." The French had had no helicopters and no aircraft carriers and no political backing at home and Ho Chi Minh could deal with *them,* all right. But when it came to the full might of the U.S.A.—when God's country struck with the righteous wrath of freedom aroused—surely then it would be Glory, Glory Hallelujah! as it had been in every war in American history. And that symbolic flag of George Frisbie Hoare's fervent oratory again would be "terrible as a meteor."

It seemed then that it might not even be necessary to send in American troops, although Ball, dissenting as usual, had argued that if there was to be an intervention it ought to be on the ground in the South, where he thought the war would be won or lost. But that would guarantee ugly casualty lists, for one thing. For another, a generation of Americans had been brought up on the proposition that never again should their troops get embroiled in a land war on the continent of Asia, as they had been in the stalemate in Korea.

Air power was cheaper. It was what the South Vietnamese officers wanted. It was most acceptable in Congress, where for

years airmen had lobbied assiduously and well. It would engage a Navy impatient for a piece of the action, with its carriers already steaming in the Tonkin Gulf. Air and sea power,
after all, were the great American assets in the Pacific area;
why not fight one's own war rather than Giap's?

Kept away from sensitive areas along the Yunnan border,
moreover, air raids also were less likely than a troop commitment to alarm the enigmatic Chinese into the kind of massive
retaliation they had launched when American forces in Korea
had approached the Yalu River in 1950.

Besides, the enemy in North Vietnam had not yet felt the
sting of war. It cost Hanoi little to sponsor and support terror-
ism and guerrilla action in the South. If the scourge of war
could be carried to Ho Chi Minh and the zealots of his government—not just to their troops and agents far off in the
South—they would get a clear and painful idea of what their
ambitions could cost. There would be "no sanctuary" in North
Vietnam and that would make it an entirely different war.

All in all, air power appeared on its face to be the quickest
way to meet the main need of the moment, which was bolster-
ing the morale and prestige of the anti-neutralist South Vietnamese army and government factions and keeping them in
control in Saigon. This was necessary if the war was even to
be continued, let alone concluded advantageously.

Still, as Inauguration Day passed and Johnson—President
at last in his own right—recovered quickly from a cold he had
caught while taking his oath and reviewing the mammoth
parade (despite what he called the "electric underwear" he was
wearing), he had made only a characteristically limited commitment to the air power advocates. They had put him under
heavy pressure in an effort, joined by the influential General
Taylor, to strike back with air power after the November mortar attack on American planes at Bien Hoa; for political
reasons, he had refused to do so, and he rejected another such
chance just before Christmas. But at some point during these
turn-of-the-year months, he had agreed with his military ad-

visers that deliberate attacks on Americans (as distinguished from attacks on South Vietnamese which might incidentally kill Americans) would be answered with air strikes against the North.[18] That was no more than implementing the pledge of the Tonkin Gulf Resolution, and the action would be modeled on the Tonkin Gulf retaliation, which had pleased the President with its blending of power and restraint.

This limited commitment again was predictable, given Lyndon Johnson's political *modus operandi*. He was under military pressure to bomb; he was under political pressure for restraint; every instinct derived from his lifelong war of political survival told him to alienate neither force but to placate both with half a loaf for each. In his retaliation decision, he found the middle ground, that comfortable territory on which he saw no reason not to stand in Vietnam, as he had always stood in Texas and in the Senate.

A more sweeping policy of bombing the North, in general punishment for what it was supposed to be doing in the South, had long been advocated by Walt W. Rostow, among others. The President, although deeply concerned at the possibility of a South Vietnamese collapse, was not willing, as February began, to undertake such a portentous campaign. McGeorge Bundy was in Saigon, however, on a mission partially designed to determine whether general air attacks as recommended by Rostow ought to be launched.

The question was never answered. On February 7, vicious Viet Cong mortar fire came down on the American special forces camp at Pleiku, and Viet Cong infiltrators breached the South Vietnamese security perimeter to blow up several aircraft. Eight Americans were killed and 108 others were injured.

This case fitted the circumstances under which Johnson had decided to retaliate against North Vietnam enough so that, on the same day,[19] with Bundy urging him on by overseas telephone, air strikes were launched by forty-nine carrier planes against staging areas and base camps around Dong Hoi in

North Vietnam, just above the Demilitarized Zone. A second wave of South Vietnamese planes, escorted by American jets, struck the Vinh Linh communications center, even nearer the DMZ, on February 8.

These raids against the North, according to the official White House statement, were "in response to provocations ordered and directed by the Hanoi regime" which had been reported by American intelligence as ordering "a more aggressive course of action against both South Vietnamese and American installations."

The statement also contained the official rationale for attacking the North Vietnamese in response to Viet Cong attacks in the South: "These attacks were only made possible by the continuing infiltration of personnel and equipment from North Vietnam. This infiltration markedly increased during 1964 and continues to increase."

Official after official, in public and in private testimony, explained at the time that the Pleiku raids had been an open and direct challenge of American will and purpose, ordered by Hanoi and carried out on Hanoi's orders; the resulting air raids had been a "limited and fitting response." Even George Ball, no doubt reflecting sadly on his hundred-page memorandum of October, 1964, testified loyally at a news conference that the Administration had had no choice but to respond, so that Hanoi could not mistake American intentions, so that American lives could be protected.

"Secret intelligence," of course, was adduced to prove that Hanoi had planned and precipitated this test. Nevertheless, Charles Mohr, a reporter who had spent enough time in Vietnam to have a sense of its complexity and who was in February, 1965, the White House correspondent of *The New York Times* (later, he returned to Saigon), analyzed the Administration explanations skeptically in a *Times* article on February 8:

The Administration contention clearly is that North Vietnam made possible the attack on Pleiku. But the questions about the incident grow out of the apparent fact that a small Vietcong unit, armed with captured [American] weapons and protected by a lack of field intelligence on the part of the South Vietnamese Army, succeeded in creeping onto the American base and dealing a bloody blow.

Thus the final question is how much of the responsibility for Pleiku can be laid not just to Hanoi but to a failure to prosecute the antiguerrilla war in South Vietnam itself in a more vigorous and successful way.

And one Administration official, asked why Pleiku had been considered more of a North Vietnamese challenge than Bien Hoa (two days before the election), replied: "There's a limit to America's patience. When the attack was repeated, and repeated under those circumstances, there was no alternative."

Another official put it more bluntly. "They were hitting us," he said, "and we asked ourselves, 'why the hell don't we hit them one?' "

Still, there was something ambiguous about this first attack on the north. There was unquestionably an element of retaliation about it, just as advertised. The attack on Pleiku was certainly the latest of a series, and the usually imperturbable McGeorge Bundy, who was on the scene shortly after the night battle, gave an emotional telephone report on the carnage; he followed this with on equally emotional memorandum, written while he was on his way back to Washington. Weeks later, in his White House office, he could still speak to me with obvious feeling of the President's right and duty to protect American boys against being butchered in their tents. Soviet Premier Kosygin also was in Hanoi at the time, and there were those in the Administration who believed that to suffer the Pleiku attack without response would only permit Hanoi to argue to him that American power in Southeast Asia was a paper tiger; hence Kosygin might be more inclined to help along the Communist war effort, scornful of American response and moving *ipso facto* nearer Peking in the process.

The rationale of retaliation, however, was subject to serious doubt from the start. For one thing, only twelve hours elapsed between the beginning of the Pleiku attack and the American strike on Dong Hoi; many critics doubted whether a policy determination as well as a combat operation could have been put together so quickly.

These doubts have been greatly strengthened in many minds by subsequent events. On February 14, for instance, while the headlines still glared, General Taylor said in an interview on C.B.S. television that future attacks on the North would be determined "by the behavior of the Hanoi government." Adlai Stevenson had already said, in a letter to the United Nations Security Council President, Roger Seydoux of France, that despite the retaliatory attacks the United States had no intention of carrying on a general air war over North Vietnam.

Yet, writing for his book, published two years later, in February, 1967, General Taylor never mentioned retaliation. Explaining the origins of the bombing, he wrote:

> The first reason was to let the people of South Vietnam feel that for the first time, after eleven years of bitter warfare, they were striking back against the source of all their troubles . . . The second reason for our use of our air power was a military one. It was to utilize superiority in the air to strike military targets which, if destroyed, would have the effect of restraining or making more difficult the infiltration of men and supplies from North Vietnam to South Vietnam . . . The third reason for the air campaign . . . was to remind the leadership in Hanoi, the men who were directing the war in the South, that little by little through the progressive, restrained application of force by bombing, they would pay an ever-increasing price for a continuation of their aggression in the South.[20]

And when a member of the White House staff, later in 1965, asked McGeorge Bundy for a guidance memo on why the bombing of the North was necessary, Bundy's reply cited the first two reasons advanced by Taylor in his book, and added another—to convince Hanoi that the United States intended to make good its commitment to South Vietnam.

By the spring of 1965, moreover, there were plenty of officials in the Administration who would confide that the *real* value of the bombing was as a "bargaining card"; that is, they said, it was something that could be traded at the proper time for value received. The destruction being wrought on North Vietnam could be used in a negotiation to offset the military superiority then enjoyed by Communist forces in the South. Barely three months after the Pleiku response—on May 13— President Johnson ordered the first "pause" in the bombing, an obviously diplomatic move; nothing happened and the bombers went back to work on May 19.

There was a glaring weakness, in fact, in the Administration's own statements about retaliation for direct attacks on American troops. McNamara inadvertently made that weakness public on February 7 when, in response to a news conference questioner who asked how the Viet Cong had been able to penetrate the base defenses at Pleiku, he said he did not believe "it will ever be possible to protect our forces against sneak attacks of that kind."

The hard-hitting Viet Cong quickly confirmed this. On February 10, three days after the Pleiku attack and the first wave of "retaliatory" raids, against Dong Hoi, the guerrillas launched another assault, this time against American barracks at Qui Nhon. They blew up the barracks, killed nineteen Americans, wounded thirteen more, and got away.

The next day, 160 American and South Vietnamese planes bombed barracks and staging areas in Chan Hoa and Chaple, North Vietnam, again in "retaliation." The essential absurdity of the scheme could not have been made plainer. McNamara had pointed out that there could be no base security in the South, while the guerrillas were free to operate; yet, once retaliation had been publicly pledged after Pleiku, for every attack on Americans there would have to be a response di-

rectly against North Vietnam. If that was not so, whatever
deterrent value, whatever credibility for American determination, whatever boost for South Vietnamese morale had been
gained at Pleiku would have been dissipated and, in effect, a
gigantic American bluff would have been called with impunity.
Such a "paper tiger" effect would surely generate even more
attacks against Americans.

On the other hand, to strike back only when struck was
ridiculous and impossible. It handed the enemy the initiative.
It made the lives of American boys a sort of trigger for American air raids. It gave over to the Viet Cong the decision
whether an American air raid could be launched against North
Vietnam. Retaliation was simply untenable and even the word
could be justified only if it were a "cover," a sugar coating, for
the launching of a general air bombardment of North Vietnam; and only then if that bombardment could ultimately be
shown to be a justified, logical and feasible military strategy
designed to bring the war to a close.

But the bombing was not that, either. The Pleiku raids were
neither purely spontaneous retaliation, as the Administration
at first fatuously insisted; nor were they, as this lack of candor
suggested to so many critics, the first step in a long-planned,
carefully conceived air campaign against North Vietnam, a
campaign the launching of which had only awaited some such
pretext as Pleiku.

The truth is characteristically Johnsonian; it lies somewhere
between these poles. Johnson *had* decided that air strikes were
needed, primarily to boost South Vietnamese morale and con-
fute the neutralists, secondarily to protect American troops,
and incidentally to make life and war more difficult for Ho
Chi Minh and his government. But with a wary eye on public
opinion in the United States and a healthy respect for the
potency of peace as a political issue, in his established pattern
of going two ways at once, as a man of restraint as well as
power, he had not been willing by the time of Pleiku to order
a general air bombardment—to order the bombing of the

North, in a phrase Richard Nixon was then using, "day by day, and for that matter, night by night" until its collapse.

The raids, then, were both agreed upon in advance *and* retaliatory; just as Stevenson wrote Seydoux, Johnson then had not ordered continuing overall aerial warfare. In his first great test as a war President, he was relying upon his tried and true method. He would bomb, all right, but he would not really turn the bombers loose. He would retaliate but he would not initiate. He would show his muscle but only suggest how tough he could be if he really tried; as Taylor said in his February 14 broadcast, the raids were "deliberately planned . . . to suggest the possibility of other and bigger forms of reaction."

Wars are not elections in Texas, however, and what suffices in one theater will not necessarily do in the other. A former official who participated in the post-Pleiku discussions has privately described what happened on February 7, 1965:

> We began the bombing with no philosophy of what we were doing. We didn't necessarily even intend to start a campaign. We ignored the difficulty of halting the natural growth of something once started, and we considered the whole thing too much in terms of immediate effect and not enough in terms of long-range problems.

A policy, by definition, is a course of action intended to produce a desired end at an acceptable cost. Bombing the North might have formed such a policy had it been believed in the Johnson Administration, however erroneously, that the assault eventually would cause Hanoi to sue for peace on terms advantageous to the United States; but *that* policy would have required the difficult, dangerous and repugnant decision to launch the "strategic bombing" of populations and cities, as well as the tactical bombing of "military targets."

Bombing might also have been a policy, in the true sense, had it been aimed at interdicting every route from the North into the South—stopping at the border or beyond every man and ounce of material coming down in aid of the N.L.F., sealing off the indigenous part of the war from any outside aid and sponsorship. But the bombing was never so aimed, and no military man was foolish enough to maintain that air power could close mountain and jungle trails to men carrying mortar shells on their backs or to old women trotting under chogi sticks loaded at both ends with sacks of ammunition—much less to battalions of determined, hardy soldiers slipping one by one through the hills to a prearranged rendezvous in the South. McNamara, for one, never contended that air power could cause any worthwhile reduction in the amount of supplies and the number of men being sent from North to South; he said only that it would make it more difficult and costly to get them there, and no doubt it has.

In either case, however, the bombing would have been aimed at ending the war at an acceptable cost, and that would have been a policy, however bloody or futile it might have proved. So would Ball's alternative suggestion of a commitment of combat troops to help the South Vietnamese army. Control of the South Vietnamese populace, after all, was what the war was about. Johnson might have taken a real step forward in that struggle by making a troop commitment before the full weight of the North Vietnamese intervention cited by Taylor could have been brought to bear. He might even have staved off a major part of the ultimate infiltration of North Vietnamese troop units, by giving Hanoi a clear signal of his determination to fight, and by getting superior forces on the scene "fustest with the mostest." A troop commitment at that time, moreover, might have been defended against adverse American and world opinion; the troops would have been fighting *in the South,* in defense, against men who could be clearly pictured as invaders.

If North Vietnam actually was responsible for the war in the South—and, with the political campaign over, the Administration insisted that Hanoi was responsible—it perhaps made some sense to "raise the price of aggression" to Ho Chi Minh. But to punish him for what he was supposed to be doing would not necessarily make him stop it, unless the punishment was total; and vengeance is not a worthy or sensible reason for making war.

Moreover, meting out punishment in this world of sin and sadness demands such an Olympian regard for one's own purity that bodes it ill for one's judgment; and it is a dubious psychological proposition, anyway. A nation assaulted by another, with whatever justification, is likely to feel aggrieved—particularly an underdeveloped, formerly colonized, often invaded, Communist, Asian country bombed from the air by a powerful, capitalist, white, Western, occasionally imperialist nation. It could just as well have been argued that bombing the North would create a fierce will to fight on and win in a people who had borne the worst of the nationalist struggle against the French and who, almost alone among Asians, had mounted an underground resistance against the Japanese occupation in World War II.

Finally, bombing the North in any systematic, planned way was seen, even in 1965 and by many high in the Johnson Administration, as a largely irrelevant war, what McNamara would later describe to me as a "diversionary effort," that would only nibble at the edge of the fundamental problem of coping with the guerrillas in the South. McGeorge Bundy, returning from Saigon and Pleiku, just after the retaliatory raids, reminded reporters that "the primary contest is in South Vietnam."

So no bombing campaign to bring the North to its knees was planned or intentionally started. The bombing began because Lyndon Johnson, in the ebullience of his power and in the fatal grip of an irrelevant experience, wanted to strike and thought he needed to strike and found in the rationale of retaliation the political stance required to fit his lifelong method of operation. The result was the third largest war in American history.[21]

15 *Master of Nothing*

Almost four years earlier, when the Kennedy Administration was young and Lyndon Johnson had believed he could play a part in it, he had written on his return from Asia that the United States must be ready to decide whether it was willing to commit major forces to the defense of South Vietnam.

"We must remain master of that decision," he told Kennedy.

Johnson lost that mastery on February 7, 1965. He lost it because the event he set in motion that day—the "retaliation" he launched in such confidence of both its power and its restraint, in such certainty that it was both "limited" and "fitting" —acquired a life of its own, ugly and growing. From it flowed consequences no one had foreseen, consequences foreign to American experience and expectation, demanding new responses, permitting no evasion, imposing their own realities, until in the end Lyndon Johnson was not the master of anything; he was the creature of personality and circumstance.

The following chronology of air action and related developments in Indochina in the months after February 7 will suggest how hesitantly and reluctantly the air assault began—as if those who had loosed the beast tried at first to restrain it, only to find its innate power greater than theirs, and at last uncontrollable:

Feb. 9 —500 U.S. Marines, manning a Hawk anti-aircraft Missile unit, arrive near Danang.

Feb. 11 —160 American and South Vietnamese planes attack Chan Hoa and Chap Le, in retaliation for Viet Cong attack on Qui Nhon.

Feb. 18 —American-piloted planes, for first time, attack Viet Cong positions in South Vietnam.

Feb. 24 —American attacks of Feb. 18 disclosed in Saigon and new American sorties against Viet Cong flown in Binhdinh province.

Feb. 25 —This day and the two following, there were American air attacks against Viet Cong concentrations near Saigon.

March 2 —More than 160 United States and South Vietnamese planes bomb ammunition depot at Xombang and naval base at Quangkhe, both in North Vietnam.

March 3 —More than 30 American planes from Danang bomb unspecified targets in Eastern Laos.

March 8 —This day and the next, 3,500 U.S. Marines come ashore near Danang; the first American combat troops in South Vietnam, they were assigned to guard the Danang air base.

—Air attack on North Vietnamese border village of Cobai.

March 14—This day and the next, Tiger Island naval base and ammunition dump at Phuqui bombed; attack on Phuqui, 100 miles south of Hanoi, is deepest aerial penetration of North Vietnam.

March 19—From this day until May 13, American and South Vietnamese air raids increased in numbers and intensity. They were resumed May 19, after a five-day "pause."

The March 2 raids marked the end of the retaliation scheme, less than a month after it had been unveiled following Pleiku. The Saigon government and American authorities in South Vietnam said that the installations at Xombang and Quangkhe were hit because they were "being used by Hanoi to support its aggression." They also cited a number of Viet Cong depredations in South Vietnam; but there was no pretense that the raids had been ordered in response to a direct attack on American forces or installations. In fact, American air power had been turned loose in both North and South Vietnam.

The next day, the State Department issued a statement in Washington. The air strikes against North Vietnam, it said, represented "collective defense against . . . armed aggression" and were sanctioned by the United Nations Charter and the Tonkin Gulf Resolution of the previous August. Attention at last was drawn to those grim but overlooked phrases of the Resolution that gave Lyndon Johnson sanction in advance for military action "to prevent future aggression"; but it was too late to stop the onrush of events.

The essential fact was that, once the Dong Hoi and Vinh Linh raids had been followed by those at Chan Hoa and Chap Le, North Vietnam had come under American air assault, no matter what Johnson chose to call it, no matter how he intended to limit it. His own generals recognized that fact; Hanoi knew it; the world could not mistake it. An effort had been opened and it could neither be closed nor expunged from the record, neither sustained as it was, nor undone. It had to grow.

Above all, the bombardment could not be sustained, as we have seen, on the untenable basis of retaliation. But because the North had been bombed, it would have to continue to be bombed; the bombardment therefore would have to be placed on some more militarily sensible footing.

The very considerations that had led Johnson to "retaliation" meant that he could not put an end to the bombing even if he wanted to. He would have seemed to have bowed either to his fears or to pressures, and in either case, that reputation for toughness as well as restraint which he believed necessary would have been destroyed. The morale of the Saigon anti-neutralists, so far from being boosted, would have been dashed to pieces by such a retreat and their neutralist opponents would have been entitled to paint the American ally as a paper tiger indeed.

Johnson had said the bombings were designed to protect American troops; what would happen to those troops if he stopped bombing, once having started? Undoubtedly, the Viet Cong would have been further encouraged to descend on those American installations which McNamara had said could not be defended against sneak attacks. In home-front politics, every American death in Vietnam would then be pictured by hawkish political opponents as the price of Lyndon Johnson's timidity.

Even the men around Johnson, and nominally subject to his wishes, provided pressure against halting the bombings, once started. Those who wanted to do more than retaliate, anyway, felt themselves near enough to their goal to redouble their effort; those who saw the inherent impossibility of the retaliation approach urged the military common sense of a planned and controlled American bombardment; and those concerned with the credibility of American power feared that a cessation of bombing would appear in Moscow, Peking and Hanoi as irresolution.

Besides, air power was America's most potent weapon. It was cheap, relatively clean, technological; it had real fire-power. It just might make Ho Chi Minh realize he could not win. As McNamara said, it would make the infiltration of men and supplies more difficult; and the more bombing, the more these effects would be increased. At the least, bombing was an antidote to American frustration; at long last, American power was coming into play. Even such moderates as Senator Mike Mansfield of Montana defended the air strikes, and Lou Harris reported on February 22 that eighty-three per cent of the American people approved Johnson's decision to order "retaliatory bombings."

But there was a note of caution in Harris's report; his respondents, he said, clearly wanted to "use retaliatory air strikes only when extreme guerrilla activity warrants it . . . a plurality of four to three believes it important to keep the targets limited to Southern Communist bases."[22] But the devouring logic of war had already made it clear that Johnson could not long limit the bombardment either to retaliation or to a small group of targets, any more than he could stop it altogether.

It was not only the air war, moreover, that, after February 7, slowly went out of the control Lyndon Johnson had prided himself upon exercising. Robert McNamara, at his news conference, had put his finger upon a fact that had crucial effect on the entire nature and course of the American involvement in Vietnam.

Air bombardment requires aircraft; aircraft require pilots, crew, maintenance; and these in their turn require air bases. Air bases require security—and McNamara had said there could be *no real security against guerrilla attack*.

By March 7, one day less than a month after the Pleiku response, two battalions of Marines—3,500 men—became the first organized American combat units in South Vietnam, the forerunners of an Army of a half-million men. They would have, said McNamara that day at a news conference, defensive duties only; they would guard air bases, not "tangle with the Viet Cong."

But escalation is seldom a one-way street, and the supply routes, the jungle, the hills and the night favored North Vietnam. Down from the North in their black pajamas and bare feet, on their bicycles, carrying vital goods slung from their chogi sticks, wraithlike, dogged, implacable, came the men, the boys, even the old women dispatched in response. Manpower was abundant in the North, and as the Americans continued to come ashore, as their air power came to the aid of the South Vietnamese Army, a lethal game of leapfrog was under way. North Vietnamese infiltration was tripling to an estimated rate of 5,000 monthly. By early June, there were 50,000 American combat soldiers on hand. Each arriving increment on either side, every American air sortie, increased the certainty of ground combat involving Americans; and the conflict inevitably came. American units were deliberately committed to battle on their own, rather than in support of South Vietnamese operations, on June 28, beginning that ground war in Asia that a generation of Americans had learned to dread.

On July 28, 1965, Johnson held a White House news conference to announce a vast buildup of combat forces; that day, as if to underscore the colossal mushroom of war that had sprung from February 7, American jets bombed an installation of Soviet-made SAM missiles in North Vietnam, only forty miles from Hanoi. Retaliation was a hazy memory, a long word in old newspaper files.

From the first input of Marines for defensive duty guarding air bases, the American involvement was certain to become gigantic. A decade earlier, Richard Russell had warned Eisenhower that if he sent 200 men into the maw of Indochina he would inevitably have to send 20,000 after them; and George Ball had similarly warned Kennedy in the fall of 1961. They understated the case. By the end of 1965, more than 200,000 Americans were on the ground in Vietnam; by the end of 1967, the number was almost half a million. From air base security, through air support and then limited ground assistance to the South Vietnamese Army—"when requested," of course—to the bloody "search and destroy" strategy that finally, at such places as the Ia Drang Valley and the Iron Triangle, made it an American war—all of this followed Pleiku and the retaliatory raids with monstrous and kaleidoscopic irresistability. From the beginning, the American air campaign in the North and in the South invited Viet Cong attacks on American air bases, thus demanding American security forces to guard the bases and guaranteeing the ultimate engagement of those forces in combat. It could not even be defensive combat, for no American commander could be required to sit still and wait to be attacked, with all the advantages such a requirement would give to ruthless, disciplined, trained guerrillas. And so the war came, and grew.

Instead of providing a "quick fix" for the disadvantageous Vietnamese involvement Johnson had found himself in at the beginning of 1965, the bombing had put the nation irrevocably on the road that would lead to an army of half a million men bogged down in that land war in Asia against which he had joined Russell in warning Eisenhower in 1954. And more than that: When the planes soared from their carriers that day, they put the United States upon the diplomatic defensive, and arraigned the land of the free and the home of the brave before the world as a brutal and powerful bully attacking a small and unprivileged nation. Even air support missions in South Vietnam supported this damaging charge; the attacks, particularly those using napalm, inevitably added to the mounting total and the gruesome nature of civilian deaths. Johnson and his commanders, like Brer Rabbit stuck to the Tar Baby, found that they could not easily stop bombing voluntarily, once they had started; in a war of intimidation and psychology, that would only signal weakness to Hanoi, would only egg the other side on; and so it became an article of faith in the Johnson Administration that except for brief and fruitless propaganda "pauses," there could be no letup in the bombing, no matter how useless or unpopular, unless Hanoi would reciprocate in some unspecified way. The bombing gave Moscow and Peking and other capitals of expediency a dramatic and shocking example of that American militarism they once had had to invent in order to make propaganda to the world. They used the bombing adeptly to conceal their own inability or unwillingness to work toward peace in Southeast Asia, and to place the responsibility for war on the United States.

And for all these disadvantages, the bombing still evaded the main question—how to win the bloody, grinding ground warfare in the South? Infiltration continued—even increased —by McNamara's own figures; no one appeared at the bargaining table; ghastly battles continued to rip apart the Southern countryside. The bombing could not make something American and technological out of the war, which was profoundly Asian and intensely human.

The effects of the bombing in the United States were more important than they were in North Vietnam. In the minds of millions of Americans, the air war against the North, more than anything else, confirmed their belief that Lyndon Johnson was not to be trusted, that he was, after all, "just a politician" as originally advertised—a manipulator, an artist of power and guile. He had promised not to "go North," or at least that was the way it had sounded in the campaign; he had said he would only retaliate for attacks on Americans. Herblock, happily in opposition again after the Kennedy years, dipped his pen in napalm and drew a cartoon of Johnson at the mirror; but it was Goldwater who stared back.

As the war wore wearily on, escalating almost automatically, its costs mounting, the casualty lists coming in, the risks ever more apparent, the end seeming to recede in the distance, Americans turned in droves from the man they had elected by the greatest margin in history. Doves deplored his war; hawks said he wasted American lives by not winning it. By late 1967, the Harris poll reported that only twenty-three per cent of Americans thought he was doing a good job; less than three years after the great landslide and the almost limitless political prospect of early 1965, Lyndon Johnson was one of the most unpopular Presidents in American history.

The dollar costs of the war rose to more than two billion dollars a month; this was only a sliver of the Gross National Product, but the combination of the actual cost with war psychology and Johnson's personal unpopularity ruined the Great Society program after its early triumphs. After the Democratic setback in the 1966 elections, Republicans and anti-Johnson Southerners could control the House. Using the cost of the war as an excuse, these myopic opportunists hacked away at a budget that Johnson had already held down drastically, on the same excuse; never adequately financed, the Great Society programs took the brunt of the reductions.

Inevitably, too, as first the gravity of the war and then his political situation came home to him, Johnson's attention moved away from domestic reform. In June, 1965, eight months after the landslide, four months after Pleiku, he delivered at Howard University what can now be identified as the last of the Great Society speeches. Perhaps it was fitting that it should be a moving and powerful address, one of the great Presidential speeches of our time, Lyndon Johnson at his best, expounding on his country's most profound problem—the "other nation" of poverty-stricken and embittered Negroes.

That was the end of a moment, an elegy for the dream; after the Howard speech, Johnson was only occasionally a reformer and never a leader who could weld national unity, mobilize national purpose. One by one, the men who had had the most to do with the Great Society vision, upon whom its success so greatly depended, began to leave the Administration. Against his every intent, Lyndon Johnson had become a war President.

If the performance of a war leader has to be judged by the extent to which he was able to mobilize in his people the spirit of sacrifice and commitment needed if any modern nation is to support a modern war, Johnson's war leadership was largely ineffective, too. He never found a clear line that dramatized and justified the American participation in the war. Defending small nations, guaranteeing their integrity and self-determination, sustaining American commitments, combating wars of national liberation—all of these may be American interests and may be worth fighting a war for. But divided nations—Korea, Germany, Vietnam itself—are commonplaces of the postwar world; the Communist subversion of the "free people" of Cuba by something like a "war of liberation" was accepted by the United States, save for the farcical convulsion at the Bay of Pigs; the American commitment to defend the territorial integrity of Middle Eastern nations against aggression was ignored by Johnson himself in the Arab-Israeli war of 1967; and a coalition agreement with known Communists was found to be the better part of good policy in Laos in 1961, and has been lived with ever since.

Circumstances, not abstract value, make such propositions "vital interests" of the United States or any other country. Defending the freedom of Hungarians was not an American vital interest in 1956 because there was no way to do it without making war on the Soviet Union, for which the Republican crusaders of 1952 properly had no stomach. The circumstances that made these propositions vital American interests in Southeast Asia in the 1960's were, first, Johnson's belief in the "domino theory" and the shibboleths of the Cold War, and, second, the fact that he had got into a hot war he later had to justify.

Now, a belief in the "domino theory" suggests that the American involvement in Vietnam is fundamentally in pursuit of an *American* interest, the containment of what Dean Rusk calls "Asian Communism" and the maintenance of a balance of power in Asia. This is precisely the view Johnson set down in his report to Kennedy in 1961.

It was precisely what McNamara told the House Armed Services Committee on February 18, 1965, eleven days after the raid on Dong Hoi:

> The choice is not simply whether to continue our efforts to keep South Vietnam free and independent, but rather whether to continue *our struggle to halt Communist expansion in Asia*. If the choice is the latter, as I believe it should be, *we will be far better off facing the issue in South Vietnam*. (italics added)

The loss of South Vietnam, McNamara said, would "greatly increase the prestige of Communist China among the nonaligned nations and strengthen the position of their following everywhere."

But on March 13, less than a month later, President Johnson told a news conference, in discussing Southeast Asia:

> In that region there is nothing that we covet. There is nothing we seek. There is no territory *or no military position or no political ambition.* Our one desire and our one determination is that the people of Southeast Asia be left in peace *to work out their own destinies* in their own ways.

"No political ambition" and a determination to enable Southeast Asia to work out its own destiny are positions that simply do not square with an American struggle "to halt Communist expansion in Asia" or with military action aimed at damaging China's position among non-aligned nations.

As President, up to the end of 1967, Johnson never found the political candor or the necessary facts to make the case for a war to contain Chinese Communism; whatever its substantive validity, such a war would have had the virtues of simplicity and probably of honesty on Johnson's part. Presenting the war rather as a noble American effort on behalf of a "small nation" and its "free people," dubious as that description is, he had to accept the consequences: South Vietnam's autonomy, political contrariness and control of its own manpower and economy, none of which helped much to improve the military situation or to effect those social and economic advances for which Johnson had seen the need in 1961. He also had to accept the effect of South Vietnamese political instability, recurring military rule, corruption, lack of effective reform, and combat weakness on American and world opinion. He had neither the benefits of controlling absolutely a fully American war for what he saw as American interests, nor of fighting disinterestedly on behalf of an obviously admirable and worthy ally. This kept alive and virulent in his own country the questions of what the war was all about; whether it was justified; why Johnson could not "get it over with"; what his real purposes were in Southeast Asia. And it dug ever more deeply the so-called "credibility gap" that afflicted the Johnson Administration from 1965 onwards.

What made it even more difficult for the President to mobilize support for the war was the way it had come about it; it was a sudden *fait accompli* which Johnson had been elected, in part, to avoid, and in which he later abjured his constituency to acquiesce as a matter of national honor and commitment. But so far from its having derived from a concerted national impulse or a confident national understanding, the sad and terrible—perhaps tragic—truth is that the war that erupted in 1965 was not even the result of a deliberate, calculated, clearly seen policy, which had boldly accepted necessary risks. One who served Johnson in those crucial days of 1965 looked back upon them long afterwards and mused emotionally upon the ways things had turned out.

> The President believed the American people wanted him to protect American boys. He wanted to let Hanoi know he could get tough and he wanted to give a boost to Saigon. We had no idea in those days about strategic bombing or stopping infiltration or bombing as a negotiation card. The President didn't choose this war, he didn't really want this war. He stumbled into it blind.

The carrier planes darting North on February 7 might have met Johnson's superficial political needs and fitted his deepest personal experience, but they could not meet the situation in Vietnam. They could only change it irrevocably, in ways that nothing in the American political and military experience was likely to foretell. The response to Pleiku was not a policy designed to deal with reality; it was only the interplay of personality and circumstance; it was not the mastery of man over event but the yielding of choice to instinct.

So, Lyndon Johnson, trusting what he knew and confident of his country and kind, drifted into war. He had seen the people of which he was so intrinsically a part—"the farmer in Iowa, the fisherman in Massachusetts, the worker in Seattle, the rancher in Texas"—all harboring the same hopes and fears, all gathered before him in the Great Tent he had erected in his vision and his dreams. He had carried out a rainy night's pledge at the University of Texas and achieved a Consensus that, for a moment, really did "end obstruction and paralysis and liberate the energies of the nation for the work of the future." He had gone a long way, from the dust of the hill country to the loneliest peak of American political power and opportunity. And then, like Roosevelt before him, he had reached too far, believed too much, scaled the heights only— in the blindness of his pride—to stumble and fall.

He could call upon history to vindicate him, and in the rich and recurring irony of the endless adventure, perhaps it would. But not history nor all the king's men could give back to Lyndon Baines Johnson of Texas that moment for which he had waited all of his life.

An Epilogue

This book was completed before Lyndon B. Johnson announced on March 31, 1968, that he would neither seek nor accept the renomination of the Democratic party for President of the United States. I was never among those prescient few who foresaw that this proud and resourceful man would retire at the end of a term both so troubled and so productive; quite the opposite.

Nevertheless, looking over the pages devoted to him in this book, I have seen no need to change them; and that would be so even if happy results should flow from the peace overtures the President announced simultaneously with his political intentions.

I did not address, after all, the questions whether Johnson could win another term or settle the war. I was concerned, instead, with a particular moment of both power and glory, how he uniquely achieved and then remarkably dissipated it, and how all this had been affected if not determined by Johnson's personality and experience, and by circumstances he could not control.

As long as historians ponder the eventful Johnson years, of course, they are going to have to grapple with the question why so considerable a man was not, in the final analysis, able to sustain the great political power the people conferred upon him in 1964.

That is the question I raised, in the broadest sense and perhaps prematurely, in the latter half of this book. I am not entirely satisfied with my answer, but I will stand on it—

adding here only what I wrote for *The New York Times* the day after the President told us he would not run again:

"The overriding cause for Lyndon Johnson's decline from the peaks of 1964 and 1965 is the war in Vietnam—too confidently entered upon, too little understood, too costly for any gain he could make men see, too complex either to win or to end by the kind of direct and straightforward action that Americans favor.

"And that is the ultimate, perhaps tragic, irony. Lyndon Johnson came into office seeking a Great Society in America and found instead an ugly little war that consumed him."

Washington, D.C.   Tom Wicker
April 3, 1968

Author's Note on Sources

This book emerged from a reporter's routine work, and that origin imposes certain handicaps upon its documentation. This is particularly true of Part II, "Johnson Loses His Consensus," since many of its events so recently occurred and since some new light is almost constantly being shed on them.

Much of my understanding of these events was obtained in confidential discussions with men still living, still active. Even so, I have assumed that a sort of statute of limitations necessarily is at work on the "off the record" and non-attributable remarks of personages of large historical importance, and I have accepted the responsibility of identifying some material of this kind if I thought it permitted by the passage of time or the changing of circumstances. This is the case, generally speaking, with all remarks noted as having been made "privately" or "to friends" or "to a group of reporters" by, say, President Johnson or other high officials.

In some other cases, for reasons that will be obvious to the reader, the protection of sources remained necessary. In these cases, as in the already mentioned cases of off-record remarks the source of which I have identified in the text, no quotations were used unless I heard the words spoken, or unless someone who did hear them and who I believed had no axe to grind—for instance, a trusted colleague or a former official with no vested interest—conveyed them to me.

For the most part, I have been able to identify quotations adequately in the text. I have used footnotes only as a last resort, and with no intention of disguising this book as one of those scholarly works that someday will march with stately tread across the same fertile ground.

My thanks are due and are here offered to Dupre Jones, the remarkable librarian of *The New York Times* Washington Bureau, and to innumerable other persons who in one way or another assisted me through the years—some of them more than they knew or desired.

Tom Wicker

Washington, D.C.
January, 1968

Footnotes

PART I | Kennedy Loses Congress

1. *'Alone, At the Top'*

    1. This is a composite of quotations from campaign speeches by Senator John F. Kennedy at Eugene, Ore., on Sept. 7, 1960; Oakland, Calif., Sept. 8, 1960; Charleston, W. Va., Sept. 19, 1960; and Cleveland, Ohio, Sept. 25, 1960.

    2. The Sorensen quotation is on page 53, and the Kennedy quotation is in the foreword, of *Decision-Making in the White House: The Olive Branch or the Arrows,* by Theodore C. Sorensen, Columbia University Press, 1963.

3. *Government of Men*

    3. The liberals were exactly right. Halleck sent the late B. Carroll Reece of Tennessee and Hamer Budge of Idaho, now a member of the Securities and Exchange Commission, to the committee; they were men who fulfilled every liberal apprehension.

    4. A twenty-one-day rule finally was approved in the liberal Eighty-ninth Congress that resulted from the Johnson landslide of 1964. It had a significant difference from the 1949 version; only the Speaker and not the committee chairmen could act under it.

4. *'No Purgin', No Packin' '*

    5. They finally did, on the nineteenth try. In 1966, Judge Smith was defeated in the Democratic primary,

in large part because the boundaries of his district were changed to include a heavy Negro vote.

6. Williams was nevertheless elected Governor of Mississippi on the Democratic ticket in 1967.

5. *Headcount*

7. For this and other transgressions, Cooley rapidly rose near the top of President Kennedy's list of least favorite Democrats. When the Rules Committee issue arose again in 1963, Cooley switched and backed the Administration position. The voters of his district switched in 1966 and chose a Republican.

6. *Look Away, Dixieland*

8. Section 8, Article One, of the United States Constitution, states that "The Congress shall have power," among other things, "to regulate Commerce with foreign nations, and among the several states, and with the Indian Tribes."

9. *The Education of JFK*

9. *Year of Trial: Kennedy's Crucial Decisions,* by Helen Fuller, Harcourt, Brace and World, Inc., 1962, p. 101.

10. *Federal Aid to Schools,* pt. 1, hearings on H.R. 4970 of the Education Subcommittee of the House Education and Labor Committee, 1961; *The New York Times,* March 17, 1961, p. 19, col. 1.

PART II   Johnson Loses His Consensus

10. *Dark Saturday*

1. "How LBJ Got the Nomination," by Philip Potter, in *The Reporter Magazine,* June 18, 1964.

11. *The First Priority*

2. This quotation, and the one above, are from an interview with President Johnson by David Brinkley, Eric Sevareid and William H. Lawrence, which was televised by the National Broadcasting Company, the Columbia Broadcasting System, and the American Broadcasting Company on March 15, 1964.

3. Meeting with reporters in the White House, July 25, 1964. A transcript of this supposedly background session was made and is available at the White House.

12. *Commitment*

4. *The Two Viet-Nams,* by Bernard B. Fall, 2nd edit., Frederick A. Praeger, 1967, p. 286.

5. *Vietnam: Between Two Truces,* by Jean Lacouture, Random House, 1966, p. 170.

6. *Ibid.,* p. 129.

7. *In the Nation: 1932–1966,* by Arthur Krock, Mc-Graw-Hill, 1966, p. 325; *A Thousand Days,* by Arthur Schlesinger, Houghton-Mifflin Co., 1965, p. 997.

8. The additional forces, moreover, were advisers and technicians, not combat units. This statement is based on private conversations with James Reston. See also *Sketches in the Sand,* by James Reston, Alfred A. Knopf, 1967, p. 86.

9. *The New York Times,* March 9, 1965, p. 4, col. 4.

10. *A Thousand Days,* p. 276.

11. I am quoting from the Johnson report as it is published in *The Professional,* by William S. White, Houghton-Mifflin Co., 1964, pp. 238–44.

12. *The Artillery of the Press,* by James Reston, Harper & Row, 1967, p. 28. Reston has given me a detailed account of his conversation with President Kennedy. See also *Sketches in the Sand,* pp. 472–73.

13. *'One Great Democratic Tent'*

13. *Following is the complete text of the Southeast Asia [Tonkin Gulf] Resolution (S J Res 189, H J Res 1145), as enacted Aug. 7, 1964:*

"Whereas naval units of the Communist regime in Viet Nam, in violation of the principles of the Charter of the United Nations and of international law, have deliberately and repeatedly attacked United States naval vessels lawfuly present in international waters, and have thereby created a serious threat to international peace;

"Whereas these attacks are part of a deliberate and systematic campaign of aggression that the Communist regime in North Viet Nam has been waging against its neighbors and the nations joined with them in the collective defense of their freedom;

"Whereas the United States is assisting the peoples of southeast Asia to protect their freedom and has no territorial, military or political ambitions in that area, but desires only that these peoples should be left in peace to work out their own destinies in their own way: Now, therefore, be it

"Resolved by the Senate and House of Representatives of the United States of America in Congress assembled, That the Congress approves and supports the determination of the President, as Commander-in-Chief, to take all necessary measures to repel any armed attack against the forces of the United States and to prevent further aggression.

"SEC. 2. The United States regards as vital to its national interest and to world peace the maintenance of international peace and security in southeast Asia. Consonant with the Constitution of the United States and the Charter of the United Nations and in accordance with its obligations under the Southeast Asia Collective Defense Treaty, the United States is, therefore, prepared, as the President determines, to take all necessary steps, including the use of armed force, to assist any member or protocol state of the Southeast Asia Collective Defense Treaty requesting assistance in defense of its freedom.

"SEC. 3. This resolution shall expire when the President shall determine that the peace and security of the area is reasonably assured by international conditions created by action of the United Nations or otherwise, except that it may be terminated earlier by concurrent resolution of the Congress."

14. By late 1967, the Senate Foreign Relations Committee was investigating whether the torpedo boat attacks in the Tonkin Gulf had actually occurred. So grave had become the doubts, resentments, and suspicions of members of the committee and its professional staff that the Pentagon was forced to state publicly that the attacks had occurred and to give corroborating evidence. It did not convince the committee investigators, who continued their attempts to prove that the entire Tonkin Gulf episode had been overstated, if not invented. In early 1967, their investigation turned toward what they considered the likelihood that the incident had been less menacing than the Administration had claimed in 1964, and that President Johnson had reacted too swiftly and too strongly, perhaps with the intent to deceive.

15. *LBJ's Inner Circle,* by Charles Roberts, Delacorte Press, 1965, p. 20.

14. *The Ebullience of Power*

16. *Responsibility and Response,* by Maxwell D. Taylor, Harper & Row, 1967, p. 24.

17. During the campaign of 1964, Johnson told me that some of the people around Goldwater were the "same old McCarthy crowd."

18. Philip Geyelin states that by the first week of February, 1965, the Johnson Administration had "made up its mind to expand the war." *Lyndon B.*

Johnson and the World, by Philip Geyelin, Frederick A. Praeger, 1966, p. 216.

19. Clocks in Saigon run thirteen hours ahead of Eastern Standard Time. Thus, action ordered "on the same day" in Washington may actually be ordered on the next day in Saigon, even with virtually instantaneous communications.

20. *Responsibility and Response,* pp. 26–27.

21. In terms of maximum American troop strength at any given time. In the Korean War, this was 281,000 men; in Vietnam, by the end of 1967, American troop strength was estimated by the Department of Defense at 478,000 men. Troop strength in World Wars I and II was, of course, much greater but, on another scale of measurement, by December, 1967, the United States had dropped more tons of explosives—1,630,500—on North and South Vietnam than it did on all World War II targets (1,544,463 tons) and twice as many tons as were dropped during the Korean War.

15. *Master of Nothing*

22. The Harris Survey, published in the Washington *Post,* February 22, 1965.

INDEX